P9-APT-208

AMERICANA TREASURES

Edited by Marian Hoffman

DODD, MEAD & COMPANY
New York

Copyright © 1972 by BPC Publishing Ltd.; copyright © 1972, 1973 by Greystone Press; copyright © 1983 by Ottenheimer Publishers, Inc.

All rights reserved

No part of this book may be reproduced in any form without permission in writing from the publisher

Published by Ottenheimer Publishers, Inc.

Exclusively distributed by Dodd, Mead & Company, Inc. 79 Madison Avenue, New York, N.Y. 10016

Distributed in Canada by McClelland and Stewart Limited, Toronto

Manufactured in Hong Kong

First Edition

Library of Congress Cataloging in Publication Data Main entry under title:

Americana treasures.

1. Americana.   2. Antiques—United States.   I. Dodd, Mead & Company
NK805.A689 1983   745'.0973   83-14031
ISBN 0-396-08279-3 (pbk.)

Contents

Introduction

When the colonists came to America, they brought few belongings with them. Soon they had to begin making articles needed for everyday life—houses, furniture, clothing, bedding, tableware. Since there was no strong American tradition as yet, they looked to Europe for design ideas. They imitated what was fashionable "back home" but added some of their own inventions, using the natural resources available in the new country. This combination of tradition and reform, of old-world heritage mixed with exciting innovations, is what characterizes Americana.

The early colonists had a spartan existence. They were working hard to build a community out of the wilderness and had no time for luxuries. Their homes were austere, and their furniture simple and functional.

By the eighteenth century, there was a greater affluence among the colonists and, consequently, a greater demand for comfort. The William and Mary style of furniture, with its use of veneer and baroque carvings, came in vogue. By 1725, this style had merged with the more elegant Queen Anne style. Chippendale style furniture was also a dominant force in American furniture of this period.

As the colonists showed some returns for their industry, they were able to enlarge their humble homes. They used the styles of England: William and Mary, Queen Anne, Georgian. Local characteristics developed, however, such as stuccoed walls in the South. In Louisiana and on the West Coast, the Spanish were influencing colonial architecture.

The eighteenth century was a time of specialization for American craftsmen. Silversmiths, cabinetmakers, potters, and glassmakers all began to thrive.

The change from the Colonial to the Federal period brought a new direction and vitality to American arts. Americans found a style consistent with the ideals of their new government—a neoclassical style that was without the elaborate ornamentation of previous periods. Thomas Jefferson was the central figure of this period, a leader in designing Federal style buildings and in planning the design of American cities.

Early Federal period furniture was influenced by the designs of two Englishmen, Hepplewhite and Sheraton. Many pieces were carved or inlaid with the American eagle. Late Federal style furniture was much heavier and bolder and is referred to as Regency or Empire, depending on whether it had more English or French characteristics. Duncan Phyfe was the most famous Regency style furnituremaker. Painted furniture was also popular in Federal America.

As life in America became more settled, there was a bigger market for luxury items. The toy-making industry grew in the first half of the nineteenth century, and from that stemmed the successful American doll industry.

Clockmaking, too, became increasingly popular; a few clockmakers practiced their craft in the colonial period, but most clocks were imported until after the Revolutionary War. By the 1830s, clocks were mass produced in America and exported in record numbers. Pillar-and-scroll, ogee, American square, Gothic, beehive, novelty, and ticket clocks were some of the nineteenth-century styles.

The War of 1812 and the British blockade of American ports made the Americans realize that they should manufacture their own fine table glass instead of relying on imports. Local glass firms began producing tableware in Bohemian style and pressed-pattern glass, and issuing commemorative glass objects.

The second half of the nineteenth century was characterized by increasing industrialization. Machine-turned furniture became popular due to its cheapness when compared with handmade furniture. Hitchcock and Belter were the leaders in high-quality, mass-produced furniture of this period.

In the early nineteenth century, John James Audubon captured one view of American life with his drawings of American wildlife. Later in the century, Currier and Ives issued prints giving a different view—one showing the popular events and personalities of the day.

The American firearms industry also started in the nineteenth century and was dominated by Samuel Colt, whose revolvers have been continuously produced from 1836 to the present. The Mexican War, the California Gold Rush, and the Civil War all created a large market for locally manufactured firearms.

Industrialization in the nineteenth century did not signal an end to fine craftsmanship. Toward the end of the century, decorative arts—such as ornate and colorfully decorated glass and decorative pottery, such as Rookwood—became a thriving industry. Louis Tiffany was perfecting his experiments in glass irridescence. And American folk artists were turning out original works such as stencil-painted furniture, carved decoy ducks, ship figureheads, and paintings.

Graphic arts developed importance at the end of the nineteenth century with the beginning of the poster movement. *Harper's, Lippincott's, The Century Illustrated Monthly Magazine* and *Scribner's Magazine* established a strong American tradition in illustration and poster design with their Art Nouveau covers and posters.

American artists and craftsmen, from colonial times to the twentieth century, looked to traditional forms and old-world prototypes for inspiration. But their willingness to try new ideas and their ingenuity transformed traditional styles into something a little different—something uniquely American.

Marian Hoffman

COLONIAL AMERICA

Colonial America

Fig. 1 (frontispiece) **The Embarkation of the Pilgrim Fathers for New England** *by C. W. Cope, 1856. Fresco, 7 ft. 2½ ins. x 9 ft. 4½ ins. (By kind permission of the House of Lords, London.)*

Spurred on by visions of political and religious freedom and of the great riches to be gained from tobacco, the early colonists came in their thousands, undeterred by the harsh living conditions of the New World across the sea

The actual date of the discovery of the New World is one of the great mysteries still to be solved by historians. Until recently the honour had been given to Christopher Columbus who, in 1492, sighted the island of San Salvador. He landed and, thinking that he had succeeded in finding a new route to the 'Indies', called the natives Indians. However, it is now certain that Columbus was far from being the first European to land in the Americas. Not long before William the Conqueror invaded England, a Norseman, Leif Ericsen, sailed westwards from Greenland in his narrow Viking ship and came upon a land rich with grapes which

Ætatis suæ 21. Aᵒ 1616.

Matoaks als Rebecka daughter to the mighty Prince Powhatan Emperour of Attanoughkomouck als Virginia converted and baptized in the Christian faith, and Wife to the wor.ᵗʰ Mʳ Tho: Rolff.

Museum Photo

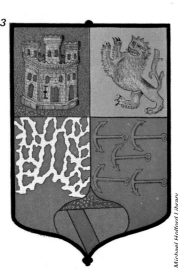

Hulton Picture Library

Fig. 2 **Christopher Columbus** *(1451–1506). Engraving. This portrait is believed to be of the great Genoese explorer who discovered America in 1492.*

Fig. 3 **Coat of Arms** *adopted by Christopher Columbus in January 1502. (British Museum, London.)*

Michael Holford Library

Michael Holford Library

Fig. 4 *Indians around a Fire by John White, early seventeenth century. Water-colour. (British Museum.)*
Fig. 5 *Pocahontas (1595?– 1617) in Jacobean dress, English, 1616. (National Portrait Gallery, Smithsonian Institution, Washington.)*
Fig. 6 *Captain John Smith (1580–1631). Engraving, 1624.*

Fig. 7 *'Pine tree' shilling, minted by John Hull, Mass., 1652. The earliest coinage from the English Colonies.*

Fig. 8 *The Landing of Columbus in the New World, 1492, from a fifteenth-century book of woodcuts. Columbus' three ships, the* Nina, *the* Pinta *and the* Santa Maria, *are seen crossing the Atlantic Ocean. Ferdinand of Portugal, patron of the expedition, is seen on the left. (British Museum.)*

he called Vinland. Thus, nearly five hundred years before Columbus, a European had stood on the soil of North America. Today, as a result of the research of Thor Heyerdahl in his papyrus boat, *Ra*, a theory exists that the ancient Egyptians sailed to the Americas four thousand years ago.

However, it was Columbus who was directly responsible for the first permanent European settlements in North America. Stories of his discovery circulated Europe, stirring the imaginations of treasure hunters, traders and persecuted religious minorities. Of these groups, the traders were in the strongest position; they had the resources, the experience and the ships. Consequently, in 1604, a highly speculative company was set up in England, which received a royal charter from James I, and small investors were encouraged to buy shares, enticed by the supposed riches of the New World.

In 1606, one hundred and twenty colonists set sail in three ships, and by May of the following year they went ashore on the coast of Virginia. The town they founded was named Jamestown after the king who had encouraged them. They planned no mere trading post but a permanent settlement, and immediately began building houses, rough but strong. Unfortunately, however, they had landed in a swampy area, and before long disease had killed more than half their number. Many returned to England with discouraging reports about the conditions and the system of government.

In 1609, a new expedition set out consisting of nine ships. The flagship was wrecked on Bermuda, providing Shakespeare with the theme for *The Tempest*. For the next ten years the settlers struggled on, enduring all forms of hardship. Eventually their life was made easier by the discovery of a plant which the Indians dried, burnt, and inhaled: tobacco. Captain John Rolfe, who had married the Indian princess, Pocahontas, took his bride and the seeds of this plant back to England. The smoking habit caught on and, in spite of strong opposition from the King, Virginia went tobacco-mad. Fortunes were made by small planters, and the consequent prosperity ensured the survival of the colony. But, in spite of this new cash crop, all was not well. The mortality rate remained enormous. Even with the arrival of more than one thousand new settlers, the population in 1621 was still only eight hundred and forty-three. By 1624 the position was so serious that the company's charter was withdrawn and Virginia became a Crown Colony. As a result, when Charles I succeeded his father, a period of prosperity began.

'The Mayflower' set sail in September with one hundred and two people aboard

Meanwhile, five hundred miles to the north of Jamestown, on the barren shore of what is today Massachusetts, a very different kind of settlement was fighting to survive, despite terrible weather and thin soil. Plymouth Plantation, as this settlement was called, had been founded in 1620 by the Pilgrim Fathers. These men had fled from Europe to find a new home where they would be able to practise their Puritan beliefs, free from the persecution which had forced them to flee from England to Holland; for even Holland, with its strange language and customs, was hardly a home.

On 6 September, *The Mayflower*, with one hundred and two people aboard, set sail from Plymouth, England. Unlike the settlers of Jamestown, most of whom were indentured labourers, the Pilgrim Fathers were predominantly middle-class artisans. They had no financial backers and nothing to rely on except their own skills and fortitude. From the very beginning they were not only well-organised

Fig. 9 *Parlour from the Thomas Hart House, Ipswich, Mass., built around 1640.*
(Metropolitan Museum of Art, New York.)
Fig. 10 *The Mayflower, seventeenth century. Drawing. No contemporary picture of The Mayflower is thought to exist, but this resembles most closely what is known of her. (National Maritime Museum, Greenwich.)*

9

Museum Photo

10

Mansell Collection

socially, but also able to provide for themselves more of the amenities of life than their counterparts in Jamestown. The characteristic Puritan values of religion, thrift and hard work ensured that in spite of rough conditions they would remain. When *The Mayflower* returned to England in 1621 not a single settler returned with her.

Virginia was Anglican. Farther north, the Dutch were settling on the Hudson River. They had pulled off the greatest property deal in history by purchasing the island of Manhattan from the Indians for sixty guilders' worth of beads. Still farther north, New England was strongly nonconformist. The Pilgrim Fathers had proved that life could be supported on 'a stern and rockbound coast'. By 1629 a royal charter had been granted to the Massachusetts Bay Company and, from then until the first rumblings of the English Civil War stopped all migration, the Bay Colony, as it was called, grew

fast. Unlike Virginia with its tobacco, New England's main cash crop was the cod which it dried and sent to Europe and the West Indies. So vital to trade was this fish that the 'sacred cod' was carved in wood and hung in the assembly chamber in Boston, where it remains to this day.

Throughout the seventeenth century the American colonies continued to expand. Connecticut, Rhode Island and New Hampshire were all being settled with varying degrees of success. The vast majority of these immigrants were middle-class tradesmen and farmers attracted by the promise of freedom and cheap land. Since there was no stigma placed on manual labour – far from it, in fact – communities grew up with their own local artisans. Throughout New England, blacksmiths, carpenters, tanners and weavers settled down to the trades they had learnt in England. Examples of their wares which survive show them to be similar to their equivalents in English villages, albeit rather cruder as a result of the scarcity of materials. The wooden houses of the period have high roofs which sweep down at the back in the style which is known as 'salt-box'. They had small leaded windows, low ceilings and tiny rooms, which could be heated throughout the freezing winters.

Contrary to what is popularly imagined, the early New Englanders did not dress in black with white ruffs and high black hats. They loved bright colours in clothes, houses and decorations. They made their own furniture and silver for both religious and domestic use. Indeed John Hull, one of the earliest silversmiths, was not only ship-owner, farmer and trader, but also a devout churchman and the Treasurer of the Colony. It was he who was responsible for the 'pine tree' shillings and sixpences, the earliest English colonial coinage, which were made from melted down Spanish pieces-of-eight and other silver objects.

Burke asked to be sent 'Two good New England Pacers'

In addition to the domestic arts and crafts, there also began the earliest forms of organised industry. In 1645 an ironworks was constructed which produced pots, pans, anchors and chains. Livestock was also bred, and with such success that when, in 1772, Edmund Burke needed horses he wrote to a friend in New York asking to be sent 'Two good New England Pacers'.

Throughout the seventeenth century, the east coast of America continued to attract settlers. Lord Baltimore, a friend of Charles I, was given what is today the state of Maryland. Unlike the other colonies, it was run extremely efficiently as a strictly commercial enterprise. Not only did it make a large fortune for his Lordship, but it also set new standards for good government and religious toleration. This was all the more surprising because the area was settled largely by Catholics.

Of all the new colonies founded during the late seventeenth century, none was more humane than Pennsylvania. The colony was founded by the Quaker William Penn, a philosopher who was later to write that 'an institution is the lengthened shadow of one man'; nowhere was this more true than in Pennsylvania. Penn himself was the son of an admiral, who left him a modest fortune. This was used to provide a refuge for Quakers who, like their

Puritan predecessors, wished to leave the corrupt and harsh English society.

In 1681 Penn obtained a charter from Charles II guaranteeing him ownership of a large tract of land. With this he launched a campaign to attract Quakers from all over Europe. His intention was not to make money, but rather to attempt a holy experiment. Unlike many of the early colonists he was just to the Indians, although his son was not averse to what some might consider to be rather sharp practice. He signed an agreement with the Indians under which he would receive a piece of land 'as far as a man can go in a day and a half'. To take advantage of this novel clause he had a track cleared and then hired the three fastest runners he could find. Together with some Indians who had come along to see fair play, he set off. The Indians tried to persuade the runners to rest, or at least to walk, but they soon gave up in disgust. As one of them said bitterly, 'No sit down to smoke, no shoot squirrel, just run, run, run all day'.

Pennsylvania was a success by any standard. Its basis of toleration, freedom and good government was the foundation on which the Founding Fathers were to build when they came to draw up the Declaration of Independence.

By the beginning of the eighteenth century there were eleven colonies stretching from New Hampshire to South Carolina, with a total population of almost three hundred thousand. The pressure for land was such that settlers were already pushing westwards across the Appalachians and Alleghenies, a process which continues today with the flood of people moving into California. Gradually the hotchpotch of colonies was brought under the direct control of England and the beginnings of unity became apparent. Economically they were still very dependent on England, and in society and

1

The Bettman Archive

12

The Bettman Archive

Fig. 11 **Capen House,** *Topsfield, Mass., built in 1683, recently restored.*
This wooden building, with its overhanging first and second storeys and small-paned windows, shows the influence of contemporary English architecture.

Fig. 12 **Scotch-Boardman House,** *Saugus, Mass., built in 1651.*
Built in the style known as 'salt-box', this steep-roofed house is typical of New England architecture in the seventeenth century. It is far rougher than the white clapboard style later to be adopted in this area.

Fig. 13 **'The manner of their Fishing'** *by John White, early seventeenth century.*
Water-colour.
This charming educational drawing is one of a large series by White depicting the customs of the Indians.
(British Museum.)

13

Michael Holford Library

the arts the settlers tended to imitate the latest styles and fads from across the Atlantic. But a few signs of independence were beginning to become clear. In most fields of design there was a time-lag of at least thirty years, especially in the sphere of silver design. But it was this uneasy dependence, both social and economic, which contained the seeds of revolt – a revolt which would re-draw the map of America before the century was out.

PLACES TO VISIT IN 'COLONIAL AMERICA'

Plymouth Rock, Plymouth, Mass. The spot where the Bay Colony Pilgrim Fathers are traditionally believed to have landed in 1620. There is also an authentic replica of *The Mayflower* moored in the harbour, which is open to visitors daily.

Jamestown, Virginia. The Historical Park with its reconstruction of the original town of Jamestown, founded in 1607, is open daily to visitors. In the harbour are replicas of the *Susan Constant*, the *Godspeed* and the *Discovery*, in which the colonists arrived in the New World.

Mystic, Connecticut. This charming colonial seaport has recently been restored and reconstructed to give an accurate idea of life in early New England.

Colonial Williamsburg, Virginia. The beautifully restored eighteenth-century capital of Virginia.

Furniture for Pilgrim Homes

Museum Photo

Transglobe

Fig. 2 *Keeping-room*, American, seventeenth century.
Of typical early colonial type, this living-room, or parlour, has a low ceiling and a scarcity of windows. Despite the enforced crudeness and simplicity of their furniture, it has a certain functional charm very attractive to modern eyes.
(The American Museum in Britain, Claverton Manor, Bath.)

Fig. 3 *Slat-back single chair*, New Jersey, c.1710.
Maple with a rush seat.
There were many different chair designs in colonial America, but all seem old-fashioned in comparison with English examples of the same period. Most single chairs were assembled from turned members, as is this example, but the seats varied. The simplest type was plain timber, which would have been softened with a cushion, but leather, held in place with large brass-headed nails, and woven rush were also popular, and undoubtedly more comfortable.
(H. F. du Pont Winterthur Museum.)

Fig. 1 *Chest of drawers* probably by Thomas Dennis, Massachusetts, 1678. Carved and painted wood, width 44¾ ins. Made for John and Margaret Staniford, this elaborate chest has the date 1678 carved in the centre of the top drawer. It is ornamented with Elizabethan strap-work carving and applied turning, and the whole is brightly painted. It was very likely made, as was the custom of the time, when the young couple were setting up home.
(Henry Francis du Pont Winterthur Museum, Winterthur, Delaware.)

Furniture in the early colonies was simple; made from local woods, it was essentially functional, although its purity of line and proportion gives it a quality pleasing to the modern eye

The first English settlers in North America attempted, between 1586 and 1603, to establish themselves in Virginia, a name given to the area in honour of Queen Elizabeth I. It was not until 1620, with the arrival of *The Mayflower* and *The Speedwell* and their cargo of one hundred and twenty dissenters, that colonisation was successfully begun.

The men and women came to a strange and hostile land with little hope of returning, and once their own small stock of supplies was expended they had to fend for themselves in every way. The settlers had the task of providing their own food, shelter, and any other requirements from the sea and the forest. Trees were felled to clear the land for cultivation and to provide timber for buildings as well as for such furniture as was essential. This latter would have been of the simplest description and has perished long ago.

Doubtless each arrival had with him a chest holding clothing and other belongings; beds would have been little more than a pile of skins on a wooden floor, while plain stools, benches and tables would have been knocked together as soon as time allowed.

The oldest surviving pieces of furniture made in the country date from the third quarter of the seventeenth century, and owe their continued preservation to the fact that they are outstanding examples in one way or another. They are complex in design involving skilful workmanship, and therefore have an artistic attraction causing them to be appreciated and cared for by successive owners.

Such pieces can be authenticated by the type of timber of which they were made. Oak was most frequently used in England for much of the century

and the same applied to America, but the species found there was lighter in colour and reveals its origin to an expert. Pine, maple and other local woods were also employed by the colonists, but being relatively soft these woods are less durable and articles made from them are not plentiful.

The appearance of pieces was dictated by the skill of the makers, by the available materials, and by the taste and wealth of buyers. The latter not only led an enforced, unsophisticated existence in the new colony, but had in many instances come from provincial homes and were unaware of urban modishness; the younger people born in New England knew little, if anything, of smart London styles.

In the seventeenth century the time-lag between town and country was a matter of several years – a city style did not influence outlying towns and villages for a decade or more. An even longer interval elapsed between the adoption of an innovation in the capital and its appearance in, for instance, far away Virginia. Thus it is frequently found that what was currently appealing to the colonists had been popular in England as much as thirty years or half a century earlier.

Boxes held Bibles and other precious possessions

The variety of articles was limited by the comparatively elementary requirements of users. Chairs which were reserved for the head of the household were outnumbered by stools and benches; tables were of various sizes according to needs; boxes held Bibles and other precious possessions. The list is completed with beds, chests and cupboards. The two last-named were the pieces to which much attention was paid. At first, as in Europe, the chest was no more than a large box with a hinged lid; then a drawer was added in the base (Fig. 6). Finally the rising lid was dispensed with and it became the chest of drawers (Fig. 1). Of all New England furniture, it was given the most distinctive appearance and is unlikely to be confused with a similar piece made elsewhere in the world.

Cupboards followed English lines, with the two-tiered Elizabethan and Jacobean court type and the enclosed buffet being made as late as 1680. Although sometimes ornamented with carving similar to that found on their prototypes, the use of American timber is a pointer to their origin. At about the same date others were ornamented with applied turned sections, split in half and painted black to provide a contrast with the background.

A further feature of chests and of some other pieces was the use of paint to emphasise or replace carving (Fig. 12). Red and yellow were popular, and their use must have helped to brighten house interiors relying for their daytime illumination on small panes of glass, or more often on sheets of semi-opaque oiled paper.

Of the men who actually made the surviving furniture little is known, and many of the attributions are to an area rather than to a person. A notable exception is a chest, on the back of which is inscribed: 'Mary Allines Chistt Cutte and Joyned by Nich. Disbrowe'. Disbrowe would appear to have been born in Essex, England, in about 1612, and by 1639 was living in Hartford, Connecticut. The chest has been dated to about 1680 when Mary Allyn was twenty-three years of age. It would have been her 'hope' chest, for holding the trousseau she was to need in 1686, on her marriage to John Whiting.

Many of the chests were made as 'hope' or 'dower' chests

No other pieces made by Disbrowe have come to light, but similar examples to the single survivor are known as 'Hadley' chests. They gained their name from the town of Hadley, Massachusetts, and are distinguished by their carved decoration of entwined flowers and leaves covering the entire front surface, often centring on the initials of their first owner. A study of the initials has shown that most of the original possessors lived in or about Hadley, where the chests were made between the years 1675 and 1740.

Comparable chests, with hinged tops and one or more drawers in the base, came from elsewhere in the Valley. They are known variously as 'Tulip', 'Sunflower', 'Connecticut' or 'Hartford' chests. Each has the upper portion of the front divided into three panels which are carved with formal representations of sunflowers or tulips and have additional ornament in the shape of split turnings, painted black and applied to relieve the otherwise plain uprights (Fig. 6).

The foregoing piece may be compared with the chest illustrated in Fig. 1. It was probably made by Thomas Dennis of Ipswich, Massachusetts, for John and Margaret Staniford; in the centre of the bottom drawer is carved the date 1678. The chest is not only carved with strap-work of Elizabethan pattern, but bears applied turning and is brightly painted. The carving and other details are accented with colour, and the overall effect may be thought to reflect the aspirations of a couple setting up house.

The fact that many of the chests were made specifically as 'hope' or 'dower' chests, and were embellished with the initials of their owners and sometimes with the date of their making, has undoubtedly led to their preservation; articles with less intimate associations have been discarded long ago. Most of these chests are now in museums where, even if they no longer have a practical function, they are kept safely for all to see.

Chairs of the time varied in their design, but again are old-fashioned in comparison with contemporary English examples. In most cases they are assembled from turned members supporting a seat of plain timber, which was made more comfortable with a cushion. Alternatively, there were seats of woven rushes (Fig. 3) or of leather, the latter held in place by large brass-headed nails.

The first Governor of Plymouth Plantation, John Carver, who came over with the Pilgrim Fathers,

4

Fig. 4 **Table or candle-stand,**
Connecticut, late seventeenth century. Maple and pine, painted red, height 23 ins.
This sturdy little stand once belonged to Peregrine White, who was born on The Mayflower *in Cape Cod Harbour in the year 1620.*
(American Museum in Britain.)

D. Balmer

5

Museum Photo

6

gave his name to one type of armchair. It has stout turned uprights and plain round stretchers joining the legs, and the back contains three horizontal turnings of which the lower two are linked by three turned uprights (Fig. 10). The seat is of rush, and the chair has a heavy throne-like appearance to be expected in the seat of someone who was in authority.

Another historic armchair is the one which once belonged to an Elder of the Plantation, William Brewster, and is preserved in Pilgrim Hall, Plymouth, Massachusetts. Like the carver it is made from lengths of turning and has a rush seat. It differs from it, however, by having the back inset with two rows of short uprights, while the same arrangement appears between the front legs

Fig. 5 **Cabinet,** *perhaps by James Symonds, Salem, Massachusetts, for Thomas and Sarah Buffington, 1676. Oak, cedar and maple, with the initials TSB. Height 17¼ ins. (H. F. du Pont Winterthur Museum.)*

Fig. 6 **Chest,** *Connecticut, 1670–90. Oak and pine, the front three panels carved with a tulip pattern and the middle one centring on the initials WSR. Width 4 ft. (American Museum in Britain.)*

and at each side. The carver and brewster armchairs were copied, usually with some variations in design, from about 1650 onwards. The principal difference lies in the number of turned uprights in the back and elsewhere, which are frequently fewer in number than in the prototypes. While both of these chairs had their back turnings running vertically, a third type featured horizontal flat strips of wood. The descriptive term 'slat-back' is usually applied to them in the United States, although comparable English versions are generally known as 'ladder-backs'. The example shown in Fig. 8 was made in New England in the last quarter of the seventeenth century, and is constructed of

Fig. 8 **Slat-back armchair,** *New England, late seventeenth century. Maple, ash and oak. Of the same design as the English chairs known as 'ladder-backs', chairs of this type were very popular in the colonies. This example, which was probably intended for the head of a household, has not only a rush seat, but also a seat cushion for extra comfort. (American Museum in Britain.)*

Fig. 9 **Armchair,** *New York, late seventeenth century. Of crude construction, this massive chair follows an English Jacobean pattern current about 1620. (H. F. du Pont Winterthur Museum.)*

7

8

9

D. Balmer

Museum Photo

Museum Photo

Fig. 7 **Chest of drawers on stand,** *Boston, c.1700. Pine wood veneered with burr maple, the legs of birch painted to match, width 40¼ ins. (H. F. du Pont Winterthur Museum.)*

maple, ash and oak.

Confusingly, present-day writers in the United States describe a normal armchair as a 'carver', and refer to eighteenth-century and later sets of chairs as comprising, say, 'six singles and a pair of carvers'. Thus the original chair belonging to John Carver has given rise to a generic term, and has kept alive the name of one of the founding-fathers of the country.

The stool was made from various woods, and does not differ greatly in appearance from those that must have been recollected by the older settlers existing in their youth (Fig. 13). No doubt they were once plentiful, but hard use over the years has resulted in scarcity today. The same remarks apply to long benches or forms, which were con-

structed in a similar manner to the stools. Both were made with mortise and tenon joints held together with wooden pegs or dowels, and both were subject to equally heavy wear and tear.

Then, as now, tables were an important feature of a room. Large ones were given sturdy bases of oak and a removable top, so that if the space was required the whole article stacked easily out of the way. The top was not always of the same timber as the base, but as it was usually covered with a cloth or carpet this disparity was of little importance.

Smaller tables followed European patterns, with turned legs united by plain stretchers and sometimes having carving on the front of the frieze drawer. Some of them were based more on Dutch

American
Colonial Furniture

Fig. 10 *Armchair of carver type,*
New England, late seventeenth
century. Named after the first
governor of Plymouth
Plantation, John Carver.
(American Museum in Britain.)

10

Fig. 11 *Chest of drawers, New*
England, late seventeenth
century. Mahogany and pine.
Width 41 ins.
(American Museum in Britain.)

Fig. 12 *Toilet Table, Boston,*
c.1700. Painted wood.
Width 31⅛ ins.
(H. F. du Pont Winterthur
Museum.)

Fig. 13 *Joint stool, Boston area,*
c.1700. Walnut, height 23 ins.
In the early colonies, the great
simplicity of household
furnishings meant that chairs
were, in general, reserved for
the head of a household. Stools
and benches were used by the
rest of the family, and few have
survived the hard daily use given
them over the years.
(H. F. du Pont Winterthur
Museum.)

11

12

13

than on English prototypes, with shaped and pierced brackets providing stability and decoration where the legs joined the horizontal members below the top. Another type, the gate-legged table, with additional legs at each side to swing outwards and support the hinged top, began to appear at the end of the century. It was made either with open swing-legs to match the remainder of the underframe, or with the gate of solid triangular form which earned it the name of 'butterfly-table'.

The foregoing does not exhaust the list of what was in daily use among the colonists. Not least was the Bible-box, mentioned earlier, which was used for holding documents and other personal property. Other minor pieces of furniture must have come and gone without leaving a trace of their existence, but a few have withstood the passage of time. An example is the simple table in Fig. 4, which once belonged to Peregrine White, who made his entry into the world in 1620 aboard *The Mayflower* in Cape Cod harbour.

Although the earliest of the arrivals in the country must have had austere homes, a greater degree of comfort became possible once a stable community was established. This largely took the form of colourful curtains, cushions and table-covers, which have now vanished. Records of them remain in inventories, and one made following the death of Major-General Edward Gibbons, of Boston, noted: 'thirty-one cushions, of which eleven were window cushions, four damask, four velvet, two leather, and two Turkey-work'. The latter was a variety of coarse work made in imitation of Turkey carpeting.

The men who laboured to furnish the homes of New England had no illusions about their skill or the unsophisticated nature of their output. The great majority of them described themselves as 'joiners', and the first record of a cabinet-maker does not occur until 1681. He was named John Clark, of whom nothing else is known except that he worked in Boston, and is the sole representative of those superior craftsmen to be so described in documents prior to 1700. By that date the population of the country was expanding very rapidly, villages and hamlets were becoming sizeable towns and the standard of living was fast catching up with that of Europe.

MUSEUMS AND COLLECTIONS

Early American furniture may be seen at the following:

Boston:	Boston Museum of Fine Arts
New York:	Metropolitan Museum of Art
	Brooklyn Museum
Sturbridge, Mass:	Old Sturbridge Village
Winterthur, Delaware:	Henry Francis du Pont Winterthur Museum

FURTHER READING

American Furniture by Helen Comstock, 1980 reprint.

American Antique Furniture by E. G. Miller, 1966 reprint.

Furniture of the Pilgrim Century by Wallace Nutting, reprint.

Furniture Treasury, 3 vols., by Wallace Nutting.

Early American Furniture Makers by Thomas H. Ormsbee, 1975 reprint.

The Look of the New World

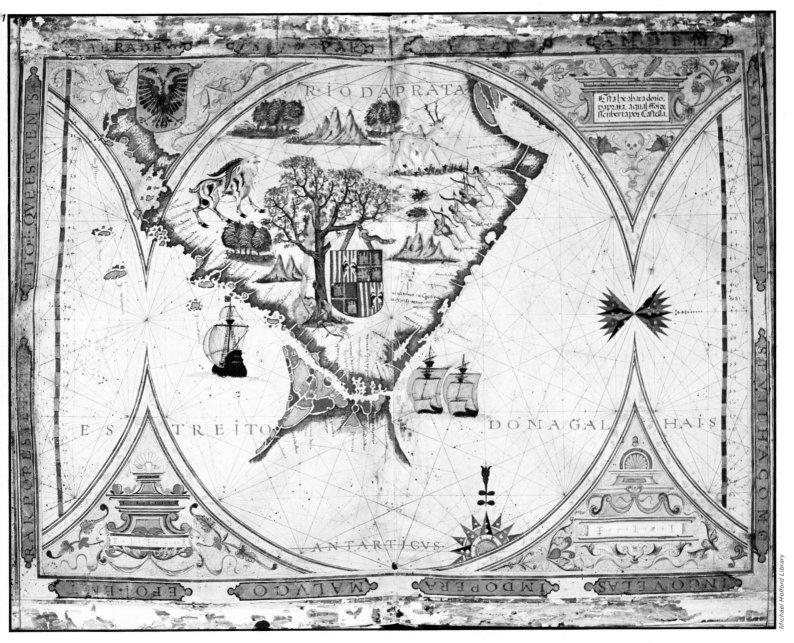

Michael Holford Library

As well as being objects of great beauty in their own right, maps played a crucial part in the explorations of the New World. Covered with fanciful drawings and references to such tantalising concepts as *El Dorado*, they must often have helped to spur the explorers on, even when times were difficult and their vigour and idealism began to fail them

Fig. 1 **Map of South America and the Magellan Straits** *by Fernão Vaz Dourado, 1568. Manuscript.*

Fernão Vaz Dourado (c.1520–80) was a Portuguese cartographer of great importance, who spent a large part of his life in Goa, a Portuguese dominion on the western coast of India. Many of Vaz Dourado's maps were engraved in Holland during the late sixteenth and early seventeenth centuries. They spread throughout Europe, and had a lasting effect on European cartography. He is known to have made seven illuminated sea atlases in manuscript form between the years 1568 and 1580. The map reproduced is from the earliest of these.
(Collection of the Duke of Alba, Spain.)

Fig. 2 **Map of New Belgium and New England** by Willem Blaeu *(1571–1636), 1635.*
Oriented somewhat confusingly with west to the top, this map shows New Amsterdam, now New York, with its rival English settlements farther up the coast. (Weinreb and Douwma Ltd., London.)

Fig. 3 **Map of Virginia and Florida** *from the Mercator-Hondius Atlas, 1635*
Gerhard Mercator (1512–94) was the most celebrated geographer of the Renaissance. He is best known for the projection named after him which was first used on a map of the world in 1569 and is still in common use. His atlas which, incidentally, was the first work to use this title, appeared in three parts. The first came out in 1585, and the last a year after his death, in 1595. At this time, America had not as yet been adequately charted, and it was left to his successor, Jodocus Hondius (1563–1611), to add detailed maps of the new continent in his expanded edition of 1606. (Weinreb and Douwma Ltd.)

Christopher Columbus, who sailed westward in 1492 under the aegis of King Ferdinand and Queen Isabella of Spain and without the help of any map, believed, on reaching the shores of America, that he had reached the golden empires of Asia. Visions of the riches of Kubla Khan had whetted his appetite for, although 'The Great Khan' had died two hundred years before, Marco Polo's tales and pictures were still vivid in the mind of Europe. Then, when the Cubans referred to 'Cubanacan', by which they meant the middle of Cuba, Columbus heard only what he wished: 'El Gran Can'. Even on his death-bed many years later he still believed that he had been within nineteen days' sailing of the Ganges before he had had to turn back.

It is, therefore, not altogether unjust that the new continent was called America rather than Columbia; for while Amerigo Vespucci, another great explorer of the period, only set sail in 1497, five years after Columbus, at least he fervently believed that he had discovered a new world.

The name America (Land of Americus, the Latin version of Vespucci's christian name) first appeared on a map by Martin Waldseemüller in 1507. He gave Columbus his due, however, by pointing out in a special note on the map that Columbus had also made a large contribution to the effort. After its publication, the name America, with very few exceptions, was adopted by cartographers.

The search for a passage through to the 'South Seas' was the major concern of most explorers, secondary only, perhaps, to the search for gold. The Spanish concentrated mainly on South America, sending expeditions under Balboa (1475–1517), Cortes (1485–1547) and Magellan (c.1480–1521), who christened the Pacific Ocean in 1520. The Straits of Magellan, named in his honour, appear on some of the earliest maps of the new continent (Fig. 1).

The discovery of a northern passage to Asia, by sailing to the north of Canada or Russia, was to daunt many explorers from the Elizabethans onwards. Although they met with no success, their incidental discoveries such as the Great Lakes and the Hudson Bay were of considerable importance.

Incorrect theories and wild projections of personal hopes led to some odd mistakes on the part of cartographers. Due to a navigational oversight, the Chesapeake Bay was thought for some years to be a vast ocean, and a large number of maps show Florida and Canada joined only by a narrow isthmus.

Many errors were as firmly rooted in medieval lore as Columbus' unshakeable belief that the Orinoco River rose in Paradise. California was felt to be a Golden Island situated very close to the Garden of Eden. Even after the arid reality of the south-west coast had been reported, the point was debated for many years. Visscher's popular map of the Americas (Fig. 4) still showed it as an island as late as 1670 or '80 and, although the error was first corrected in 1700, it persisted on some maps until the middle of the century.

In the early days maps were used to give information about new ways of life and frequently included drawings of local costumes and wildlife as well as topographical features. It is these personal touches that give the early maps their charm and elegance, as well as a contemporary view of a new civilisation in the making, and make them so desirable to the collector.

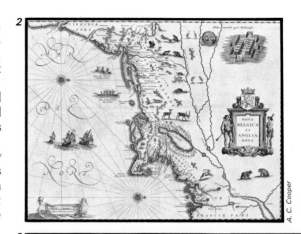

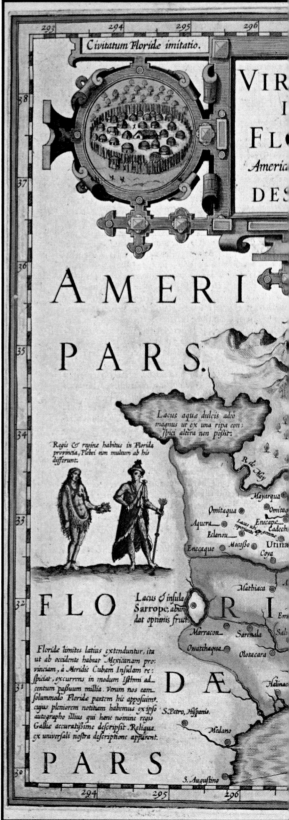

R. B. Fleming

Fig. 4 **Map of America** by Nicholas Visscher, c.1670–80.
Inserted into an atlas in the 1670s or '80s, this charming representation was popular for many years, and appeared in many versions copied from the original. Although it is billed as 'Novissima et Accuratissima' (the very newest and most accurate), it shows California as an island, a mistake which was not finally cleared up until well into the eighteenth century.
The cartouche describes the New World's celebrated 'never-fading Mines of Silver and Gold'. (British Museum, London.)

Fig. 5 **Map of the Gulf of Mexico** from De Bry's engravings, Vol. I, 1593.
Theodore de Bry (1528–98) was a Flemish engraver who, with his son Jean Theodore (1561–1623), established a printing firm in Frankfurt which did a great deal of work in cartography in the sixteenth century. (American Museum in Britain, Claverton Manor, Bath.)

D. Balmer

A. C. Cooper

Fig. 6 **Map of New Belgium** by N. Visscher, c.1655.

One of a large family of cartographers, three of whom confusingly bear the same name, Nicholas Visscher (1618–79) made many maps of the New World. He frequently signed his maps 'Piscator', the Latin word for fisher or Visscher, a charming renaissance conceit, so alien to the modern concept of scientific mapmakers, which is unfortunately not on the map illustrated. Depicting the east coast of America from the Chesapeake Bay to the St. Lawrence River, this map's most attractive feature is the fine view of New Amsterdam under the title.
(American Museum in Britain.)

Fig. 7 **Map of the World** *from the Atlas of Ortelius, the Latin name of the Flemish cartographer Abraham Ortell (1527–98), whose atlas, Theatrum Orbis Terrarum, first published in 1570, was the basis for many geographical works in succeeding years. It was the first modern atlas of the sort we know, and was based on contemporary charts and maps from many sources. In 1587, a much improved edition was brought out; this map from the year before shows South America still in an unshaped and inaccurate form, even though Ortelius had access to more correct maps by 1570.*
(American Museum in Britain.)

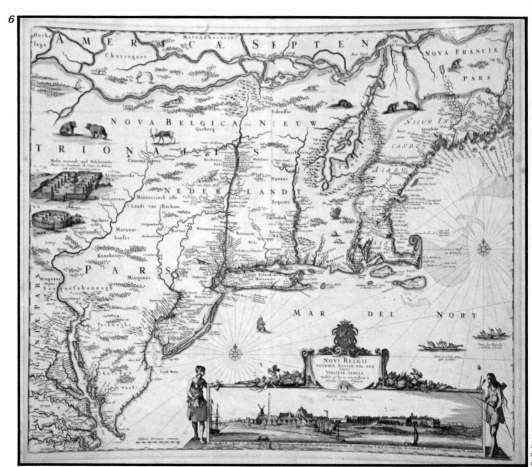

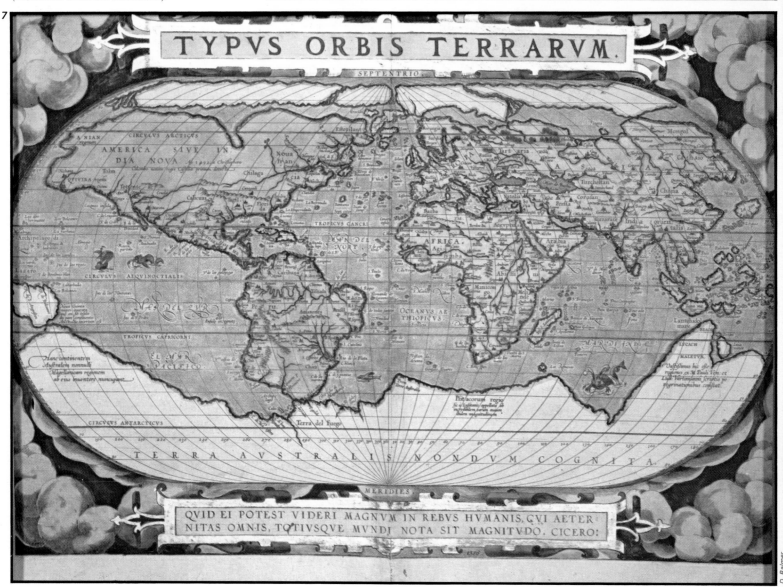

MATCHLOCKS AND BLUNDERBUSSESS

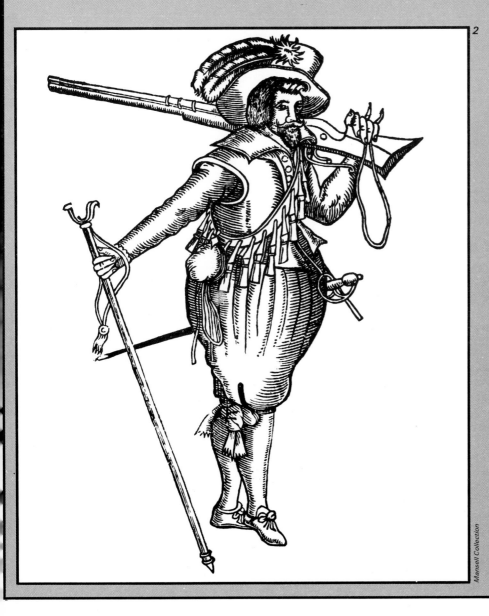

Most early arms used in the Colonies were made in Europe, though some repairs were done and new designs developed in America. Local gunmakers acquired the skill to take on serious production when the War of Independence began in 1776

In few countries have firearms played a more important part than in America; from the first arrival of the Spanish explorers, with their horses, armour and firearms, through to the Pilgrim Fathers and on to the Frontier days of the nineteenth century, firearms were an essential item of the colonists' equipment. Until the American War of Independence brought about the break with England, the majority of American firearms were, in fact, of European origin, most being imported from England, France and Germany. It needed the break of the Revolution to stimulate the growth of any real native firearms industry. That there were a number of gunsmiths in America is not to be doubted and repairs and replacements were carried out by American-born craftsmen, but the production of barrels and locks must have been on a very small scale.

Fig. 1 *Charleville Musket, French, 1777. Barrel length 42 ins., weight 9½ lbs. (Private Collection.)*

Fig. 2 *Musketeer with match lit at both ends in left hand. Woodcut after Jacob de Gheyn, 1607.*

Mansell Collection

3

Fig. 3 **Powder horn,** American,
c.1750.
*Made from cow horn and
engraved with a map of the
English forts along the Mohawk
River.*
*(H.M. Tower of London
Armouries.)*

Ministry of Public Building & Works: Crown Copyright

In the Americas of the sixteenth and seventeenth centuries the most common form of firearm was undoubtedly the matchlock, using a system of firearm ignition which had originated in Europe during the fourteenth century. This consisted of a pivoted arm, one end of which held a piece of burning cord treated with saltpetre; pressure on the trigger made the arm swing forward to press the glowing end into a pinch of powder placed adjacent to a small hole in the breech. This touch hole led through to the main charge inside the barrel which then took fire and discharged the bullet. Until the latter part of the seventeenth century this was the standard mechanism for military firearms and some of the earliest illustrations relevant to America, made during the middle of the sixteenth century, show the matchlock being used against the Indians. The flash, smoke, roar and lethal effect of the matchlock must have made a tremendous impression on the natives.

The mechanism was fitted on two main types of weapon, the musket and the caliver which, by the seventeenth century, differed only in size. Muskets were long and weighed up to twenty pounds (Fig. 4); indeed, so barrel-heavy were they that it was necessary for the musketeer to carry a rest, a pole surmounted by a U-shaped arm, which he used to support and steady the barrel of the musket when aiming and firing. Calivers were shorter and lighter and did not necessitate the use of a rest.

To ensure that the musketeer was always prepared, both ends of the match were lit

The matchlock system was simple and reliable but very inconvenient. Undoubtedly the greatest single handicap was the need to maintain a glowing end to the match; to ensure that the musketeer was always prepared, both ends of the match were lit so that a reserve means of ignition was to hand (Fig. 2). Obviously, with the presence of loose gunpowder in close proximity to glowing matches, the risk of accidental explosion was high. Even professional soldiers such as the hero of early Virginia, Captain John Smith, were not immune to such accidents; he once received severe burns when a lighted match ignited some gunpowder he was carrying loose in his pocket. The match was obviously very much at the mercy of wind and weather and there are contemporary accounts of sudden Indian attacks catching the colonists with unlit matches.

Early in the sixteenth century an alternative method of ignition, which used a mechanical means to ignite the powder, was produced. This system, known as the wheel-lock, was, in comparison with the matchlock, a complex piece of mechanism. Consequently it was expensive to produce and very susceptible to damage. As the majority of the colonists were hardly men of substance, the number of wheel-lock pistols and long arms used in early America was probably limited. There are references in inventories and accounts of the sixteenth century to wheel-locks but archaeological excavations have revealed scant evidence of their use. It is unlikely that there were any American-produced wheel-locks and it may safely be assumed that all such weapons were imported from Germany and Italy (Fig. 4, lower picture).

Although the wheel-lock was an alternative to the matchlock, its high cost limited its adoption; but there was a simpler, cheaper method of mechanical ignition available. This system operated on the principle that a piece of flint, struck sharply against a steel surface, produced small sparks of incandescent steel. A shaped piece of flint was gripped in an arm which, activated by a variety of mechanical systems, swung forward through an arc. Above the pan which held a small priming charge of gunpowder was the battery, a flat steel plate so positioned that, as the arm swung forward, the sharpened edge of the flint scraped down the steel surface to produce the required sparks. To protect the priming charge against wind and weather, a sliding pan-cover was fitted on these locks. This basic lock is known to collectors as the snaphaunce, but, apart from some produced in northern Italy, examples of such weapons are comparatively scarce. Some certainly found their way to America as proved by archaeological evidence from the sites of such long established colonies as Jamestown.

American snaphaunces, if such there were, enjoyed only a limited life, for early in the seventeenth century a simpler, more reliable and cheaper method of ignition was produced by a French gunsmith known as Marin le Bourgeoys. This type of lock differs from the snaphaunce, not in principle, but in operation; in the flintlock, the steel from which the sparks are struck is united with the pan cover into a single L-shaped piece of metal.

Second-best quality items were earmarked for the colonial market

Another innovation which appeared with the flint-lock was the incorporation of a safety position into the mechanism. The metal arm holding the flint, known as the cock, could be moved to an upright position where it was locked into place by a hook-shaped arm known as the dog, situated at the rear of the cock. Accidental, or indeed deliberate, pressure on the trigger could not activate the lock and the weapon could be carried in safety. Archaeological evidence indicates that the doglock was fairly common in America and this may well have been because English gunsmiths, who soon abandoned the system at home, exported obsolete stocks to the colonies. This was certainly the position later on, when second-best quality items were earmarked for the colonial market.

The flint-lock with its simpler internal mechanism, more reliable action and lower production costs, soon began to replace other ignition systems. There are many references which show that in the latter part of the seventeenth century the Colonial militia and similar forces were exchanging their matchlock muskets for flint-lock weapons and, by the early eighteenth century, the flint-lock was nearly supreme.

During the late seventeenth and eighteenth centuries, the expansion of the colonies and the severe fighting between French and English forces meant that the number of English troops stationed in America increased. The tremendous distances involved, and the slow methods of transport, made it difficult to maintain supplies; consequently gunsmiths working in the colonies were called upon to repair, re-stock, and occasionally make, military firearms. It is not surprising that the locally produced weapons differed little from the English-made model although there were small local differences due mainly to the predominance of some particular national community in the area. Guns produced around the Hudson Valley area,

gunmakers used maple or black walnut.

Increased immigration, from England and Europe, resulted in a larger number of resident gunmakers and led to the gradual development of a native firearms industry. This in turn led to the production of one of the most characteristic

Fig. 4 (above) *Matchlock musket and rest*, English, c.1620. Overall length 66 ins., barrel length 48 ins. Early muskets were so barrel-heavy that a rest was required in order to support and steady the gun while firing. (below) *Wheel-lock carbine*, German, c.1650. Overall length 37 ins., barrel length 25 ins. Carried by harquebusiers, or members of the cavalry, guns of this sort were hooked on to a belt over the left shoulder with a spring clip. (H.M. Tower of London Armouries.)

Fig. 5 *Ferguson flint-lock cavalry carbine*, East India Company, signed and dated, Henry Nock of London, 1776. Overall length 44½ ins. This type of rifle was developed by Captain Patrick Ferguson of the 70th Regiment and it had a very efficient breech-loading system. The trigger-guard rotates, thereby unscrewing the breech-plug. (Sotheby and Co., London.)

Fig. 6 *Two pairs of pistols.* (above) *Pair of pistols*, French c.1610. Overall length 21 ins., barrel length 15 ins. (below) *Pair of pistols*, Dutch, c.1625. Overall length 20 ins., barrel length 14 ins. The barrels of both pairs are longer than those of later pistols because gunpowder in the seventeenth century was of such low quality that plenty of time was required for it to ignite and build up pressure. The lock plates lack studs and catches, a characteristic of later pistols of this sort. (H.M. Tower of London Armouries.)

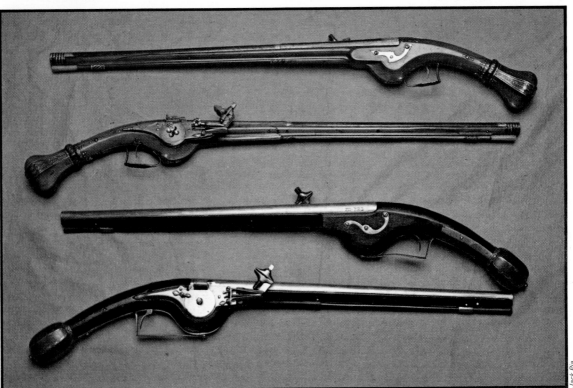

which contained a large Dutch population, seem to have been fitted with rather large, bulky stocks (the wooden body of the weapon), whilst in New England the outline of the weapon was fairly slim and graceful. English firearms were mostly stocked with walnut, but, since this wood was not so readily available in America, the native

American firearms: the so-called Kentucky, or Pennsylvania, long rifle. This weapon evolved from the German Jaeger, or hunting rifle, and had a barrel about forty to forty-five inches in length, normally octagonal in section and with the maker's name marked in some way on the top face. Some makers engraved their names in full whilst others

7

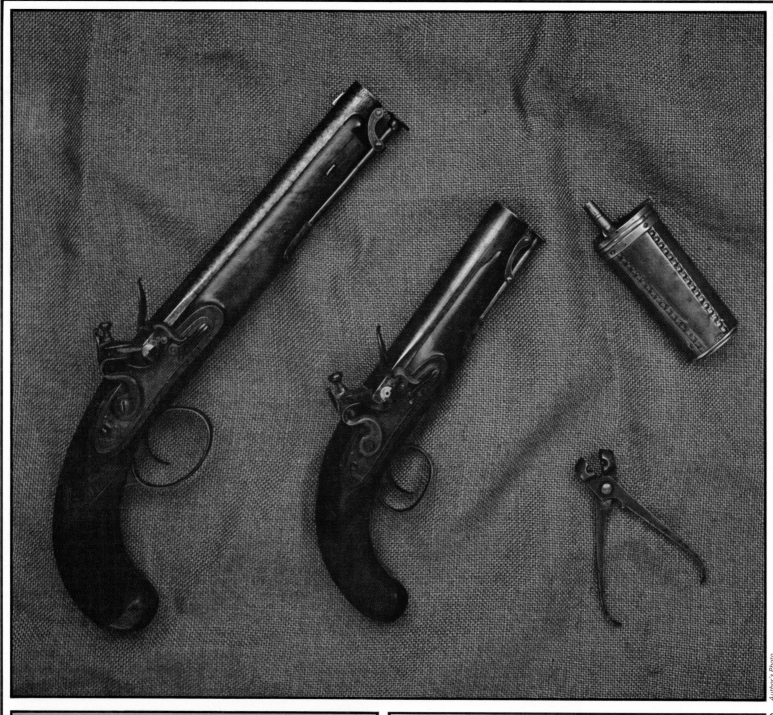

Author's Photo

8

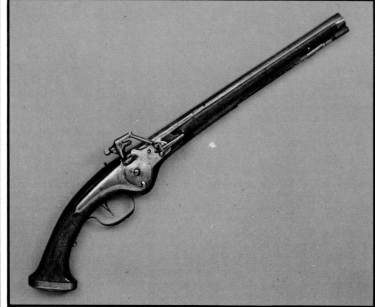

Author's Photo

9

Author's Photo

Fig. 7 (from left to right)
Pistol *by Henry Nock of London (1741–1804), late eighteenth century. Overall length 10½ ins., barrel length 6 ins., bore .8 ins.*
Pistol *by William Parker (1792–1840), English, early nineteenth century. Overall length 15 ins., barrel length 8½ ins., bore .6 ins. Like the previous pistol, this has a captive ramrod, secured by a link to prevent loss.*
Copper powder-flask *with brass pourer.*
Bullet Mould, *into which molten lead was poured. The mould was held closed for the moulding process, then opened after a few seconds to release the bullet. The clipper between the handles was then used to remove the 'tail', leaving a round pellet. Private Collection.)*

Fig. 8 **Wheel-lock pistol,** *one of a pair, Dutch, c.1640. Overall length 20½ ins., barrel length 14 ins., bore .45 ins. (Private Collection.)*

Mansell Collection

Fig. 9 **Blunderbuss** *by Smart, English, mid-eighteenth century Brass barrel, overall length 29 ins., barrel length 14 ins. (below) **Blunderbuss** by H. W. Mortimer, English, late eighteenth century. Overall length 30 ins., barrel length 14½ ins. (Private Collection.)*

Fig. 10 **Pikeman,** *protector of the musketeer while he was reloading. Woodcut after Jacob de Gheyn, 1607.*

merely used their initials. The barrel was attached to the wooden stock by pins which passed through the wood and engaged with lugs fitted beneath the barrel. Stocks were of plain maple or, occasionally, curly maple or walnut. Some were carved, but the great majority were fitted with brass inlay, the most noticeable feature of which was a cover for a recessed patch-box fitted into the butt. In this box were carried small pieces of waxed linen to wrap around the bullets before they were pushed home down the barrel. A very obvious feature of these rifles was the down-sloping, gracefully narrow butt, although this feature seems to have been far less pronounced on the earliest models and was not fully developed until the end of the eighteenth century. Genuine Pennsylvania long rifles are extremely rare and always command a very high price in the sale rooms. Many were converted from flint-lock to later systems of ignition, and such weapons are less in demand although they still realise quite good prices.

Specifications for weapons were drawn up by local Committees of Public Safety

An outstanding feature of these long-barrelled weapons was their greatly increased accuracy due to rifling, or grooving; but its use was limited during the eighteenth century because of the considerable technical problems involved in cutting grooves on the inside of the barrel. Another rifle closely associated with the American colonies, and particularly with the American War of Independence, was the Ferguson rifle (Fig. 5). This weapon, designed by Captain Patrick Ferguson of the 70th Regiment, was issued to a unit of one hundred well-trained men during the American War of Independence (1776–83). It was a weapon far in advance of its contemporaries, for it used a breech-loading system: instead of the old laborious process of pouring gunpowder down the barrel and then driving home the bullet with a long, thin ramrod (normally carried in a recess in the stock beneath the barrel), the ball and powder could be placed directly into the breech. Access was obtained by rotating the trigger guard which, in turn, lowered a specially designed breech plug which normally closed the loading aperture. Captain Ferguson lost his life in the American War of Independence at the Battle of King's Mountain in 1780. This very satisfactory weapon was never exploited and few military examples have survived.

With the outbreak of hostilities against the mother country, the colonists were cut off from their normal sources of supply. Although the French later came to their assistance and supplied large numbers of muskets and pistols the colonists were, at first, forced to fall back on their own very limited resources. If the English Army was to be defeated, the greatest need was for muskets and the specifications for these weapons were drawn up by the local *ad hoc* groups, usually known as the Committees of Public Safety, which were formed to govern the various colonies. They naturally tended to copy English models and, although these muskets were produced by individual contractors, they are all very similar to the standard English 'Brown Bess' musket.

One weapon so often associated with the first American colonists is the blunderbuss (Fig. 9). Available evidence suggests that few of these wide-muzzled weapons found their way to America before the eighteenth century. The basic idea behind the design was that a widening barrel would ensure that the shot also spread over a wide area. Experiments have shown that this is not the case and diameter of muzzle has only a limited effect. Those blunderbusses which did reach America during the eighteenth century were mostly English in origin and had barrels of brass or steel.

Prior to the outbreak of the American War of Independence in 1776, the vast majority of firearms used in America were English rather than American-produced, but the position changed rapidly after this date. Pressures of the war forced the colonists to set up their own arsenals, one at Harper's Ferry in Virginia, and the other at Springfield, Massachusetts. The design of the weapons produced there was very similar to French models, since France had supplied quantities of arms to the colonists.

Associated with these early American firearms are a number of accessories of which the most highly prized are powder horns carved with contemporary maps (Fig. 3). These articles were made from pieces of cow horn which were then engraved by some of the soldiers with maps of the area in which they fought. Unfortunately, the demand for such items has encouraged the production of numerous spurious pieces.

To sum up, it must be said that very few firearms made prior to 1776, long arms or pistols, can be positively identified as being of American origin; consequently, genuine pieces are invariably much sought after and highly priced.

MUSEUMS AND COLLECTIONS

American firearms may be seen at the following:

Mass: Armory Museum, Springfield, Pilgrim Hall, Plymouth

New York: Metropolitan Museum of Art West Point Museum

Virginia: Colonial National Historical Park, Yorktown. Colonial Williamsburg Magazine and Guard House

FURTHER READING

The Pennsylvania-Kentucky Rifle by Henry J. Kauffman, Harrisburg, Pennsylvania, 1960.

Arms and Armour in Colonial America 1526–1783 by Harold L. Peterson, New York, 1956.

Early American Gunsmiths 1650–1850 by Henry J. Kauffman, Harrisburg, Pennsylvania, 1952.

The Warner Collector's Guide to American Longarms by Michael H. Madaus, New York, 1981.

Firearms in Colonial America, 1492–1792, by M. L. Brown, Washington, D.C., 1980.

Historical Treasury of American Guns by Harold Peterson, 1966.

Fig. 1 **Porringers** by John Coney (1656–1722) and Peter van Inburgh (1689–1740). (Yale University Art Gallery, New Haven, Connecticut. Mabel Brady Garvan Collection.)

Fig. 2 **Beaker and Porringer** by Robert Sanderson (1608–93) and John Hull (1624–83), Boston, 1659 and c.1655. (Loaned by the First Church, Boston Museum of Fine Arts.)

Museum Photo

Sandak Inc.

Sandak Inc.

Fig. 3 **Standing salt, candlestick, sugar castor and tankard** by John Coney, Edward Winslow (1669–1753) and Henry Hurst (c.1665–1717), Boston, c.1700–10. (Boston Museum of Fine Arts.)

Fig. 4 **Caudle cup** by Robert Sanderson, Boston, c.1680. (Henry Francis du Pont Winterthur Museum, Winterthur, Delaware.)

Fig. 5 **Monteith** by John Coney, Boston, early eighteenth century. (Yale University Art Gallery. Garvan Collection.)

Museum Photo

Museum Photo

6

A. C. Cooper

7

Museum Photo

Fig. 6 **Sugar-box** by John Coney, Boston, c.1700. Length 7¼ ins. Only three of these very rare caskets made by Coney survive. (Christie's, London.)

Fig. 7 **Punch-bowl** by Jeremiah Dummer (1645–1718), Boston, c.1692. Height 3¼ ins., diameter 6¾ ins. (Yale University Art Gallery.)

Simplicity in Silver

The pilgrims newly arrived in America brought with them many skills, not the least of which was silversmithing. The pieces they created are some of the most interesting in the history of American craftsmanship

There was no silversmith listed among the hundred and two 'Saints and Strangers' who landed at Plymouth, Massachusetts, in the little ship, *The Mayflower* three hundred and fifty years ago, but the men and women who made that voyage to a new life in America were soon followed by many others, chiefly from England and Holland. They included farmers and labourers, artisans and merchants, who helped to create new settlements that shortly grew into towns and cities very like those that they had left behind in Europe.

Early American silver is understandably rare, confined mainly to essential pieces such as spoons, porringers and drinking-vessels, and to church plate. Unfortunately for the historian and the silver collector, American silversmiths were entrusted with making their wares to the sterling standard without the supervision of an assay office or other authority, although in some respects, such as that of apprenticeship, the colonists had hardly more freedom than they had had in Europe. In recent years there has been extensive and rewarding research into the lives and works of a notable number of silversmiths in Boston, New York and Philadelphia, and many have now been identified.

Fig. 8 **Two-handled cup** by John Coney, Boston, 1679. Height 6⅞ ins. Arms of Addington. This superb caudle cup is an excellent example of Coney's mastery of silver. (Yale University Art Gallery. Garvan Collection.)

Fig. 9 **Two-handled cup and cover** by John Coney, Boston, 1701. Height 10¼ ins. Arms of Stoughton. This magnificent cup was given to Harvard University by the Hon. William Stoughton in 1701. (William Hayes Fogg Art Museum, Cambridge, Mass.)

8

Museum Photo

9

Museum Photo

American Colonial Silver

Fig. 10 *Detail of Fig. 11, showing Edward Winslow's mark.*

10

A. C. Cooper

Silver Marks

Peter van Dyck

John Coney

Robert Sanderson

Jeremiah Dummer

In some cases, no more than a name is known, such as that of Thomas Howard, recorded as a goldsmith in Jamestown in 1620, the year of *The Mayflower's* historic voyage. Others left not only their marks and their works, but notes and diaries that invest them with as much humanity as the rarer surviving portraits.

Nothing is yet known of the work of an English goldsmith, John Mansfield, who emigrated to Boston in 1634, perhaps to escape religious intolerance, perhaps because he feared the onset of the Civil War. It was probably in that same year that the father of a certain John Hull emigrated with his family from Market Harborough to Boston, where John and his brother are known to have worked as silversmiths. John Hull later wrote how he 'fell to learning (by the help of my brother) and to practising the trade of a goldsmith' – at which he prospered. By 1652 he was so greatly esteemed that he was appointed Mint-master for the Court of Massachusetts, electing his friend, the silversmith Robert Sanderson, to act in partnership with him.

Robert Sanderson was a London silversmith who was born in 1608 and served his apprenticeship to William Rawlins. He worked for some years in London, and it is certain that the mark RS shown below a sun in splendour was his, for he continued to use it after his arrival in America. It has been found on at least three pieces of English silver – a salver of 1635 found, in fact, in the United States and recorded by Jackson (*English Goldsmiths and their Marks, 1921*), and a chalice and paten of the same year bearing the arms of Sir Thomas Myddelton and his wife.

The setting up of the Mint indicated the growing importance of Boston

In America, Sanderson first lived in Hampshire, Massachusetts, but, by 1642, was in Watertown where the first of his three sons, all later to become silversmiths, was born. By the middle of the century he had moved to Boston, which continued to grow rapidly in importance and distinction throughout the ensuing decades. Some indication of this is shown not only by the setting up of the Mint, but by the fact that by 1680 there were enough well-established goldsmiths and bankers in the colonial capital to train several apprentices each, among them 'four ministers' sons.

In 1659, John Hull records that he 'received into my house Jeremie [usually called Jeremiah] Dummer and Samuel Paddy . . . as apprentices'. Paddy was, unhappily, a failure, but the fourteen-year-old Dummer was to become one of the most notable of the early American craftsmen. Others trained by Hull and Sanderson included William Rouse (or Ros), apparently of Dutch origin, and Timothy Dwight, born in 1654, as well as the notable John Coney who had been born in 1656.

Dummer himself, who, according to Hull in 1681, lived 'in good fashion, hath . . . a good estate', probably trained Thomas Savage, born in 1664, and Edward Winslow, born five years later. Besides the young men who were truly American by birth, a number still came from the Old World, among them Edward Webb, who lived in Boston and died there in 1718, and John Edwards, brought to Boston as a young man and probably apprenticed

11

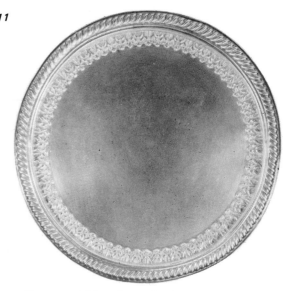

A. C. Cooper

to Dummer. Edwards worked in partnership with John Allen, and later alone, his two sons carrying on their father's business into the mid-eighteenth century.

Naturally, the first generation silversmiths from England continued to make silver in much the same styles as those used at home. A small dram cup by Hull and Sanderson, now at Yale, is one of the oldest recorded pieces of American silver, dated 1651. Its central flower motif and twisted wire handles makes it similar to many Commonwealth wine-tasters, but it should be noted that in colonial inventories, these small bowls are almost always termed 'dram cups' for drinking spirits. Another plain example by the same makers can be dated to 1673, while a beaker of about the same date, engraved with pendent drops below strap-work and with a stamped border at the foot, might almost have been made in East Anglia, where many of the immigrants once lived. A winecup, also at Yale, is typically English in style, while several bellied porringers, both plain in the East Anglian manner and with simple panelled decoration in the style of the 1650s, have been noted.

Apparently originals and patterns continued to arrive from England throughout the second half of the seventeenth century, but in many instances the American craftsmen were developing their own distinctive styles, especially in the pierced flat ears of porringers (Figs. 1 and 2) and in the scalloped bands around the bases, and even on each side of the moulded rib on otherwise conventional tankards. One of about 1690 by John Edwards features an unusual serrated square on the base of the handle echoed by similar cut-card work at the junction, a beaded spine, lion thumb-piece and two rows of gadrooning on the cap cover.

Gadrooning was perhaps the most favoured of all styles of decoration in late seventeenth-century Boston. Jeremiah Dummer is credited with having introduced it in about 1680, and it was much used by John Coney and by Edward Winslow for the borders of salvers, cups, mugs, salts, castors and sugar caskets. John Coney's grace cup for Harvard, dated 1701, shows a late survival of Stuart caryatid handles with more up-to-date fluted and gadrooned formality, while in his footed salver of about 1695 Edward Winslow has captured the new English Baroque with a border of stylised foliage below the heavily gadrooned rim (Figs. 10 and 11). These craftsmen, in fact, developed Boston silver along very similar lines, making fine gadrooned salvers,

Fig. 11 *Footed salver by Edward Winslow, Boston, c.1695. Diameter 9¾ ins. This handsome salver has a raised gadrooned rim and stylised foliage border. (Christie's.)*

the rare sugar-caskets (Fig. 6) based on Charles II styles (of which only eight have been recorded in American silver), and lace-back and other decorated spoons in the English manner.

Edward Winslow was also responsible for one of the three known standing salts from Boston (Fig. 3), the others being by Dummer, Edwards and Allen.

Tea, coffee and chocolate made their impact on New England as in Europe, chocolate apparently being the most popular in Boston, where Coney made a baluster-shaped pot about 1701, its spout curved and slender like those made in England some fifteen years earlier. It is, however, to New York that the student must look for the earliest teapots, two of them dated to about 1697, and another, by Peter van Dyck, c.1710, of pear shape with an almost straight spout. In 1960 a teapot of about the same date came to light, made by the

London-trained silversmith Simeon Soumain.

The silversmiths of New York have almost as long a history as those of Boston, but it was the Low Countries rather than England that proved the chief influence and source of craftsmen. New York silver is rich with Dutch names such as Bartholomew Schaats, Benjamin Wynkoop, Konraet ten Eyck, Jesse Kip and the noted elder craftsman, Cornelius van der Burgh. Others show their Huguenot descent – René Grignon and the Le Roux family as well as Soumain, and their silver is markedly European in flavour. This is especially true of their beakers and tankards, dram cups and two-handled bowls, often decorated in the Dutch manner.

One of New York's earliest and best-known pieces is Van der Burgh's beaker, now at Yale, with strap-work panels engraved with designs taken from Van der Venne's engravings for the poems of

Fig. 12 *Spout cup by William Cowell (1682–1736), Boston, c.1700. Probably used by invalids. (Private Collection.)*

Fig. 13 *Two-handled cup and cover, maker's mark IB, probably for Jurian Blanck, New York, c.1695. The shape of this cup is typically English, but the richness of ornament is very Dutch, as is the coat of arms. (H. F. du Pont Winterthur Museum.)*

Fig. 14 *Beaker by Cornelius van der Burgh, New York, c.1685. Height 5⅞ ins. (Christie's.)*

Fig. 15 *Tankard by Peter van Dyck (1684–1750), New York, early eighteenth century. Height 6¾ ins. (Yale University Art Gallery. Lent by F. P. Garvan '97 and Mrs. Garvan.)*

16

Fig. 16 **Sugar Castor,** *probably from a set of three, by Peter van Dyck, New York, early eighteenth century. Height 7¾ ins. Arms of Schuyler.*
(Yale University Art Gallery. Garvan Collection.)

Museum Photo

Jacob Cats. The beaker is engraved 'Robert Sanders, 1685', and dates from about the same time as another beaker by the same silversmith, also in Dutch style, charmingly and delicately engraved with three birds, strap-work and pendant flowers and foliage.

Some of the Dutch flower motifs embossed and chased on the bowls of two-handled cups, often with scroll panels and caryatid handles (Fig. 13), are reminiscent of the styles brought back from abroad by the English Court at the Restoration, and it is perhaps some indication of the provincial outlook of the town that they were still being made in New York some forty years later. As in Europe, however, it was the Huguenot-born silversmiths who helped to lift silver styles out of the seventeenth and into the eighteenth century. A two-handled cup by Charles Le Roux, for example, has formal, although very simple, strap-work and fine harp-shaped handles in sharp contrast with the little Commonwealth and Charles II style spirit cups and porringers of the period.

The New York Dutch styles were not, however, without charm, and some very pleasant effects were achieved in minor details. Cupid masks and elaborately cast flowers were both popular terminals used at the base of tankard handles (Fig. 15), while a cut-card cast lion in relief climbing the scroll handle was a conceit affected by several makers between about 1690 and 1710.

The swift colonisation of America during the second half of the seventeenth century brought silversmiths in the train of the settlers to many East Coast towns. In Philadelphia, Cesar Ghiselin and Johannis Nys were able to forge a living making spoons and tankards, cups and porringers. Francis Richardson's father took him from New York to Philadelphia as a boy, where the Irish family Syng, from Cork, also settled about 1714. Interchange of ideas and designs as well as increased travel among craftsmen seeking fame and fortune meant a gradual development of what one might call the American silver style. Boston became less 'English' and New York less 'Dutch', as the silversmiths of the second and third generations developed an affinity of thought and design to cater for a young, vigorous and increasingly wealthy nation.

MUSEUMS AND COLLECTIONS

Early American silver may be seen at the following:

Boston:	Boston Museum of Fine Arts
Cambridge:	Wiliam Hayes Fogg Art Museum
Chicago:	Art Institute of Chicago, Illinois
New Haven:	Yale University Art Gallery
New York:	Metropolitan Museum of Art
	Museum of the City of New York
	New-York Historical Society

FURTHER READING

Colonial Silversmiths, Masters and Apprentices by Kathryn C. Buhler, Boston, 1956.

American Silversmiths and Their Marks by Stephen C. G. Ensko, New York, 1948.

American Silver, 1655–1825, by Kathryn C. Buhler, Boston, 1972.

American Silver: A History of Style, 1650–1900, by Graham Hood, New York, 1971.

Museum Photo

Fig. 1 *A View of Mount Vernon, the Seat of General Washington* by an unknown artist, American, eighteenth century. (*National Gallery of Art, Washington, D.C. Gift of Edgar William and Bernice Chrysler Garbisch.*)

COLONIAL ARCHITECTURE

2

Author's Photo

3

4

Fig. 2 **The Church of San Luis Rey de Francia**, *built 1811–1815. The ninth and last mission to be founded by Father Lasuén, San Luis Rey was founded in 1798. Within two years, it had some 2,000 Indian converts in residence.*

Fig. 3 **Shirley Plantation**, *on the James River, near Williamsburg. Plantation houses were often large, and built of brick, giving a clear picture of the gracious living of those whose labours had brought them fortunes.*

Fig. 4 **Iron gates** *leading to the Governor's Palace, Williamsburg. Although Williamsburg had only about one thousand inhabitants in the mid-eighteenth century, it was the great tobacco centre, and merited, therefore, an imposing governor's palace.*

Fig. 5 **The reconstructed Governor's Palace**, *Williamsburg. The original building, of which this is a replica, was burned down in 1781. It was considered one of the finest buildings in the Colonies, and served as an inspiration for Washington's Mount Vernon (Fig. 1).*

Fig. 6 **The Coke-Garrett House**, *Williamsburg. Wood was so plentiful in the new continent that it was a popular building material, even for the largest houses.*

Fig. 7 **Wrought iron balconies** *in a New Orleans street, Louisiana. The Spanish arrived in New Orleans in 1769, to find a squalid and dirty clapboard town. During the period of their colonisation, it was developed into a beautiful Spanish city.*

Although most American colonial architecture was firmly rooted in the styles of England, new modes and variations were developed to accommodate the needs of the ever-expanding and changing Colonies

One of the essential differences between life in Britain and life in the American colonies in the eighteenth century was the absence of a rigid class structure in America. Few of the nobility became colonists, even if they had investments in Colonial enterprises, and the settlers were largely of the 'middling and lower orders'. A man could carve a plantation out of the wilderness and by the fruits of his own industry become rich and rise in the social scale. If the houses that the travelling gentry saw in the colonies often seemed small in scale, they offered a better standard of living to many a settler than he could have expected back home in England.

In their clarity and symmetry, colonial houses reflected the directness and simplicity of their builders. Often they were built only one room deep and enlarged later by the addition of a lean-to at the rear to form a 'cat-slide' roof. Many buildings had one and a half, rather than two storeys, the upper storey being partly in the roof. To offer more accommodation, the roof frequently had two pitches, forming a mansard, or in the colonial term, 'gambrel' section. Later, dormer windows would be added to the upper storey to admit more light, and often wings of one storey might be added to the dwellings. As their owners showed some returns for their industry and expertise they were able to enlarge their earlier, humble properties.

William and Mary, Queen Anne, Georgian – the styles of Colonial architecture reflected those of England with a time-lag of about three decades, evident when buildings are compared. The publication of design books showing house types and structural details made architects largely dispensable and most landowners helped with the building of their homes, and frequently directed operations. Bricks and stone were sometimes imported and local brick industries were also established. But with timber so abundant that animals were sometimes hunted by the simple expedient of burning down the forest, wood was extensively used.

As the century progressed, the simple windows that were set in the plane of the walls received an elegant trim, doorways were rusticated and had sidelights provided to illuminate hallways, and eventually pillared porticos rose to two storeys in height. Local characteristics developed: stuccoed walls in Charleston and the South; panelled shutters in the Middle Colonies.

As some of the planters became wealthy and generation succeeded generation, a large number of stately mansions were built along the Rappahannock and in the gentle hills of Tidewater Virginia: Fairfield, Ampthill, Stratford, Cleve. Among the finest was Westover, built in 1726 by William Byrd II, which is set among splendid tulip poplars. Its finely proportioned north front, its elaborate wrought iron gates and its box tree walks are testimonies of the quality of Colonial architecture.

Houses like Wilton in Henrico County or Carter's Grove in James City County with their string courses of rubbed bricks, their contrasts of dull red and vermilion-hued brickwork, their decorated water tables and finely turned timber details, give an impression of the gracious living of those whose labours brought them fortunes. Their slaves and servants did not live in the mansion houses, but in 'dependencies' and these buildings, though simple and small, were substantially built and offered more comfortable quarters than did the insect-infested log cabins of the poorer pioneers, who had plunged deeper into the woods. Carter's Grove is in the vicinity of Williamsburg, the tobacco-planter's capital, of which a first-hand report was published in London in 1724 by Hugh Jones, professor of Natural Philosophy and Mathematics at the College of William and Mary.

'The town is laid out regularly in lots of square proportions sufficient each for a house or garden', he wrote. 'They don't build contiguous, whereby may be prevented the spreading danger of fire; and this also affords a free passage of the air which is very grateful in violent hot weather. Here, as in other parts, they build with brick, but most commonly with timber, lined with cieling, and cased with feather-edged plank, painted with white lead and oil, covered with shingles of cedar, etc., tarred over at first'. The inhabitants of Williamsburg 'dwell comfortably, genteely, pleasantly and plentifully in this delightful, healthful, and (I hope) thriving city'. But thirty-five years later, the

Fig. 8 **Travis House**, *Duke of
Gloucester Street,
Williamsburg.
Sloped roofs afforded little space
for those living in the upper half-
storey, and were often replaced
by a roof with two pitches. These
formed a mansard; or, to use the
Colonial term, gambrel section.
White picket fences were a
common feature throughout
Williamsburg, as were unpaved
and very dusty streets.*

Fig. 9 **Drawing** *for the façade
of a Colonial style house.
Porticos with classical columns
became increasingly prevalent in
Colonial architecture as designs
became less strictly functional,
and the richer members of society
acquired more leisure and taste.
Verandas, as on the side of this
house, were also popular,
especially in the South, for the
shade they offered.*

Fig. 10 **Private residence,**
*Williamsburg.
A visiting professor to the
College of William and Mary in
Williamsburg, Hugh Jones,
reported of the town in 1724 that
it was 'laid out regularly in lots of
square proportions sufficient each
for a house or garden. They don't
build contiguous, whereby may
be prevented the spreading
danger of fire; and this also
affords a free passage of the air
which is very grateful in violent
hot weather.' This small but
charming house is typical of what
the professor saw.*

Reverend Andrew Barnaby, M.A., travelling through the Middle Settlements, took a somewhat less charitable view of the city. 'It consists of about two hundred houses, does not contain more than one thousand souls, whites and negroes, and is far from being a place of any consequence.' He admired the square, and the wide main street and '. . . the governor's palace, indeed, is tolerably good, one of the best upon the continent; but the church, prison, and other buildings are all of them extremely indifferent. The streets are not paved, and are consequently very dusty, the soil here about consisting chiefly of sand'. But at least it was free of mosquitoes and upon the whole he admitted it was agreeable when there were courts and general assemblies. 'On those occasions there are balls and other amusements; but as soon as business is finished, they return to their plantations and the town is deserted'.

The Governor's Palace was a source of inspiration for George Washington when he built Mount Vernon overlooking the broad sweep of the Potomac River. But the house had elements which showed his originality – in the high-columned piazza which extended the full length to trap the breeze and the shade, or in the 'rusticated boards', which he had bevelled to look like stone and which were sand-cast on the wet paint to give the appropriate texture. Much of the building may have been of his own design, even of his own workman-ship. 'Mr. Saunders not coming according to expectation, I began with my own people to shingle that part of the Roof of the House wch. was stripped yesterday, and to copper the Gutters &ca.', runs one diary entry. It was, like other plantation homes beyond the towns, a 'little empire', in the words of Washington Irving, with the mansion house the 'seat of government, with its numerous depen-dencies, such as kitchens, smoke-house, workshops and stables', supporting about two hundred and fifty persons on the entire estate.

So a certain freedom was enjoyed to design according to one's inclinations, and the influence of England, while always present, was being shrugged off when it was inapplicable. Further south, in Charleston, with its early settlers coming from the then declining sugar plantations of the West Indies, the style of architecture was more in character with that practised in Barbados. Its plan was based on a grid bound by fortifications, for Lord Ashley, in founding it, insisted that it be divided 'into regular streets, for be the buildings never so mean and thin at first, yet as the town increases in riches and people, the void places will be filled up and the buildings will grow more beautiful'. Such optimism was justified there, but with the British firmly entrenched on the whole eastern seaboard to the Appalachians, the other nationalities had to seek territories that were sometimes less promising for development. Though the British burnt down the Spanish missions in southern Georgia and Florida, the French held on to their Gulf Coast forts, and tried to settle.

By a royal grant in 1717, John Law's Company of the West gained control of the whole French province of Louisiana and appointed the explorer Bienville to act as Governor. Bienville supervised the plans of the engineer Pauger for a grid-iron city of Nouvelle Orléans, four thousand feet long. But there were less than a hundred little log cabins by 1722 and a third of these were blown down in a

hurricane a year later. The city was built on such a swamp that the dead could not be buried below ground, as the graves filled with water. Subject to alternate droughts and floods, mosquitoes and even a plague of mad dogs, it remained a squalid and dirty clapboard town until the arrival of the Spanish, improbably led by Don Alexander O'Reilly, in 1769. A couple of disastrous fires swept away most of the French buildings but the Spanish, in a local phrase more colourful than accurate, 'found a town of hovels and left it a city of palaces'. Hardly that, but the iron lattices, the balconies and jalousies, the gratings and arches, the inner court-yards with parterres, the fountains and statues – all these were Spanish innovations, and even the French market was Spanish throughout.

Out on the west coast of the continent, the

8

Spanish were also establishing a foothold, deter-mined to challenge the Russian intention to colonise California. In charge of the missionaries, under the King of Spain's personal agent for New Spain, was Father Junípero Serra. He had sailed from Mallorca for America in 1749 and had spent a score of years in Mexico before riding the seven hundred and fifty miles on mule-back, while suffer-ing from a leg infection, up the desert strip of Baja California, to found the first Franciscan Mission at San Diego. During the next dozen years, he estab-lished eight more in the coastal region, including San Luis Obispo, San Juan Capistrano and his beloved San Carlos Borromeo de Carmel. Built by Indian labour, as the folk quality of the interior decoration often reveals, the missions were indisputably Spanish colonial. Their simply expressed forms and economical use of decorative modelling, their adobe, brick and stuccoed walls, Roman tiled roofs, arched cloisters and shaded tropical gardens, are superbly adapted semi-desert architecture. After Father Junípero Serra's death in 1784, his successor, Father Fermin Lasuén, built a further nine missions in California, but the Mexican secularisation of the missions and later American occupation brought many of them to a state of disrepair and neglect.

Though the French settlements had spread right up the Mississippi around the Great Lakes, and linked with the St. Lawrence by the mid-1770s, most of them were forts and military outposts. The vast region of Spanish Louisiana was ceded to Spain by the French in 1763 and only St. Pierre and

Roger-Viollet

Paul Popper

Miquelon in Newfoundland remained in French possession. From the former French territories east of the Mississippi, George III formed an Indian Reserve and, a decade later, the Quebec Act of 1774 extended the Province of Quebec to complete the ring of territories around the thirteen colonies. By this time, Boston had grown from a city of seven thousand to one of sixteen thousand; Philadelphia had multiplied its 1690 population ten-fold, to four thousand, and New York had twenty-five thousand people. Newport, Norfolk and Charleston were also principal ports in the colonies and, if the other towns and cities were smaller, their establishment was a positive indication of the resoluteness of the Americans.

The houses, the mansions, the plantations and the towns may have owed much in their architecture to England, but they had also shown that a new and different culture on the continent of America was a fact. The colonists wanted autonomy and the Revolution was the result. 'The history of the present King of Great Britain is a history of repeated injuries and usurpations, all having in direct object the establishment of an absolute tyranny over these States'. So ran the 'Minor Premise' of the *Declaration of Independence* of 4 July, 1776, which concluded that its signatories 'solemnly publish and declare That these United Colonies are, and of Right ought to be Free and Independent States'. When the dust of battle had cleared, the Georgian exterior gave way to a new and severe Classicism. American architecture had come of age.

Redware and Other Pottery

Fig. 1 *'Money Wanted'*,
*American. Redware with slip
motto, length 14 ins.,
width 10 ins.*
*The unusual motto on this
large dish was probably intended
for display in a shop window.
Money was very scarce in early
America as most trade was done
by barter, and the shop would
have wanted to advertise its need
of this precious commodity.
(Shelburne Museum, Vermont.)*

Fig. 2 *Oblong dish*, *American.
Redware with slip decoration,
length 19 ins., width 12¾ ins.,
depth 3¾ ins.*
*Dishes of this sort were used
commonly throughout the
Colonies as imported English
wares were very expensive.
Pottery was needed to
supplement local supplies
of pewter and treen.
(Shelburne Museum.)*

Fig. 3 *Spill holder*, *American,
1789. Redware with yellow slip
decoration. Height 5 ins.*
*This spill holder would
have hung on the wall by the fire.
(American Museum in Britain,
Claverton Manor, Bath.)*

Fig. 4 (opposite) *Cup and dish*,
*American, the cup, 1780,
4½ x 3½ x 2¾ ins.; the dish with
slip decoration and glaze,
diameter 6 ins. Redware.*
*Slip was the creamy liquid clay
used to decorate a great deal of
early redware. It was poured from
the holes in a cup like that on the
right to create patterns of the
type seen on the dish. The pure
lead glaze used gave the slip its
yellowish colour.
(John Judkin Memorial, Bath.)*

Pottery was such an everyday art
in the Colonies that few pieces
have survived from the seventeenth
and eighteenth centuries, but
those pieces of redware which we
still have are charming in their
unsophisticated simplicity

The manufacture of redware, the first pottery
made in the American Colonies, began in the
late 1600s and continued well into the nineteenth
century. From New England to Georgia, a familiar
sight in Colonial towns and villages was the
potshop, where the potter, alone or with the more
promising village lads as apprentices, turned out
redware for house and dairy.

The long list of redware includes such useful
articles as dishes, bowls, cups, mugs, basins,
jelly and cake moulds, herb pots, crocks, milk pans,
churns and flower pots. Occasionally, especially
in the Pennsylvania area, fanciful or decorative
pieces were made.

In addition to the full-time potter, there was the
seasonal potter, who worked at the craft when other
activities, usually of attending to his all-important
food crops, permitted. After enough stock was
accumulated, he loaded it on to a wagon and
peddled it through the countryside. As in most
Colonial transactions, money rarely changed hands
and payment was made by barter, acceptable items
being such useful things as tobacco, meat, corn and
tar.

Several factors accounted for the vast output of
redware. First, the clay used was the same as that
in red brick and roof tiles and a bountiful supply
was available practically everywhere. Then, the
potting process was so simple that almost anyone
could use it for basic products. Essential equipment called for a horse-powered mill for grinding
and mixing clays, a home-made potter's wheel
and kiln, a few tools, inexpensive materials, and
wood fuel, usually available for the taking.

Two more persuasive influences helped to boost
the production of redware: it was urgently
needed to supplement pewter and treen, and it was

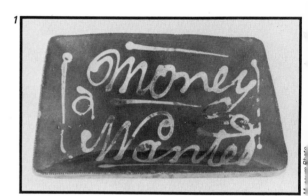

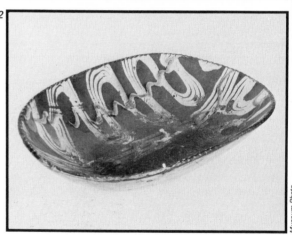

Fig. 5 *'Mind Your business'* dish, American, late eighteenth century. Redware with notched rim and slip decoration, diameter 13 ins.
Mottos, some of which sound rather strange to modern ears, were a popular form of decoration.
(American Museum in Britain.)

Fig. 6 **Bowl**, American, eighteenth century. Redware with dark brown glaze and stylized bird decoration. Diameter 14 ins.
Manganese, used in varying proportions to create tan, brown, or black, formed an inexpensive and common glaze.
(American Museum in Britain.)

cheaper than imported English wares.

The basic colour of redware came from traces of iron oxide in the clay. When fired, this substance produced varying shades of red. Sometimes the red colour was retained in the finished piece by using a pure form of lead glaze – actually glass – which is transparent with a yellowish tinge. The pottery could be given other colours when something was deliberately added to the glaze. Green was produced by adding copper oxide, but the colour was costly and used sparingly. Inexpensive manganese, in varying amounts, provided tan, brown and mirror-black glazes (Fig. 6). Interesting decorative effects occurred accidentally through unsuspected impurities in the clay or unusually high temperatures in the kiln during burning. Under these conditions, pieces might develop attractive streaks or mottling in brown, green, orange or red. For intentional decoration, the potter often relied on coloured glazes, applied in an endless variety of ways, to create

unpretentious designs. The piece then received a conventional glaze before being fired. Bands of colour were a popular finish for the edges of bowls. In the heat of the kiln the decoration ran a little, producing a flowing effect (Figs. 9 and 12).

Slip, or liquid clay, offered another type of redware decoration (Fig. 4). Using a clay cup, the potter poured slip through one or several quills inserted in the liquid to make simple designs, such as scrolls, dots, or names of national heroes or the piece's intended owner (Fig. 13). Over this decoration, glaze was applied, intensifying the colours and producing a lustrous surface. Sometimes a whole redware object was immersed in cream-coloured slip (Fig. 9).

Slip had another, less obvious, use. When bright green motifs were desired, they were first executed in white slip, then covered with green glaze. If the transparent green glaze had been applied directly to the redware surface, the resulting colour would have been olive green.

American Redware

Fig. 7 *'Apple Pie' plate,*
probably made in Pennsylvania.
Redware with slip motto.
Diameter 11 ins.
The so-called Pennsylvania
Dutch, who were actually
German settlers (Deutsch), *had*
two specialities: apple pie and
apple butter. Special dishes were
made for both in redware, often
identified by a motto.
(Shelburne Museum.)

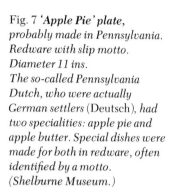

Fig. 8 **Keg,** *American, nineteenth*
century. Redware speckled with
black, height 8½ ins.
Although redware was porous, it
was used for the short-term
storage of many things,
including liquids.
(American Museum in Britain.)

Fig. 9 **Jug,** *American, nineteenth*
century. Redware coated with
cream slip and decorated with
brown and green glazes.
Height 9 ins.
Entire pieces were sometimes
immersed in slip to give them a
more refined, creamy appearance.
The glazes applied as decoration
often ran in the heat of the kiln,
producing the attractive flowing
effect seen on this jug.
(American Museum in Britain.)

Fig. 10 **Water-carrier,** *American,*
early nineteenth century.
Height 8½ ins.
Bottles of this sort were used
by farm labourers during the
harvest. They were slung over
the men's arms to leave their
hands free for carrying tools.
(American Museum in Britain.)

11

Museum Photo

Fig. 11 **Shallow bowl**, *American.
Redware, top diameter 17½ ins.,
bottom diameter 9¾ ins.,
depth 5½ ins.
Simple wares of this sort could
be made by almost anyone with
the proper equipment. All that
was needed was a horse-powered
mill for grinding and mixing
clays, a home-made potter's
wheel and kiln, a few tools,
inexpensive materials, and wood
fuel, usually available for the
taking. As the necessary red clay
was plentiful, it is not surprising
that redware was made in large
quantities throughout the
Colonies.
(Shelburne Museum.)*

Little is known about the earliest potters and in many cases their work in red and other local clays has completely vanished. At the time, silver-smiths had a certain prestige, but no-one attached any importance to preserving the commonplace work of the familiar potter.

The meagre records indicate, however, that pottery was made as early as 1625 at Jamestown, Virginia, the first permanent English settlement in America. Another early southern venture was undertaken by Andrew Duché (1710–78), a Huguenot who left Philadelphia to make pottery in South Carolina from 1731 to 1737. Moving on to Savannah, Georgia, and materially encouraged by General James Oglethorpe, founder of the Georgia Colony, he made pottery and experimental por-celain until 1743.

Pottery became a popular and lively trade in the Colonies

Two more efforts were launched in North Carolina. One was by a colony of Moravians, who, from 1756 to 1768, made redware, stove tiles and clay pipes in the village of Bethabara. The pottery was moved to North Salem, North Carolina, in 1768, where it continued to make wares of improved quality until about 1830.

The other North Carolina enterprise was the so-called Jugtown Pottery at Steeds, a mid-eighteenth-century settlement made up of colonists from Staffordshire. In spite of encourage-ment given to the pioneers, they seem to have con-fined their efforts to making the plainest of wares.

The number of eighteenth-century potters in the north must have been enormous. To give only one example, the small town of Peabody, Massachu-setts, sent twenty-two potters to the nearby Battle of Lexington in 1775.

Because there was a lively trade in pottery among the Colonies, the place where a piece is found is not necessarily its place of origin. However, regional characteristics sometimes help to identify New England and Pennsylvania pottery. New England, mindful of its Puritan heritage, tended to produce sober, useful objects for workaday purposes. One of the only concessions to frivolity was the use of richly coloured glazes.

Often in distinct contrast was the pottery made by the Pennsylvania Dutch, who were actually *deutsch*, or German. The immigrants from the Palatinate arrived in the eighteenth century and, with Swiss Mennonites, settled in Pennsylvania's so-called 'Dutch' counties.

Redware made by these German colonists, more capable of a relaxed enjoyment of life than their New England counterparts, reflected the potters' imagination, sense of fun and love of colour. Among their products, along with the customary house-hold and dairy items, were bird-shaped whistles, money-boxes in charming designs, and puzzle jugs. They also made articles for two typical Pennsyl-vania Dutch foods: flat dishes for fruit pies (Fig. 7) and pots for apple butter.

While slip decoration was used everywhere, Pennsylvania potters employed it for the superb *sgraffito*, or scratched, designs that they alone among the colonists produced. A thin slip coating on a piece was scratched through to show the redware body, the intricate designs perhaps being enhanced with additional colours.

A hundred miles of the beautiful Shenandoah Valley in Maryland and Virginia became the site of a number of late but notable potters. Most interesting was the Bell family. Peter, the founding father, worked in Hagerstown, Maryland, and Winchester, Virginia, from 1800 to 1845. His sons and grandsons carried on his work, making both redware and stoneware. Finally, the factory, which had been moved to Strasburg, Virginia, closed in 1908. In a breakaway from Pennsylvania Dutch tradition, to which they were accustomed, the Bells developed a style of their own. Their distinctive flowing designs, such as birds in browns and subdued greens, were almost Oriental in feeling. In addition to practical redware, they made appealing animal figures and other ornaments.

American Redware

Fig. 12 **Basin**, *American.
Redware coated inside with slip
and decorated with coloured
glazes, diameter 15 ins.,
depth 4½ ins.
The insides of vessels were often
coated with slip and glazed in .
order to make them waterproof;
the redware itself was porous and
was eventually supplanted by
stoneware for this reason. Even
the glazes on redware were
unreliable, as can be seen by the
faults in the finish of this basin.
Its attractiveness, however, is
undeniable, and explains its
long-lasting popularity.
(Shelburne Museum.)*

Museum Photo

Museum Photo

Fig. 13 **Bowl**, *probably made in
Pennsylvania, 1796. Redware
with slip decoration, diameter
13¼ ins.
The gaiety and lightness of touch
is characteristic of the
Pennsylvania Dutch potters. As
on the apple pie plate in Fig. 7,
the decoration is applied without
self-conscious planning,
probably through a slip cup or a
quill. The initials are probably
of the original owner.
(Shelburne Museum.)*

As early nineteenth-century settlers moved westward, especially into Ohio, potters travelled with them. They produced pottery blending the traditions of New England and Pennsylvania from whence these pioneers came.

With all its merits, redware also had its faults. It was brittle and chipped or broke easily. It was also porous, and therefore unsuitable for many of the items necessary in a kitchen. Even worse was the suspicion, debated at leisure in England and in the Colonies, that the lead glaze was poisonous. This fear eventually helped the introduction of stoneware at a time when redware was still able to put up a fight against it.

HINTS FOR COLLECTORS

Marks or signatures on early American pottery are rare. The few seen appear on the works of master potters; no-one bothered to identify commonplace pieces.

Fakes exist, particularly in redware. A few signs of age in redware (unfortunately imitated by the faker) include darkening of the piece (that is, darkening of the glaze) from acids in food and cooking heat and minute scratches made by knives. Use through the years turns the unglazed bottoms of baking dishes black. Impressed marks, which must be made while the clay is still damp, command more respect, though not always acceptance, from experts than scratched marks which can be added at anytime.

It is interesting to remember that pottery, unlike antiques in many other categories, is inert. This means that if a new piece was never used but was wrapped up and put away in a trunk or drawer, it emerges, even after centuries, as fresh as on the day it left the potter's hand. A few great treasures in American redware are fine objects that have been so discovered.

FURTHER READING

Early New England Potters and their Wares by Lura Woodside Watkins, Cambridge, Mass., 1968 reprint.

American Potters and Pottery by John Ramsay, Boston, Mass., 1976 reprint.

Early American Pottery and China by John Spargo, New York, 1974 reprint.

The Pottery and Porcelain of the United States by Edwin Atlee Barber, 1979 reprint.

Marks of American Potters by Edwin A. Barber, 1976 reprint.

MUSEUMS AND COLLECTIONS

Eighteenth-century American pottery may be seen at the following:

Dearborn, Michigan:	Henry Ford Museum
New York:	Brooklyn Museum
	New-York Historical Society
	Metropolitan Museum of Art
Philadelphia:	Philadelphia Museum of Art
Reading, Penn:	Public Museum and Art Gallery
Shelburne, Vermont:	Shelburne Museum
Sturbridge, Mass:	Old Sturbridge Village

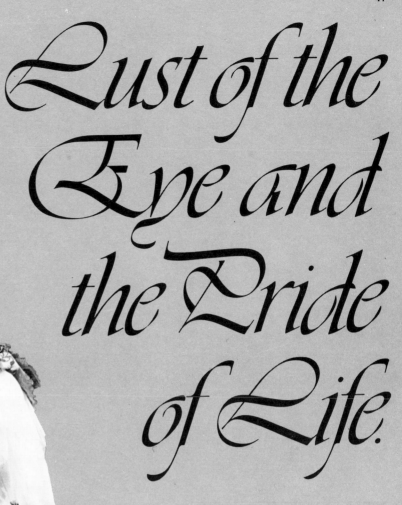

Lust of the Eye and the Pride of Life.

Fig. 1 **Wedding dress** *worn by Mary Beck for her marriage to Nathanial Carter in 1742, at Newburyport, Massachusetts. Spitalfields brocade. (Boston Museum of Fine Arts.)*

Fig. 2 **Mrs. Wynant van Zandt** *by an unidentified Hudson Valley artist, c.1725. Oil on canvas. (New York Historical Society.)*

Museum Photo

N.Y.H.S. Photo

3

4

Museum Photo

5

Derek Balmer

6

Derek Balmer

The fashions of the American Colonies were still the fashions of England; despite the political and religious extremes at work in the Colonies, freedom in dress was as important to the early settlers as liberty of conscience

The conventional picture of the early settlers of America is that of the 'gray old gospeller, sour as midwinter'. Such an impression is misleading, for the first planters, whatever their religious or political sympathies, dressed as well as their counterparts at home. There is evidence, too, that remoteness from Whitehall led to the adoption of extremes in fashion by some of the wealthier planters: a succession of sumptuary laws attempted to put some limits on this extravagance. In 1639 the General Court of Massachusetts was

7

obliged to forbid the use of 'immoderate great breeches, knots of riban, broad shoulder bands and ragles, silk roses, and double ruffles and capes', and John Pory of Virginia recorded that 'our cowe-keeper . . . goes accoutred all in freshe flaminge silk'.

The Cavalier element persisted long after the Puritan revolution in England; even in 1650 the Connecticut magistrates were unable to exercise any very strict control and had to be content with a law which forbade any man with an estate of less than £200 to indulge in 'costly or gay attire'. Such an estimate was unlikely to prove accurate, for the general currency was still tobacco; a complete suit, including 'ribbonin and stiffinin', cost something in the region of 378 lbs. of tobacco in 1643.

The majority of the colonists were, however, of the 'yeoman sort', and their clothes were identical to those worn in England: leather doublets, linen shirts and breeches of tanned hide were the usual working clothes, supplemented by boots or shoes of untanned leather and a beaver hat. This costume, although simple, was decorative in the extreme, the jerkins of 'phillymort' (feuillemorte, or dead leaf colour) and cloaks of ginger 'lyne' contrasted with the red worsted stockings and black beavers to produce an impression of considerable richness and style.

There is a wealth of evidence about the wardrobes of these humbler settlers, both from the *Lists of Apparell* furnished by the companies carrying passengers to America, and from the inventories of personal estates. The variety and number of clothes thought necessary for life in the Colonies were such that 'it became verie hard to know who is noble, who is worshipful, who is a Gentleman and who is not; for you have those who are neither of the nobilitie, gentilitie or yeomanrie goe dailie in silks, velvets, satens, damasks notwithstanding they be base by birth, meane by estate and servyle by calling'.

Even the avowed Puritans did not shun richness and ornament in their clothes: in 1639 Jasper Mayne wrote of a lady, 'she is a Puritan at her needle: she works religious petticoats, besides my smock sleeves have such bold embroideries and are so learned, that I fear in time that all my apparel will be quoted by some pure instructor'. Although the dress of the Puritans was designed to show disapproval of the follies and extravagance of the Caroline Court, it did so by its simplicity of style, rather than the abjuring of fine materials.

She exchanged her hat band for four young cows . . .

In America, the Puritan style was more severe, partly because it seemed a needless extravagance to spend money on silver buttons when a horse or farm implement was of greater necessity and worth, and partly because of the existence of the sumptuary laws. These laws were passed to encourage the growth of a native fashion industry – only imported silks and damasks were forbidden – but the enormous number of prosecutions suggests that many people 'psisted in fflouting', despite all the efforts of preachers and magistrates. The dress of Puritan women, too, did not differ markedly from that of country women in England:

'The good old dames among the rest
Were all the most primitively drest
In stiffen-bodyed russet gowns
And on their heads old steeple crowns
With pristine pinners next their faces
Edged round with ancient scallop laces'.

The one item of extravagance in which these Puritan ladies seem to have indulged was the hat band: in July 1650, Susan Mosely 'in a great want of cattle' exchanged her Dutch-made hat band for four young cows, one older cow and four oxen. This hat band, she recorded, 'were made for me at Rotterdam and I paid in good Rex dollars sixty gulders for ye juell and fivety and two gulders for ye ring, which comes in English money to eleven pounds fower shillings'. Another Puritan lady, Jane Humphrey of Massachusetts, died in 1668 leaving 'a red kersey, a blemish serge, a red serge, a black serge and a green linsey woollsey petticoat – five in all; a sad grey kersey, a white fustian, a green serge, a blue and a murry waistcoat – five waistcoats to correspond; two jumps; a blue short coat; a green coat; a kersey coat; a fringed whittle; a cloak;

Fig. 3 *Isaac Royall and his family* by Robert Feke, 1741. (*Harvard Law School, Cambridge, Mass.*)

Fig. 4 *James Badger* by Joseph Badger (1708–65). (*Metropolitan Museum of Art, New York. Rogers Fund, 1929.*)

Fig. 5 *Breeches,* American, first half of the eighteenth century. (*American Museum in Britain, Claverton Manor, Bath.*)

Fig. 6 *Night cap,* American, eighteenth century. Cotton. (*American Museum in Britain.*)

Fig. 7 *De Peyster Boy* by an unidentified New York artist, c.1720–40. Oil on canvas. (*New York Historical Society.*)

George Rainbird Ltd.

N.Y.H.S. Photo

American
Costume

Fig. 8 **Mrs. David Chesebrough**
*by Joseph Blackburn (c.1700–
after 1765), signed and dated
1754. Oil on canvas.*
*This is a fine example of the
'Watteau' dress with a lace
ruche and ribbons tied in 'a very
tasty manner'. Dresses of this
type were worn with only minor
variations from the 1720s until
the Revolution, a monotony
relieved only by the richness and
variety of stuffs used in their
making.*
*(Metropolitan Museum of Art.
Gift of Sylvester Dering, 1916.)*

Fig. 9 **Mrs. Thomas Boylston** *by
John Singleton Copley (1738–
1815), 1765. Oil on canvas.*
*In the early days in New England,
the older women were the most
richly dressed in the community.
By the eighteenth century the
reverse was the case, although
women of advancing years like
Mrs. Boylston made use of fine
linen and lace to ornament the
simplicity of dress.*
*(Fogg Art Museum, Cambridge,
Mass.)*

black silk, calico and holland neckclothes; white, blue, holland and green aprons; quoifes and queues and hoods and muffs'. Such a wardrobe belies the legend of Puritan asceticism.

One variant on the Puritan theme was the dress of the Dutch settlers in the New Netherlands: the Dutch ladies were renowned for the richness of their jewellery and the sparsity of their underwear. Vronentje Ides Stoffelsen died in 1641 leaving a whole collection of gold and silver medals, rings and chains, 'two pairs of old stockings and one purple shift'. The Dutch ladies also perpetuated their distinctive hair style, 'untortured by the abominations of art, pomatumed back from their foreheads with a candle, and covered with a little cap of quilted calico'.

The coming of the Restoration made very little impact on most of the American colonists, few of whom kept up definite links with their home country. Just as the New England Puritans had refused to give way to the excessive zeal of the Cromwellian era, so the Colonial Governors remained largely unimpressed by the sartorial splendours of Charles II's Court.

At the upper end of the social scale, the lives led by Provincial Governors were very similar to those of country families in England: hunting, racing and other sporting amusements took up much of the time, and good living in every respect was encouraged. It was a matter of pride for the local American gentry to dress well, keep a good table and appear to be *au courant* with the latest fashions and styles from Europe. Many late seventeenth- and early eighteenth-century portraits testify to the comparative splendour of these 'colonial aristocrats'. Nathaniel Hawthorne, surveying the age, wrote that 'there are tokens everywhere of a style of luxury and magnificence we had not associated with our notions of the times'.

The letters of the brothers Winthrop give a good impression of the importance of male fashion in early eighteenth century Boston: John Winthrop wrote in June, 1706, that 'since my last, I have picked up at severall shops in towne a parcell of patterns which are enclosed. There is no choice of anything. Everything very ordinary and extravigantly dear. It was an accidental thing I litt upon the camblett: as soon as ever I saw it in Bunnisters' shop I thought it was the genteelest thing I had seen anywhere'. His brother replied desiring him to 'bring me a very good cloak lined with what you like except blew. It may be purple or red or striped if so worn suitable and fashionable'.

There are fewer records for female costume in the late seventeenth and early eighteenth centuries. It appears, however, that the fashions of the English Court were adopted in a modified form: the low necklines were partially filled by borders of muslin or lace, and it was usual to leave the hair unpowdered. Sleeves, too, were worn longer than was the fashion in England, although the variety of materials and colours was just as magnificent. Indeed, the ready availability of materials from the West Indies and the Spanish colonies often gave American ladies an advantage over their London cousins, who had to pay more for these items, when they could be had at all.

Outside the circle of the Provincial Governors, there was little to inspire an independent movement of fashion. There were spinning matches, singing schools, gatherings on royal birth nights and 'consorts'. Such forms of entertainment did not call for gowns of highest mode; the richness and variety which so many travellers noted, stemmed from the materials used rather than from the design of the dresses. The gradual opening up of the East Indian trade brought to America a whole range of materials and motifs. Alice Morse Earle,

8

9

American
Costume

Fig. 10 *Nicholas Boylston
(1716–71) by John S. Copley.
Oil on canvas.
Dr. Boylston is wearing a
negligé dress consisting of a
banyan of blue brocade, scarlet
morocco slippers, and a scarlet
turban. This was the fashionable
form of informal dress from the
1740s on to the Revolution.
Consciousness of this fact may
account for the doctor's
complacent air.
(Harvard University Portrait
Collection, Fogg Art Museum.)*

Fig. 11 *Child's dress, American,
mid-eighteenth century. Linen
and cotton with wool embroidery,
approximate length 27½ ins.
This is an example of one of the
enduring American traditions: a
child's dress embroidered in wool
crewel-work with a simple
pattern of flowers and fruit.
(Metropolitan Museum of Art.
Rogers Fund, 1954.)*

in her monumental *Customs and Fashions in Old New England*, lists over one hundred names of Oriental stuffs, 'whose exact definition cannot now be indicated'.

Throughout the first three quarters of the eighteenth century, women's dresses were all conceived on the same pattern, loose, worn over hoops or panniers. There were many different variants – polonaise, levites, negligé, were names given to what was, in effect, the same dress. The most popular name was the 'Watteau', called after the prevailing French fashion of the mid-century. In 1753, this receipt for modern dress described the current fashion.

'*Let your gown be a sacque blue, yellow or green,
And frizzle your elbows with ruffles sixteen,
Furl off your lawn apron with flounces in rose,
Puff and pucker up laces on your arms and toes
Make your petticoats short, that a hoop eight
  yards wide,
May daintily show how your garters are tied'.*

The influence of Indian art and design seems to have been negligible at this time. The frontiersmen of pre-Revolutionary days tended to adopt the Indian hunting shirt and moccasins for the sake of convenience, but that is the only perceptible use of Indian styles. The hunting jerkin, or wamus, was a loose tunic with close-fitting sleeves and an immense collar or hood attached. Such garments were made of elk skin, kneaded till it was 'soft and white as milk', often decorated with leather or stitching. The tunic was worn with hide breeches and leggings and either a felt hat or a cap of coon, fox or squirrel fur. The frontiersman's dress hardly changed from the earliest days through to the era of Davy Crockett and Kit Carson.

One other important element in the history of American costume was the Quaker movement. 'Come out from among them and be ye separate', was their watchword, and they insisted on severity of dress as 'one of the testimonies of an earnest people'. The figure of the Quaker with the white bands and broad black hat has become as much a part of the American myth as the buckskin-clad frontiersman.

The Dartmouth Monthly Meeting of 1722 recorded that one R.D., 'hath given way to the lust of the eye and the pride of life in following some of the vain fashions and customs of the times, especially that of wearing his hair long, which is a great shame, according to the Apostles' declaration; for this we have laboured with him'.

This willingness to labour with unconventional forms of dress still seems to be an American, and not merely a Quaker, characteristic. Now the strands of America's sartorial history are being disentangled to produce a medley of Indian, Early Colonial, and cowboy costumes, alongside the newer forms of Puritanism.

MUSEUMS AND COLLECTIONS
American costume may be seen at the following:
Boston: Boston Museum of Fine Arts
New York: Metropolitan Museum of Art

FURTHER READING
Early American Costume by E. Warwick and H. Pitz, New York, 1929.

Historic Dress in America, 1607–1870, by E. McClellan, Boston, 1970 reprint.

Costume of Colonial Times by A. Morse Earle, New York, 1975 reprint.

Two Centuries of Costume in America by Alice Morse Earle, 1974 reprint.

English Styles in Colonial Furniture

Fig. 1 Fall-front desk by
Edward Evans, Philadelphia,
1707. Walnut, red pine and white
cedar.
This magnificent desk is the
earliest known piece of signed
and dated Philadelphia furniture.
(Colonial Williamsburg,
Virginia.)

The increased demand for elegance and comfort in the Colonies during the eighteenth century led to the production of handsome, well-proportioned furniture based on English designs

In England, the eighteenth century witnessed a brilliant flowering of all the arts aided by the expansion of commerce and trade in addition to political and social stability. While England moved into this period of graciousness, the Colonies followed, but at a slower pace. New wealth on both sides of the Atlantic assumed a material form in stately houses furnished in an elaborate and refined manner.

At the beginning of the century, a third generation of Americans was already living in the Colonies, still retaining many of the basic traditions of their ancestors in matters of taste. However, the rural arts and crafts of the seventeenth century were transformed into a culture which was now urban in character. In Philadelphia, Quaker traditions were in evidence and in New York could be seen a strong Dutch influence. In New England, the Puritan standards which had been established soon yielded as trade and ship-building industries flourished. Cities such as Boston, Newport, New York and Philadelphia grew and developed rapidly as commercial shipping centres. Trading with England, especially in tobacco, brought many goods, including furniture, directly to the southern states. It seems apparent, therefore, that styles were not at first transmitted from within the Colonies, but reached separate regions through various commercial means.

Eighteenth-century houses were based on the spacious architectural plans of the Renaissance. Although the frontier vigour of earlier houses was no longer evident, the resulting benefits in spaciousness and comfort more than offset this loss. These symmetrically planned houses now contained several rooms, including a central hall, a dining-room and two parlours. One of the parlours was usually formal, containing chairs, sofa, mirror,

several small tables and perhaps a desk (Figs. 6 and 9). The second parlour was for the family and would often contain a day-bed, chairs, pine tables, a cradle and general family furniture (Fig. 4).

The settlers of the previous century had, of necessity, to be adept at a variety of crafts. This versatility was responsible for a type of furniture which involved no special skills. In contrast, the eighteenth century was an age of specialisation. Along with the builder and the silversmith, the cabinet-maker was now able to devote all his time to his particular trade. However, unlike the silver of this period, which was stamped with the maker's mark, attributions of furniture to a single maker cannot be readily made as the labelling of furniture was not yet in practice. A single exception to this is a fall-front desk by Edward Evans of Philadelphia. His name, and the date 1707 branded on one of the drawers, establishes it as the earliest signed piece of Philadelphia furniture (Fig. 1).

The eighteenth century was an age of specialisation

The William and Mary style, based on the application of veneers, required professional skill far beyond that of a mere joiner. Fortunately, by the early eighteenth century sufficient numbers of skilled cabinet-makers were already working in the Colonies. Without these trained cabinet-makers to interpret the new styles from England it would have taken a much longer time for earlier Jacobean styles to be replaced.

As oak was the wood best suited to seventeenth-century furniture, so walnut was best suited to the baroque forms of the William and Mary and Queen Anne styles. Walnut is close-grained and lends itself to carving while veneers can be cut from it to give splendid surfaces to desks, tables and chests. Since walnut is not attacked by worm, does not splinter easily, and takes a fine finish, especially when burled, much of this wood was brought to England from the Colonies. By 1730, the South Sea Company had established trade with England for black walnut from the forests of Pennsylvania. Other native woods used were pine, maple and a variety of fruit-woods – pear, apple and cherry. Mahogany was introduced into America in the 1700s; however, it was only used occasionally for

2

Fig. 2 **Bonnet-top highboy** by *John Pimm, Boston, c.1740–50 Maple and pine with japanned decoration.*
This masterpiece of American furniture was made by,Pimm for Commodore Joshua Loring of Boston. The decoration is in imitation of Oriental lacquerwork, and was probably painted by Thomas Johnson. (Henry Francis du Pont Winterthur Museum, Winterthur, Delaware.)

Fig. 3 **Highboy,** American, c.1700–20.
This piece has trumpet legs.

Museum Photo

Fig. 4 *Room from the Samuel Wentworth House*, Portsmouth, New Hampshire, built 1671, panelled c.1710. (Metropolitan Museum of Art, New York.)

Fig. 5 *Gaming-table*, American, c.1740–50. The oval hollows are for gaming counters.

case furniture in the American Queen Anne period and did not become of major importance until the second half of the century.

The introduction of a new style meant additional changes in the construction of furniture. Interiors of case pieces were more accurately joined and particular care was taken in the dovetailing of the drawers. Usually the grain of the wood provided sufficient ornament, but this did not preclude embellishments of scrolls and foliage. Metal hinges, handles and back-plates were mainly imported. In addition, a few pieces of furniture were decorated to simulate Chinese lacquer.

The use of veneer was only one of the innovations employed with William and Mary furniture; carving also became bolder. The vigorous carving of baroque details was incorporated into the existing rectilinear furniture shapes producing visual contrasts of light and shade. The Spanish foot, resembling a semi-flexed fist resting on knuckles, was a move away from the unsophisticated feet common to the period (Fig. 8).

For America, the William and Mary style was significant in that it introduced many new furniture forms: the highboy, the lowboy, the slope-top or slant-top desk, the upholstered easy chair and a

great many types of utilitarian tables. It should be remembered that pattern books were scarce and that, from the beginning, the American craftsmen took fundamental furniture forms and proceeded from there to develop an indigenous style.

One of the most notable innovations of the period was the upholstered arm-chair. The entire frame except for the legs and feet was covered with perpetuana (a durable wool and silk material much favoured in eighteenth-century America). Upholstery improved the appearance of these chairs as well as their comfort. Some dining-rooms contained sets of side-chairs and matched arm-chairs which were either caned or upholstered, and carving on the back, arms and feet gave added grace to these pieces. Sofas and settees were also introduced.

The storage chests of the earlier period underwent a considerable change. There were still the simple chest of drawers, but now the drawers were veneered, the divisions of the front were accented by mouldings and the whole piece rested on ball or turnip feet. A further practical innovation was the raising of the chest upon a framework of legs and stretchers from which resulted the earliest form of high chest. In America, it is more commonly called

Museum Photo

Museum Photo

8

Parke-Bernet Photo

Fig. 6 *The Readbourne Interior.*
The Philadelphia scroll-armed
easy chair dates from the 1730s.
Note also the shell-carved
Philadelphia chairs and the
New York tea-table with ball and
claw feet. The Boston highboy
is seen in Fig. 2.
(H. F. du Pont Winterthur
Museum.)

Fig. 7 *Armchair, Philadelphia,*
c.1740–50. Walnut.
(H. F. du Pont Winterthur
Museum.)

Fig. 8 *Lowboy with Spanish feet*
and deeply scrolled and arched
skirt, New Jersey area, 1730–50.
Maple.
(Parke-Bernet Galleries,
New York.)

(Fig. 1). This desk was essentially a chest of drawers, topped with an additional section containing small drawers, pigeon-holes and a writing surface. Occasionally, a cupboard with panelled doors was added on top of the desk, creating another form called the 'secretary'. The increased space allowed for storage of books as well as papers.

The import of ceramics, with their utilitarian and decorative appeal, increased the demand for other new forms of furniture for storage and display. Corner-cupboards, as well as several varieties of table, were used to fulfil this need.

By 1725, the fundamentally baroque character of the William and Mary style had merged with the more sophisticated Queen Anne style. For the most part, there was little change in the basic types of furniture although, as might be expected with the increasing wealth and complexity of Colonial life, more specialised types of furniture were also made. In addition to the greater skills exhibited in furniture construction and finish, there was a new concern for the co-ordination of all the elements of interior design.

A respect for the natural qualities of the wood

Queen Anne furniture at last lost the stiffness of the furniture of earlier periods and a clear and distinct elegance emerged. Although American models were based on English styles, they were simpler than their counterparts. Whereas English furniture relied on carving and gilding for decoration, American furniture craftsmen always had a respect for the natural qualities of the wood, and sought to achieve delicate and graceful forms through simplicity.

The most important element of Queen Anne design was the cyma curve – the elongated S-shape called by Hogarth 'the line of beauty'. The use of this curve went beyond decoration; it was part of the structure itself. The cyma curve is ubiquitous throughout the furniture of this period and is most noticeable in the serpentine cabriole leg. Complementing the cyma curve legs were the curved seats, chair-backs, table aprons and scroll tops of the highboys.

The Queen Anne style is epitomised in the chair, in that it required a variety of skills – those of the upholsterer, the joiner, the carver and the turner – and is capable of reflecting Colonial tastes of this period on its own. It is the side-chair which best serves to illustrate regional differences. In general, American Queen Anne chairs are smaller than those of England. They possess an organic unity which makes use of both a bold outline and a subtle interplay of curves (Fig. 6). New England chairs were tall, square-seated, and usually had stretchers connecting the legs; the pad foot was commonly used. New York chairs were broad and heavy, also with a square seat; in addition, there was an early adoption of the ball-and-claw foot, in the Queen Anne style. This feature was not adopted fully by other regions until around the middle of the century. The stiles (back posts) had reversed curves which matched the vase splats. Carving on the back cresting of New York chairs had strong Dutch characteristics.

The most important centre at this time was Philadelphia, and it was here that the Queen Anne

the 'highboy'. This form lost favour in England after the Queen Anne period, but remained popular in the Colonies throughout the period 1700–80. From the beginning, the highboy was built in two pieces for convenience of moving, with both upper and lower portions containing drawers (Fig. 3). The finest William and Mary highboys exhibit a beautiful use of burled walnut, whereas others were painted black and decorated with colour imitating Chinese motifs. Many variations occured in the turning of the legs and the scrolling of the stretchers. Some earlier pieces had turned legs, usually six, with bell, cup, or trumpet turnings (Fig. 3). The façade of the highboy also underwent several modifications involving the moulding around the drawers, the curving of the apron and the elaboration of the cornice. Crossed stretchers between the legs were sometimes used instead of the customary connecting stretchers. Tear-drop handles first, and later, bail, or half-loop, handles were used on the highboy drawers of the William and Mary period. The lowboy, which was at first a support for the high chest, was also used as a separate piece.

Another piece of furniture which developed in this period was the slant-top, or slope-top, desk

Fig. 9 ***The Perley Parlour,***
Boxford, Massachusetts, 1763.
Built for the leader of the
Boxford Minute Men, Captain
Perley. The panelling is painted
in imitation of grained cedar, and
the pilasters are marbled. The
furniture is all of the period.
(American Museum in Britain,
Claverton Manor, Bath.)

Fig. 10 ***Corner, or roundabout,***
chair, *Philadelphia, c.1740–50.*
Walnut.
(H. F. du Pont Winterthur
Museum.)

chair achieved its greatest refinement. The straight line was completely eliminated: the square seat was replaced by the horse-shoe or compass seat, which was in further harmony with the curving splat and stiles; and the elimination of stretchers gave the chair a continuous undulating line. Another Philadelphia characteristic was the chamfered stump leg and the trifid or drake's foot. The Philadelphia arm-chair shows an integrated blending of the arms with the back and the seat (Fig. 7). The carving of shells on the back cresting and knees of Philadelphia chairs was naturalistic, emphasising the alternation of concave and convex shell radials. An innovation in chairs of the period was the corner, or roundabout, chair with the back curving around two sides and a corner pointing to the front (Fig. 10).

The cabriole leg adapted well to the popular highboy. Regional differences included long slender legs on pieces from New England (Fig. 2), as compared with the shorter legs of the Phila-

The lasting popularity of the Queen Anne style in America cannot wholly be attributed to a provincial time-lag. It is evident that the Colonial cabinet-maker as well as his client preferred the style. In fact, American Queen Anne furniture rivalled those styles which followed as late as the third quarter of the century.

No discussion of American furniture of this period would be complete without mention of the familiar Windsor chair. Brought from England in the early 1700s and established by the 1730s, the Windsor chair remained popular with all classes throughout the Colonies. Simple, utilitarian, and made of the most readily available woods, the Windsor achieved a lean elegance, combining lightness with strength. The chairs were frequently painted green, with coloured lines added as decoration. Like other styles brought to America from outside the Windsor chair was developed and modified, with new forms emerging which were totally unknown in the land of its origin.

delphia highboys. The flat tops of highboys of the William and Mary period gave way in the Queen Anne period to scroll-top and bonnet-top pediments above the cornice.

In tables, other significant changes were made. The drop-leaf table with cabriole legs replaced the gate-leg. Tea-drinking, fashionable in America as in England, gave rise to a variety of tea-tables, some with marble tops and others with a protective moulding round the edges. This use of a heat-resistant surface on a table can be considered as a forerunner of the popular sideboard. Another notable form was the gaming-table which could be folded in half and moved about easily (Fig. 5). Smaller pieces of furniture, such as candle-stands and fire-screens, were now placed on cabriole tripod stands, but retained their characteristic columnar form.

Museum Photo

MUSEUMS AND COLLECTIONS

American furniture may be seen at the following:

Boston: Boston Museum of Fine Arts
New York: The Metropolitan Museum of Art
Philadelphia: Philadelphia Museum of Art
Winterthur, The Henry Francis du Pont
Delaware Winterthur Museum

FURTHER READING

American Furniture by Helen Comstock, 1980 reprint.

American Furniture of the Queen Anne and Chippendale Periods by Joseph Downs, New York, 1952.

Furniture Treasury, 3 vols., by Wallace Nutting.

American Silver in the 18th Century

Silversmiths' shops sprang up and flourished in the Colonies, producing valuable wares of great beauty which applied the American ideal of simplicity to the influential designs of English imported wares

One hundred years after America was settled, every major centre of population had a number of silversmiths' shops to supply the needs of the wealthier colonists who wished to turn their accumulated coins into objects which were useful, and identifiable in case of loss or theft. The New World silversmith generally patterned his work after English styles, following the designs that were current in the late renaissance style of the seventeenth century and, at the turn of the eighteenth century, indulging in the extravagances of elaborate baroque designs.

The richness and heaviness of the baroque style were bound to give way to greater simplicity, lightness of line, and restrained ornamentation. By 1720, the modifications of baroque elements had been introduced into American silver and were beginning to form themselves into a style distinctly their own. With an emphasis on contour, plain surfaces and rhythmic curves, objects became basically circular with little decoration other than engraving.

The octagonal shape shows graphically the transition from rectilinear to circular forms. The candlestick in Figure 1, one of a pair made by Nathaniel Morse of Boston, is devoid of surface decoration, relying upon the contours of the shaped shaft and the facets of the octagonal base for success. Variety was achieved by dividing the shaft into many sections of unequal lengths, ranging from a wafer-thin disc to an elongated ogival curved section. The faceting of the base is repeated lightly in the slight faceting of the central section of the shaft, creating a pleasing repetition to unite the variations.

The octagonal shape was one of the most popular features of early eighteenth-century silver. An 'Eight square Tea-Pot' was spoken of as 'the newest Fashion' in 1727, when it was offered in the *New York Gazette* as part of a prize made by Simeon Soumain. Such a teapot, with an S-shaped spout and a C-scrolled handle, was also fashioned, in about 1725, by the silversmith Peter van Dyck (Fig. 7).

A contemporary of Van Dyck, William Hogarth (1697–1764) of London, summarized the fundamental principles of the current style in his *Analysis of Beauty*. Published in 1753, this study of aesthetics is of particular interest because Hogarth was himself trained as a silversmith as well as being an excellent engraver and a painter. One of

Fig. 1 (previous page) *One of a
pair of candlesticks by
Nathaniel Morse (1685–1748),
Boston, c.1720. Height 6⅛ ins.
Engraved with the arms of
Faneuil.*
(Henry Francis Du Pont
Winterthur Museum,
Winterthur, Delaware.)

Fig. 2 *Salver by Jacob Hurd
(1702–1758), Boston, c.1730.
Diameter 12½ ins. Engraved with
the arms of Clarke.*
(Yale University Art Gallery,
New Haven, Connecticut.)

his chief theories was that there was a fundamental
'line of beauty' which was S-shaped, with just
the proper amount of curvature; a line which
was not too straight and not too exaggerated a curve.
This line appears repeatedly in silver made in the
second quarter of the eighteenth century.

It was important that the material should be suited to both purpose and design

Another aspect of beauty which Hogarth discussed was the quality of fitness. There must be a
fitness of the material for the purpose of the object.
This is particularly true of the minor arts, where
usefulness is a primary factor. There must also be a
fitness of the material for the design; that is, the
properties of silver should be considered and not
violated, a·principle voiced earlier by Shakespeare:
'o'erstep not the modesty of nature'.

Silver ·was well suited to the brewing of tea.
Sometimes teapots were made in a pear shape. This
was done to ensure that the tea would steep
better because a maximum amount of water
would be in contact with the tea leaves when they
settled at the bottom of the pot. Tea was precious
and the early teapots were necessarily small so that
small quantities could be brewed. However, the
handle of the teapot had to be of a certain size in
order to be gripped by the normal hand and a curved
handle fits the grip better than a square handle.
Since silver is a great conductor of heat, it was not
suitable for handles, and wood was usually
substituted. All these factors of fitness to function
and beauty of line had to be taken into consideration
by the silversmith (Fig. 7).

To achieve variety in design, several different
curving lines were often joined together to form a
continuous, smoothly flowing line. Engraved
borders and embellishments of infinite variety were
added. A salver made by Jacob Hurd (Fig. 2) has a
border composed of many different motifs and
textures, 'to lead the eye a wanton chase', as

2

Hogarth put it. Chief among these motifs were the delicate C-scroll, diapering (engraved lozenge-shaped patterns, enclosing dots or flower-heads), lightly curved leafage and flowers, and the scallop shell, which, with its many lobes, epitomised the desired roundness and united curved lines.

Engraved ciphers were well suited to the dictates of freely curving design with their circular and foliated script shapes of initials. Simeon Soumain made the cipher the chief form of embellishment on a sugar dish . . . a sugar dish now in the Mabel Brady Garvan Collection, Yale University Art Gallery. The engraving of the initials EC, for the original owner, Elizabeth Cruger, contained within a circle on the side and just above on the lid, accentuates the roundness of the form itself and the circular form of the foot and reel top. The shape of the dish was taken from that of Chinese porcelain tea bowls, and Chinese design and decoration played an increasingly important part in the mid-eighteenth century.

One of the most impressive and lasting forms of

this period is the covered cup made on several special occasions by Jacob Hurd for presentation to outstanding men (Fig. 5). Although a large piece of silver, it has grace because of the simplicity of its curvilinear form. The expanse of the body is broken up by an elaborately engraved cartouche in the upper section, and by the proper placement of a mid-band, dividing the sections into pleasing proportions.

Jacob Hurd (1702–58), who was a prominent second-generation American silversmith, was a master of proper details and cohesive design. In the coffee-pot in Figure 6, he accentuated the roundness of the body with a domed lid and a round finial. Beneath the spout he added a drop, which is the same shape as the finial but only half-round. The same silhouette, cut from a flat piece of silver, was soldered just under the top of the handle. It is this thoughtful repetition of the same shape in different dimensions which gives the design originality, interest and unity in American silver of the age of Hogarth.

Fig. 3 **Teapot** *by Jacob Hurd, Boston, c.1738. Silver and wood. spherical teapots of this type became common early in the eighteenth century and changed very little through the years except for minor features such as the higher foot, broken spout and elaborate finial on this pot. (Yale University Art Gallery.)*

Fig. 4 **Milk jug** *by Adrian Bancker, New York, c.1740. Height 4⅛ ins. Pear shapes of this sort were popular for many purposes in eighteenth-century silver, both English and American. It was frequently used for teapots, as it allowed the maximum amount of hot water to come into contact with the rare and expensive tea-leaves when they settled to the bottom of the pot. For jugs, the pear shape was less obviously sensible, but it created a practical, steady form which was hard to tip over, and easy to pour from. Although this jug is almost plain, it has the moulded rim, elaborately curved handle, and hoof feet with shell tops which are frequently seen as details on rococo pieces. (H. F. Du Pont Winterthur Museum.)*

Fig. 5 **Covered cup** *by Jacob Hurd, Boston, 1744. Height 13⅞ ins. Inscribed to Richard Spry, Commander of the Comet Bomb which captured a privateer, and presented to him by several Boston merchants. (Private Collection.)*

Fig. 7 *Teapot by Peter van Dyck,*
(1694–1750) New York, c.1725.
(Yale University Art Gallery,
Mabel Brady Garvan Collection.)

Fig. 8 *Salver by Joseph*
Richardson, Snr., made for
Mary Grafton, 1746.
(Yale University Art Gallery,
Mabel Brady Garvan Collection.)

Fig. 9 *Sauce boat by Jacob*
Hurd, Boston, mid-eighteenth
century.
(H. F. Du Pont, Winterthur
Museum. Gift of C. K. Davis.)

MUSEUMS AND COLLECTIONS

American Silver may be seen at the following:

Boston:	Boston Museum of Fine Arts
New Haven:	Yale University Art Gallery
New York:	Metropolitan Museum of Art
	Museum of the City of New York
	New-York Historical Society
	Brooklyn Museum
Philadelphia:	Museum of Art
Winterthur, Delaware	Henry Francis du Pont Winterthur Museum

FURTHER READING

Early American Silver for the Cautious Collector by Martha Gandy Fales, New York, 1970.

Early American Silver by C. Louise Avery, New York, 1968.

Historic Silver of the Colonies and its Makers by Francis Hill Bigelow, New York, 1948.

American Silver, 1655–1825, by Kathryn C. Buhler, Boston, 1972.

Colonial Silversmiths, Masters and Apprentices, by Kathryn C. Buhler, Boston, 1956.

6

7

8

9

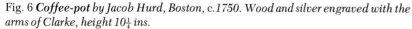

Fig. 6 *Coffee-pot by Jacob Hurd, Boston, c.1750. Wood and silver engraved with the arms of Clarke, height 10¼ ins.*
Note the unity of design seen in the accentuation of the roundness of the body by the dome, and the repetition of the finial shape under the spout.
(H. F. Du Pont Winterthur Museum.)

Funk & Wagnalls

Museum Photo

Museum Photo

Museum Photo

The Emergence of a National Style

Sandak Inc.

Sandak Inc.

Fig. 1 **'Greek' design** for the Bank of Pennsylvania, Philadelphia (subsequently destroyed), by Benjamin Henry Latrobe, 1798. Water-colour perspective. (Maryland Historical Society.)

Fig. 2 **Miles Brewton House**, Charleston, South Carolina, attributed to Ezra Waite, 1765–69.
Waite, a London-trained architect, builder and carver, derived this house from Palladio's Villa Pisani.

Fig. 3 **The Brick Market**, Newport, Rhode Island, by Peter Harrison, 1761–62.

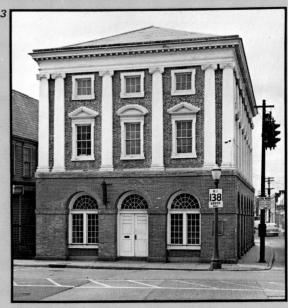

Sandak Inc.

As the Atlantic seaboard strip of colonies became a nation stretching to the Mississippi and beyond, American architecture moved from a provincial Palladianism to a creative role in the emerging international neo-classical style

When Dr. Alexander Hamilton of Annapolis – the charming port and capital of Maryland – made the 1744 seaboard journey which was to be reported in his *Itinerarium*, he travelled through dense forests of virgin timber, calling in at the small ports, county towns and plantations which then constituted the North American communities. William Penn's 'greene countrie towne', Philadelphia, was well on its way to becoming the largest city in the British Empire after London. Surpassing all other towns of the Empire, including those of the home islands, it boasted such institutions as the internationally renowned American Philosophical Society.

Apart from Philadelphia, the towns were small and pleasantly provincial and bustling with trade which would provide the means for the erection of fine houses and buildings. The people were impatient for the establishment of their own manufactures, prohibited under the Empire's mercantile

system. This would come with independence, which was to bring to Federal America a whole new range of building ideas. In 1744 Dr. Hamilton saw much architecture in the traditions of England, Holland and Sweden and a number of provincial buildings expressing earlier architectural ideas of fifty years or more. He could hardly have known how up to date the cities and towns on his wilderness route would look two generations later.

The towns, though small, had a surprising number of cultivated people among the newly emerging merchant traders. Many of the landowners, divines, lawyers and merchants had received excellent educations, both in America and abroad. Massachusetts had a higher percentage of college graduates than England and the plantation owner of the South, or the merchant of a middle Colonies port, attached great importance to the tutor, the library and the latest cultural intelligence from London papers and magazines. First the Palladian movement was reflected in Colonial architecture and then, while the events surrounding the American Revolution and Independence brought the great cities to their first flourishing, a new architecture, the Federal Style, was introduced in which were created important monuments of the international neo-classical style.

The Lindens, built in Danvers, Massachusetts, in 1754, is a Jonesian-Palladian English house type, translated to the American setting. The façade is entirely in wood, cut and sand-painted to imitate ashlar masonry and quoins. The house was built by the merchant Robert Hooper (called 'King' Hooper owing to his wealth and manners), and it

Sandak Inc.

Sandak Inc.

Old Salem Inc.

Mansell Collection

8

Paul Popper

Fig. 4 ***Prize-winning design*** *for the United States Capitol, Washington D.C., by Dr. William Thornton, 1790. The present building retains the original walls of this design. (Library of Congress, Washington.)*

Fig. 5 ***Parlange Plantation***, *Mix, Pointe Coupée Parish, Louisiana, 1750. This porticoed, hip-roofed, 'raised' type of French plantation house was built throughout the eighteenth century and into the nineteenth.*

Fig. 6 ***Old Salem***, *Winston-Salem, North Carolina. The buildings are in a German tradition, built by Moravian settlers in the 1770s and 1780s.*

Fig. 7 ***Monticello***, *near Charlottesville, Virginia, home of Thomas Jefferson, designed by him and built in two major phases, 1768–78 and 1796–1809.*

Fig. 8 ***Independence Hall***, *the State House, Philadelphia, Pennsylvania, 1731, steeple 1751–52, later changes. Here the Colonial delegates voted and proclaimed Independence in 1776.*

points to the cultural aspirations of the merchants, the 'new' men of the time. The skills at hand in Massachusetts in the middle of the century are suggested in the rich finishing of the house. The portico-like feature indicated by a pedimented central bay of rather vertical proportions became part of the typical New England Palladian façade. This marvellous house was moved to Washington D.C. in the 1930s.

These aspects of English Palladianism are reflected also in many public buildings of this period, of which the best-known example is the State House in Philadelphia, today called Independence Hall, as it was here that the colonial representatives voted and proclaimed Independence in 1776. As with many civil structures, this building has had numerous changes and additions over the years, as well as seven major campaigns to restore it to its condition of 1776. The basic structure, rather like an enlarged house or meeting-house, was built by the Philadelphian Andrew Hamilton in 1731, but the steeple was only completed in 1751–52. The steeple was taken down as rotten in 1781 and rebuilt along the original lines in 1828; the wing buildings of Congress Hall and City Hall, together with the connecting 'hyphen' arcades, were added in 1787–91, the hyphens being remodelled in the early nineteenth century and subsequently restored to their earliest form.

The full influence of the Palladianism of Jones, Gibbs and Burlington was felt in the Colonies only from about 1740 onwards, and it continued to play an important role even at the end of the century, when it had been long overtaken in England by the architecture of Chambers, the Adam brothers, Dance and the later neo-classicists.

A plate from Colen Campbell's *Vitruvius Britannicus* was the original source for the Brick Market at Newport, Rhode Island, one of a group of important Palladian buildings by the gifted amateur Peter Harrison. Harrison was a merchant who often captained his own ships, taking the opportunity when abroad to buy the books which were to give him an architectural library second only to that of William Byrd of Westover. The Redwood Library at Newport (based on an illustration to a 1736 London edition of Palladio), King's Chapel in Boston and the Touro Synagogue in Newport are the other major known works of this gifted man. For the Brick Market, he adapted the plate showing the river elevation of the Great Gallery of Jones' Old Somerset House, rendering it in brick and painted wood, and without rustication in the arcades, but creating a superbly regular market house in this important eighteenth-century port.

Gibbs' influence cannot be mentioned without evoking the image of the City of London churches, imitations of which arose all over the American coast. In Philadelphia, Dr. John Kearsley designed Christ Church, built 1727–44 (tower and spire 1752–55). In Charleston, the magnificent St. Michael's Church, which has sometimes been attributed to Peter Harrison, was built in 1752–61. In Providence, Rhode Island, Joseph Brown built the First Baptist Meeting House in 1775, with a steeple based on one of the alternative designs by Gibbs for St. Martin's-in-the-Fields. Even in the midst of the towers of Wall Street today, one of these Gibbsian churches stands, St. Paul's Chapel by Thomas McBean, built 1764–66, with the portico and spire added in English style by the

Fig. 9 **Mount Pleasant,**
*Philadelphia, Pennsylvania,
1761–62.
The Burlingtonian Palladian
house (including dependencies)
became a principal theme of
American architecture in the
second half of the eighteenth
century, especially in versions
developed from Gibbs' plates.*

Fig. 10 **St. Paul's Chapel,** *New
York City, by Thomas McBean,
1764–66, portico and spire
attributed to Pierre Charles
L'Enfant, 1794–96.
The Gibbsian City-church type
appeared throughout the
American cities in the later
eighteenth century.*

Fig. 11 **The Lindens,** *built in
Danvers, Massachusetts, in 1754
and moved to Washington D.C.
in the 1930s.
This is a classic example of the
Jonesian-Palladian style in
America. It employs the central
pedimented portico-like bay
which became a typical feature of
New England Palladian houses.
It was built for the merchant
Robert 'King' Hooper (so called
owing to his wealth and manners)
and points to the cultural
aspirations of the prospering
merchant class.*

Fig. 12 **Prize-winning design**
*for the President's house (later
called the White House) by
James Hoban, 1790.
As with the Capitol (Fig. 4), the
White House has been much
altered in the course of its one
hundred and eighty years'
existence, but the walls built to
this design are still its basic frame.
(White House Historical
Association, Washington D.C.)*

French architect-engineer Pierre Charles l'Enfant, in 1794–96.

Although the Palladian style had important effects in the north, it is most clearly seen in the country houses, and some important town houses, of the middle and southern Colonies. Two are illustrated here: Mount Pleasant, near Philadelphia, and the Miles Brewton House in Charleston. Mount Pleasant, a Gibbsian house with a pedimented central bay which projects, and two curved-roof dependencies balanced on each side, was built for a Scottish privateer and sea captain, John MacPherson. Its rich detailing and clustered chimneys with arcaded tops mix English and Scottish influences from the century preceding its construction. The Brewton House, built 1765–69, is attributed to Ezra Waite, who advertised as 'Civil Architect, House-builder in general, and Carver, from London'. The Brewton House elevation appears to be derived from the illustration in the works of Palladio of his Villa Pisani at Montagnana, but the lack of detailed information about Waite and his English background, as about that of his client, indicates the research into American architecture which has yet to be done.

A whole new set of needs in the form of buildings and in architectural symbolism

Parlange Plantation and the view of Old Salem are reminders of the French and German traditions which, in addition to the Dutch, the Spanish and the Indian, continued to have an important role in the buildings of North America throughout this period. These houses also remind us that, although we are dealing in the main with the most up-to-date works, traditional forms and methods of building persisted. It is probable, for instance, that half of the buildings erected in the English colonies in the Colonial period were built of the squared-log construction.

The change from the late Colonial to the Federal period brought a whole new set of needs in the form of buildings and in architectural symbolism. Although relatively conservative designs won the prizes for the Capitol and the President's House (the White House), they emphasise the diverse sources from which the inspiration came: a French-inspired classicism in the design by the gifted amateur Dr. William Thornton for the Capitol, and a very Gibbsian influence in the Irish architect James Hoban's design for the White House.

Both these buildings, although they remain central to the plan of the capital city of Washington, and to the national symbolism, have been very substantially changed over the years. Thornton was not a professional architect, and Hoban was engaged to erect the Capitol as well as the White House, and he had the opportunity to make his own modifications to the Thornton design. At the behest of General Washington, the Thornton plan was resumed, but it was subsequently revised by Benjamin Henry Latrobe in 1803–17, further changed by Charles Bulfinch, and enlarged to its present form, with added wings and great new dome, by Thomas U. Walter in 1855–65.

The grounds and terraces were also remodelled over the years (the original plan for the city had called for a grand water staircase down the Capitol Hill to a canal across the Mall to the President's park) and many other changes have been made inside and out.

The White House has been rebuilt time and again, since the laying of its cornerstone in 1792. Latrobe redesigned it between 1803 and 1812, before it was first finished, but Hoban rebuilt it on the original plan after it was burnt down by the British armies in the war of 1812. Extensive additions and renovations occurred repeatedly during the nineteenth century, though the major efforts of the twentieth century have been to return the house to something like its original character.

But the striking examples of the new architecture of the Federal period, and of the development of an American neo-Classicism of innate vitality, are the works of Latrobe and of that universal man, the third President of the United States, Thomas Jefferson.

Latrobe, an English-trained architect who first worked in the London office of S. P. Cockerell, brought the new architecture of the younger Dance, Holland, Soane and the German neo-Classicists to America. He is well represented by his stunning water-colour design for the Bank of Pennsylvania, the first use of a Greek order in the United States of America in a prostyle temple which, despite its Roman features, Latrobe would have regarded as Greek in character. This judgment has caused it to be given the place of the first building in the American Greek Revival. Latrobe visited General Washington, but received no official work through him; in the years after 1803, however, President Jefferson appointed him Architect of the Capitol and Surveyor of Public Buildings, from which positions his influence was as enormous as his talent. Among other greater and lesser works he created three successful 'American orders': one based on the maize plant, which the Congressmen promptly dubbed the 'corn-cob capital'; one based on the tobacco plant; and a third on the cotton plant.

Finally, this look at America's eighteenth-century architecture must end with Jefferson, as must any review of her eighteenth- and early nineteenth-century achievements. While drafting the Declaration of Independence, carrying out his numerous official duties including those of the Presidency, overseeing the acquisition of a quarter of the continent in the Lousiana Purchase, and generally forming much of Federal America, he still had the time to be a great amateur architect. In France he had come to know Clérisseau, who while a member of Piranesi's Rome circle had tutored Robert Adam. With Clérisseau, Jefferson designed the State Capitol for Richmond, Virginia, as a temple-form structure based on the Maison Carrée at Nîmes. But his greatest achievement architecturally was the highly personal creation on his mountain-top lands near Charlottesville, Virginia, of his own Palladian house, Monticello. He first built it as a double-porticoed house in 1768–78, remodelling it into the present domed villa in 1796–1809. Here he combined a general Anglo-Palladian conception with details from French and English neo-Classicism to create the greatest personal monument of the Federal period, and a great individual work of art of any period. Monticello is a beautiful and just summation of the Palladian and neo-classical currents in architecture seen in America during the second half of the eighteenth century.

Sandak Inc.

11

Sandak Inc.

Charles Baptie

Association Photo

Early Glass:
Wistar & Stiegel

2

Museum Photo

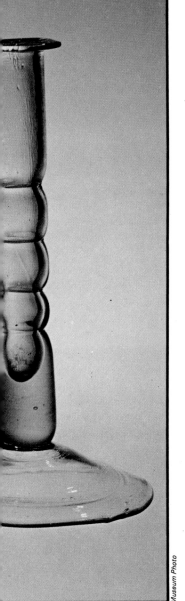

Museum Photo

It was not until the middle of the eighteenth century, with the factories of Wistar and Stiegel, that the Colonies began to develop a true glass industry of their own

In 1608 and again in 1621 attempts were made to establish a glass factory in Jamestown, Virginia, giving rise to the claim that glass-making was the first industry in English-speaking America. But both failed. Several other attempts were made in the seventeenth century to establish glass-works elsewhere in the Colonies, but these, too, were abortive. It was not until the eighteenth century, when about a dozen more attempts were made, that some degree of success was achieved. The most noteworthy and best-known glasshouses of that century were those established by Casper Wistar, Henry William Stiegel and, later, John Frederick Amelung.

Casper Wistar was not a practical glass-maker, but a successful brass button manufacturer in Philadelphia who had come there from the Palatinate in 1717. In 1739 he employed his capital to purchase a large tract of land and build a glass-house in what came to be called Allowaystown, or Wistarberg, about thirty miles to the south east of Philadelphia (Fig. 6). Wistar imported his glass-makers, the first four coming from Rotterdam, as shown by an agreement dated 7 December, 1738. As their names suggest – John William Wentzell, Casper Halter, John Martin Halton and Simon Kreismeier – these men were Germans or Dutch.

Later he imported other skilled workers from Germany.

Wistar's glasshouse produced primarily window-glass and bottles but, while these necessities were the basic products of his factory, his workers also made limited quantities of tableware from the same material from which the window-glass and bottles were made. These 'off-hand' pieces, made primarily for the workers' own families and for the local market, are characterised by individuality and were influenced by the Germanic tradition with which the workers were familiar. They were utilitarian and bold in form, sometimes almost crude, and were often decorated with applications of the same glass in the form of threading, gadrooning, prunts, trailing patterns and sometimes even bird-shaped finials (Fig. 1).

These pieces from Wistar's factory and later South Jersey glasshouses are referred to today as 'South Jersey Type' glass and the general style, which gradually spread to window- and bottle-glasshouses in New England and New York State, is called the 'South Jersey Tradition'. The Germanic influence on these glasses can be readily noted by comparing the two sugar-bowls shown in Figure 7. The origins of the South Jersey Tradition, however, may be traced well beyond the eighteenth century to the *Waldglas* produced in the small glasshouses of central Europe in the fifteenth, sixteenth and seventeenth centuries.

After Casper Wistar's death in 1752, his glass-house was carried on by his son, Richard. The following advertisement from the *Pennsylvania Gazette*, of 28 September, 1769, suggests the nature of the products of this fairly successful glasshouse. The difficulty of competing with imported wares is also suggested by Richard Wistar's plea for support of American manufacture:

Fig. 1 *Left: **Covered sugar-bowl with chicken finial,*** *German, last third of eighteenth century. Colourless glass. Wistar imported many of his glass-blowers from Holland and Germany. With them they brought their old traditions, and many pieces with animal finials were made after prototypes such as this.*
*Centre and right: **Covered sugar-bowl** and **candlestick,*** *attributed to a South Jersey glass-works, possibly Wistar's, c.1760–80. Olive green and aquamarine glass. Height of candlestick 6½ ins.*
(Corning Museum of Glass, Corning, New York.)

Fig. 2 ***Pattern-moulded glass*** *attributed to Stiegel's glass-works, Manheim, c.1769–74. From the left:*
Salt-cellar. *Cobalt blue glass.* ***Covered sugar-bowl.*** *Cobalt blue glass, height 6⅛ ins.* ***Creamer.*** *Amethyst glass.* ***Creamer,*** *English, third quarter of the eighteenth century. Pattern-moulded glass.*
A comparison of the Stiegel creamer with the one of English origin on the right indicates the difficulty of distinguishing Stiegel's work from contemporary English or European glass.
(Corning Museum of Glass.)

3

Fig. 3 *Two enamelled tumblers
with inscriptions, probably made
in Europe and enamelled
at Stiegel's glass-works,
Manheim, 1772–74. Height 4 ins.
(Corning Museum of Glass.)*

Fig. 4 *Bottle of the type
produced in Wistar's glasshouse,
probably of English origin,
dated 1767. Height 9 ins.
(Corning Museum of Glass.)*

4

'Made at subscriber's Glass Works between 300 and 400 boxes of Window glass consisting of common sizes 10 x 12, 9 x 11, 8 x 10, 7 x 9, 6 x 8. Lamp glasses or any uncommon sizes under 16 x 18 are cut on short notice. Most sort of bottles, gallon, 1/2 gallon, and quart, full measure 1/2 gallon case bottles, snuff and mustard bottles also electrofying globes and tubes &c. All glass American Manufacture and America ought also encourage her own manufacture. N.B. He also continues to make the Philadelphia brass buttons noted for their strength and such as were made by his deceased father and warranted for 7 years.

RICHARD WISTAR.'

It has always been assumed, on the basis of his 1769 advertisements, that Wistar produced all of the glass he offered for sale, but manuscripts in the possession of a descendant include letters from Richard Wistar in which he ordered crown window glass from Bristol in 1759 and later, and enquired about the pieces of 'hollow ware' in 1767. Thus, a degree of caution must be used in interpreting his advertisements.

Richard Wistar continued to operate the glasshouse in Allowaystown until 1780, when he offered the business for sale. There were apparently no takers, and glass-making operations ceased. Despite its importance in the history of American glass-making, no products are known which can definitely be attributed to it. An English bottle of a type which was probably made there between 1740 and 1780 is illustrated in Figure 4. The South Jersey Tradition continued until about 1860, and found its fullest expression and development in New York State glasshouses during the period 1835–50 (Fig. 7).

Henry William Stiegel, born in Cologne in 1729,

came to America in 1750 and settled in Shaefferstown, near Lancaster, Pennsylvania, where many of his fellow countrymen were living. He was an iron-worker by trade, married to the daughter of iron-master Jacob Huber, the successful owner of a local forge. In 1758, after the death of his father-in-law, Stiegel took over the iron works, rebuilt it and named it Elizabeth Furnace, after his wife. He later built another iron furnace at Charming Forge, and apparently both prospered. With profits from his iron furnaces, Stiegel established a small glass-works at Elizabeth Furnace which began producing bottles and window-glass in September 1763. In November 1765, together with Philadelphia partners, he established a glasshouse in Manheim, a small town near Lancaster which he founded. Here, tableware as well as bottles and window-glass were produced. A third glasshouse, also located in Manheim, was begun in 1768 and completed in 1769, to which additions were made in each of the next three years.

Stiegel specialised in the production of fine tableware

Stiegel's advertisements referred to the firm as the American Flint Glass Works. Here he produced colourless and coloured flint glass and fine tableware of many varieties, including engraved and enamelled glasses. This was the first glasshouse in America to specialise in the production of fine tableware, which emulated both English and Continental glasses. He employed, at the peak of his production, about one hundred and thirty men who had come primarily from England and Germany. Stiegel advertised fairly widely and his products

Early American Glass

Fig. 5 **Mug**, *possibly made at Stiegel's glass-works, Manheim, c.1770. Free-blown of almost colourless glass with applied strap handle and decorated with sketchy engraving. Height 6¼ ins. (Corning Museum of Glass.)*

Fig. 6 **Map** *showing the sites of early glass-making centres in Colonial America.*

Fig. 7 **South Jersey Type glass:**
Left: **Sugar-bowl**, *Suncook Glass Works, New Hampshire, 1839–50.*
Centre: **Sugar-bowl** *with 1829 silver coin in stem, probably Redford or Redwood Glass Works, New York, 1835–50. Height 10½ ins.*
Right: **Mug**, *South Jersey, 1835–60.*
(Corning Museum of Glass.)

were marketed as far away as Boston. At the time of his failure on 5 May, 1774, Stiegel listed unsold glass with dealers or agents in York, Hanover and Carlisle, as well as Manheim (Pennsylvania), Hagerstown, Fredericktown and Baltimore (Maryland), and New York City. He probably also sent some glass to the West Indies. The bankrupt Stiegel was thrown into a debtors' prison in the autumn of 1774 but was released by Christmas. He died at Charming Forge on 10 January, 1785.

The 'Stiegel Tradition' flourished in the Midwest

Although Stiegel was not a practical glass-maker, he was very successful in emulating the various types of English glass in demand in the Colonies at the time, as well as the common engraved and enamelled Germanic wares with which his fellow Pennsylvania-Germans had been familiar in their homeland. With a few exceptions, it is impossible to distinguish between products which may have been made in one of his glasshouses and those produced in England or on the Continent during this period. Stiegel imported glass-blowers and enamellers from Germany and glass-blowers from the Bristol area of England. Because the output of his workmen was closely controlled, the products from Stiegel's factories were far less individual in character than those produced in the South Jersey Tradition. Pattern-moulding as a decorative technique was widely used in his glasshouses. The use of

this technique was continued in many of the glass-houses established in the early nineteenth century west of the Allegheny Mountains, an area termed, in American glass-making parlance, the 'Midwest', of which Pittsburgh was the centre (Fig. 6). This presumed Stiegel influence resulted in what is called today the 'Stiegel Tradition'.

Though many of his pattern-moulded glasses cannot be distinguished from their counterparts in England or Europe, pocket-bottles, which were once found largely in Pennsylvania bearing a diamond daisy or a daisy in hexagonal pattern, appear to have no European counterparts or prototypes and may be attributed with a degree of certainty to Stiegel. They were probably made in his second Manheim factory between 1769 and 1774. With these exceptions, it is impossible to distinguish Stiegel's products, but we know from his advertisements and his account books, which are still extant in the Historical Society of Pennsylvania, Philadelphia, that his factories produced a wide range of tableware and other glass. A partial listing in one of his account books '. . . for glass sold and sent out' to various stores and agents for the months of November and December 1769 included 'Quart Moulded Decanters, Pint Decanters of all sizes, half pint ditto, Quart, Pint, half pint and gill and half gill tumblers, Wine and Water glasses, Wine and Beer Glasses, quart, Pint and half pint Mugs, Bowls, Specie Bottles, half pint Cans, Cream Jugs, Smelling Bottles, Vinegar Cruets, Sugar boxes with covers, Chain Salts, Mustard Pots, Pocket Bottles, Jelly, sillabub and Free mason glasses, Phials of all

8

Museum Photo

Fig. 8 *Decanter, possibly made at Stiegel's glass-works, Manheim, c.1770. Free-blown of colourless non-lead glass and engraved, height 9⅞ ins. (Corning Museum of Glass.)*

Sorts, Candlesticks, Fine Wine glasses, common tail wine glasses, and Toys of all Sorts'. One can speculate that the entries for 'Chain Salts', 'Sugar boxes with covers', and 'Cream Jugs' are of the types illustrated in Figure 2, which are indistinguishable from English glass of these types.

Stiegel produced enamelled glasses for the local German inhabitants

Presumably some of the tumblers and mugs produced were sketchily engraved with floral and geometric designs in what we term today a 'peasant' or 'folk' manner, like the mug in Figure 5 and the decanter in Figure 8. Such glasses were widely produced on the Continent and those thought to have been made by Stiegel must be referred to today as 'Stiegel-type' glasses, rather than 'Stiegel glasses', because of the uncertainty of their origin. The same terminology must be applied to enamelled glasses like those in Figure 3, which Stiegel began producing in 1772, undoubtedly to supply the local Pennsylvania German market. They closely imitated the same type of enamelled peasant glass with which these people had been familiar in their native land. About a dozen enamelled tumblers are known bearing English inscriptions with a Germanic flavour expressing the following sentiments: 'We Two will be True', and 'My Love you like me do' (Fig. 3). While these glasses, too, may have been made in Europe for the American market, they are likely to have been enamelled in Stiegel's factory.

MUSEUMS AND COLLECTIONS
Early American blown glass and English prototypes may be seen at the following:

Boston: Boston Museum of Fine Arts
Corning, N.Y.: Corning Museum of Glass
Dearborn, Mich.: Henry Ford Museum and Greenfield Village
New York: Metropolitan Museum of Art
Philadelphia: Philadelphia Museum of Art

FURTHER READING

Chats on Old Glass by R. A. Robertson, revised with a new chapter on American glass by Kenneth M. Wilson, New York, 1969.

Two Hundred Years of American Blown Glass by George S. and Helen A. McKearin, New York, 1950.

Stiegel Glass by Frederick William Hunter, New York, 1966 reprint.

American Glass by George S. and Helen A. McKearin, New York, 1941.

Henry William Stiegel and His Associates by George L. Heiges, 1976.

American Historical Glass by Bessie M. Lindsey, 1966 reprint.

Stiegel Glass by Frederick W. Hunter, 1966.

THE PORCELAIN TRADE OF AMERICA

Museum Photo

Although there were attempts at producing true porcelain in the Colonies before the Revolution, most wares were imported from England and China until 1825

The material culture of colonial America was, quite understandably, complex. Such varied factors as geographical isolation, English colonial policy and an ever expanding frontier contributed to the composition of a society which differed in many ways from that of England. However, by the mid-eighteenth century some parts of the Colonies had developed to the point where a respectable emulation of English social patterns was possible. In such places as Boston, Philadelphia and the great plantations of tidewater Virginia, a rather high level of material culture was maintained by the well-to-do. Porcelain was included in the many possessions that enabled the prosperous Colonial American to live in a style comparable to his counterparts in England. Two broad generalisations serve to describe the situation. First, virtually all the porcelain in use was imported. Second, this porcelain was predominantly Chinese, though some English porcelain was imported at the end of the Colonial period.

In recent years, archaeological research has enabled American scholars to arrive at firm conclusions about the type of Chinese porcelain imported by Americans during the period from about 1725 to 1775. Excavations of widespread Colonial sites reveal a remarkably consistent pattern. Blue and white Chinese porcelain decorated with stylised landscape scenes or with foliate motifs was predominant. Of course these porcelains, decorated only in under-glaze blue, were cheaper than the more elaborate over-glaze enamelled pieces. Wasters from Colonial sites indicate that much of this simple blue and white porcelain was of reasonably good quality – thinly potted and well painted. In general, pieces from tea- and dinner-services have been most frequently found in archaeological sites, but punch-bowls and mugs are not uncommon. Contemporary newspaper advertisements provide further evidence of a substantial and well-established trade in Chinese porcelain by the middle of the eighteenth century. For example in 1767 a New York china vendor advertised 'India China, enamelled and blue and white Bowls, Caudle Cups, etc., . . . Nankin China Mugs, Salt Cellers, etc., etc.'

Though blue and white Chinese export wares comprised the main body of porcelain used in Colonial America, more expensive porcelains were not uncommon. Archaeology, documented pieces and literary sources all establish that some fine over-glaze, polychrome-enamelled Chinese porcelains also were present in limited quantities. More modestly decorated polychrome wares were present in greater numbers, and fine punch-bowls seem to have been in common use by the time of the Revolution. It should be remembered that during the Colonial period there was no direct American trade with China, and that imported Chinese goods came in via England.

On a considerably smaller scale, English porcelain, especially the cheaper blue and white wares, was imported after the middle of the century. As with the Chinese porcelain, tea- and coffee-services or part-services and dinner wares were predominant. Much of the blue and white English porcelain found during archaeological excavations is from Worcester or from the several Liverpool factories. This is significant, as Bristol (near Worcester) and Liverpool were the two chief English ports serving the American trade. Even on the frontier in the midst of the American wilderness, some of the English seem to have maintained a relatively high material culture. In the wealthier parts of the Colonies, it is quite probable that fine English porcelain was present in limited quantities. For example, the documentary sources relating to Colonial Williamsburg, Virginia, mention Chelsea figures.

Though Colonial Americans imported nearly all of their fine ceramics, local potteries soon appeared in the settled areas. Supplying nearby markets, these small potteries made coarse earthenware and stoneware for everyday use. Little was attempted in the way of better ceramics, though some creamware and possibly some delftware was produced before the Revolution. Ambiguous documentary sources

Fig. 1 (Previous page) *Jug*, Tucker factory, Philadelphia, c.1830. Height $8\frac{1}{2}$ ins. As with most Tucker wares, the decoration on this jug is in the French manner. (Smithsonian Institution, Washington D.C.)

Fig. 2 *Mug and bowl*, Chinese export, c.1800. Decorated with the Great Seal of the United States, the borders of the Nanking pattern. Height of mug 6 ins, diameter of bowl $7\frac{5}{8}$ ins. (Smithsonian Institution.)

Fig. 3 *Sweetmeat-dish*, Bonnin and Morris factory, Philadelphia, c.1771. Height $5\frac{1}{2}$ ins. (Smithsonian Institution.)

Fig. 4 *Plate*, Sèvres, 1785. Cornflower pattern, length 10 ins. This was used as state china by John Adams, the second President. (Smithsonian Institution.)

Fig. 5 *Bowl*, Niderviller, c.1780–82. Diameter 10 ins. This bowl is from a dinner service presented to George Washington by the Comte de Custine of Niderviller. (Smithsonian Institution.)

Fig. 6 *Plate*, Chinese export, c.1775–90. Decorated in blue and white with a standard landscape. Length 14 ins. This blue and white service also belonged to George Washington. (Smithsonian Institution.)

2

suggest the possibility that porcelain was made at an earlier date, but the first proved manufactory was established in Philadelphia in 1770 by Gouse Bonnin and George Morris. This pioneering commercial effort was short lived, the factory surviving only two years. The blue and white soft-paste porcelain made by Bonnin and Morris was roughly in the style of Worcester. From the fewer than twenty pieces that have been identified to date, it appears that this porcelain was of reasonably satisfactory quality and that the modelling and painting were better than might be expected. The diminutive sweetmeat-dish in Figure 3 is representative of Bonnin and Morris porcelain. Sauce-boats, baskets, covered jars and cups and saucers are also known. But, with the one minor exception of Bonnin and Morris of Philadelphia, all pre-revolutionary American porcelain appears to have been imported.

With the conclusion of the Revolution and the advent of the new republic, the situation did not change to any great extent. Possibly one might have expected the immediate, full-blown birth of an American porcelain industry. Such was not the case. The technology, the impetus and the know-how simply were not present. Rather, the pre-revolutionary situation persisted. Chinese porcelain was imported in even greater quantity, but now directly from Canton in American ships. The dominance of the English in the overall American ceramic market was interrupted only by the Revolution. After 1785 an increasing stream of creamware, pearlware, stoneware and porcelain poured across the ocean and England's profitable ceramic trade with the newly born United States has continued to the present time.

During the Revolution a fine Niderviller service was presented to George Washington

In the particular area of porcelain, the only notable change was a minor one. The French, who had assisted the Colonies during the Revolution, were able to sell some porcelain to America. This trade was limited, and it appears that a good proportion of the surviving French porcelain owned by Americans during the early republic was purchased by Americans in France or imported to special order. One of the more important French porcelain services acquired during this period is the Sèvres dinner-service purchased by John Adams, the second President of the United States. Adams acquired this service before 1800 (it has 1783, 1784 and 1785 date-letters in the mark) and used it as his state china when he became President. The rather commonplace cornflower pattern on the service shown on the plate, in Figure 4, perhaps reflects New England restraint.

In fact, as early as 1782, while the Revolution was still in progress, the Comte de Custine, proprietor of the Niderviller factory, presented a fine porcelain service to George Washington (Fig. 5). Thus, contrary to the general trend in which English and Chinese porcelains dominated, American Presidents from Washington until Lincoln frequently exercised an option for dinner-services of French porcelain. Sèvres, Niderviller, Rue d'Angoulême, Dagoty and Nast are all represented in what survives of the presidential china of the early republic. Presidential taste was not necessarily

7

Museum Photo

8

Derek Balmer

9

Derek Balmer

10

Derek Balmer

Early American
Porcelain Imports

Fig. 7 Vase, *Chinese export,*
c.1850. Decorated with
polychrome painting in the
'rose medallion' style.
Height 15½ ins.
After about 1825, the quantity
and quality of Chinese export
porcelain declined. A new form
of decoration became popular,
called 'rose medallion' which
was characterised by
compartmentalised foliate
motifs, exotic birds and scenes
with figures.
(Smithsonian Institution.)

Fig. 8 Vase, *Tucker factory,*
Philadelphia, c.1830. Painted
and gilt decoration.
Height 14⅛ ins.
Started in about 1825 by
William Ellis Tucker, this
factory produced the first true
porcelain in America, and the
factory continued, under various
names, chiefly Tucker and
Hemphill, until 1838. The style of
decoration on the white, hard-
paste wares was much influenced
by French designs, as seen on this
neo-classical urn which owes its
inspiration to Sèvres products of
this period. The establishment of
the Tucker factory marked the
beginning of a flourishing
porcelain industry in the United
States.
(American Museum in Britain,
Claverton Manor, near Bath.)

Fig. 9 Cup and saucer, *Tucker*
factory, c.1830. The cup,
twelve-faceted and decorated
with a stylised vine motif.
Height 2½ ins. The saucer
sixteen-faceted and picked out
in gilt. Diameter 5¼ ins.
Made during the Tucker-Hulme
partnership, this cup and saucer
are part of a service made for the
Hulme family. The saucer has an
incised mark on the base.
(John Judkyn Memorial,
Freshford Manor, near Bath.)

Fig. 10 Jug, *Tucker factory,*
1828. Painted with polychrome
flowers and gilt. Height 9 ins.
The initials 'ES' painted in gilt
under the spout are believed to
be for the original owner,
Elizabeth Slater.
(American Museum in Britain.)

reflected in the American market. Advertisements by china sellers in late eighteenth-century American newspapers were common, but in nearly every instance only Chinese and English porcelain were mentioned. Occasionally it is possible to discover an advertisement such as one in a New York paper in 1796 offering 'a few French China table sets'. Thus, the conclusion must be that the market for French porcelain in the early republic was relatively limited.

Larger amounts of English porcelain were imported, and most of this was probably blue and white until after 1800 when polychrome porcelain became somewhat less expensive. Though specific references are unusual, some of the post-Revolutionary advertisements do provide helpful information. For example in 1791 a Baltimore china vendor reported that he had for sale 'Liverpool China, in Boxes'. The various Liverpool manufactories had a slight competitive edge in that they were located in a seaport engaged in the American trade.

As a matter of logic, it would seem likely that the early years of the nineteenth century saw some incursion into the American market by the burgeoning porcelain factories of Germany, but such was not the case. Contemporary literary sources, business records and archaeological investigations all indicate that practically no German porcelain was exported to the United States during this period. A notable exception – again pointing to the fact that the White House was atypical – was a Meissen/Berlin family service belonging to John Quincy Adams, the sixth President (1824–28). This service, decorated in under-glaze blue with the decoration known as 'onion pattern', once again indicates a certain predilection for blue and white.

William Ellis Tucker was the pioneer of the porcelain industry in the U.S.A.

All contemporary evidence indicates quite strongly that Chinese export porcelain continued to be the porcelain most commonly in use during the years after the Revolution. As with the other types previously discussed, blue and white was predominant, but the quality of paste, glaze and decoration was generally inferior to pre-revolutionary imports. Though the trade was primarily in American ships after 1785, little else differed. America's China trade was essentially the same as that conducted from Canton by various European countries or their trading companies.

Most wares were decorated in stock patterns and imported for sale by china dealers in the coastal cities or for sale at dockside auction. An example of this sort of ware can be found in a large blue and white platter decorated with an unexceptional Chinese landscape scene (Fig. 6). This plate was part of a service owned by George Washington. Of more interest were services made or decorated specially to order in Canton. Sometimes these contained patriotic scenes or symbols. A bowl and mug (Fig. 2), decorated with polychrome versions of the Great Seal of the United States, typify this genre. Other services were made with standard patterns and borders, but individually embellished with the owners' monograms.

A number of pieces of exceptional Chinese export porcelain made especially for the American market have survived. Most have more historical interest than aesthetic merit. In this category are pieces from George Washington's 'Society of the Cincinnati' service. The Society of the Cincinnati was a select fraternity made up of ex-officers who had served in the Revolution. Several services of Chinese export porcelain were decorated with versions of the Cincinnati emblem, and one was acquired by Washington. Although the iconography is pedestrian and the border common for that time, the association with Washington seems compelling, and pieces from this service command exceptional prices.

After about 1825, as the China trade declined and as the quality of Chinese export porcelain also declined, a new decorative style termed 'rose medallion' became popular. The large vase in Figure 7, dating from the middle of the nineteenth century, is typical of this class.

After 1820 English and, to a lesser degree, French porcelains maintained a substantial share of the American market. As the China trade fell off, the United States made tentative steps towards establishing its own porcelain industry. As noted earlier, an abortive venture – that of Bonnin and Morris of Philadelphia – had endured for only two years, about 1770–72. After the Revolution, a few more inconsequential attempts seem to have been made, but it was not until 1825 that a degree of commercial success in porcelain manufacturing was achieved. Again, the place was Philadelphia. There, William Ellis Tucker, the son of a successful china seller, established a factory which continued until 1838. Both in form and in decoration, Tucker porcelain was inclined to be influenced by the French (Figs. 1, 8, 9 and 10).

After the breakthrough by Tucker, American porcelain manufactories began to establish themselves, and by 1875 the United States had a true porcelain industry. But, as has been shown, this was slow in coming. The history of porcelain in America – both before and immediately after the Revolution – is essentially the history of porcelain imported from China and Europe.

MUSEUMS AND COLLECTIONS

American porcelain and imported pieces may be seen at the following:

New York:	Metropolitan Museum of Art
Washington, D.C.:	Smithsonian Institution
Williamsburg, Va.:	Colonial Williamsburg
Winterthur, Del.:	H. F. du Pont Winterthur Museum

FURTHER READING

Chinese Export Porcelain for the American Trade by Jean M. Mudge, Newark, Del., 1980.

The Pottery and Porcelain of the United States by Edwin A. Barber, New York, 1979 reprint.

The Warner Collector's Guide to American Pottery and Porcelain by Bert and Ellen Denker, New York, 1982.

Early American Pottery and China by John Spargo, 1974.

Author's Photo

ROCOCO SILVER IN THE COLONIES

Fig. 1 *Teapot by Benjamin Burt (1729–1805), Boston, 1757. Chased and engraved silver with wooden handle. Height 5⅛ ins. Engraved 'M:ʸ Derby' for Mary Derby on the base, this pot commemorates her marriage to George Crowninshield in 1757. (Private Collection.)*

Fig. 2 *Whistle and bells by Daniel Christian Fueter (active c.1754–76), New York, c.1760–70. Chased gold set with coral. Length 5¼ ins. (Mabel Brady Garvan Collection, Yale University Art Gallery, New Haven.)*

Following closely the fashions of English design, silver in eighteenth-century America blossomed into a profusion of surface ornament

The fashions of Hogarth's day prepared the way for the rococo style which emerged in the middle of the eighteenth century. While the emphasis in American silver had previously been on form and line, attention now became fixed on detail and surface ornament. Many of the old basic forms remained but they were lightened by naturalistic flowers, leaves and ruffles, which gave a gay, fanciful, feminine effect to the designs.

Lines that had been singly curved before became doubly curved. C-scrolls became broken C-scrolls. The early symmetrical scallop shell was replaced by an asymmetrical or tattered shell. Where there had been smooth surfaces and some engraving, there was now repoussé work, gadrooning and cast ornament, all in great profusion. Hardly a spot of surface survived without some embellishment.

Because of its malleability, silver was very well suited to the enthusiasm for abundant decoration. A teapot (Fig. 1) made by Benjamin Burt shows the addition of the chased and engraved ornamentation over the top surface of the body, spilling right over from the shoulders on to the flat lid and hiding the flush hinge. Instead of a simply turned type of finial, a fat pineapple has been added. While the most popular shape for the earlier bodies of vessels was a pear or globe,

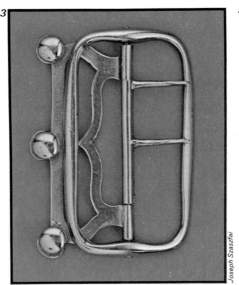

Fig. 3 **Stock-buckle** by Joseph Richardson Sr. (1711–84), Philadelphia, c.1750–70. Length 1¾ ins, one tine missing. (Gift of W. M. Jeffords, B.A. 1905, Yale.)

Fig. 4 **Snuff-box** by Joseph Richardson Sr., Philadelphia, c.1750–70. Chased and engraved silver. Length 3⅛ ins. (M. B. Garvan Collection, Yale.)

Fig. 5 **Snuffers and stand** by Myer Myers (1723–95), New York, c.1755–70. Silver with cast decoration. Length 7⅛ ins. (M. B. Garvan Collection, Yale.)

teapots and other forms now became apple- or inverted-pear-shaped. This did away with the heavy, substantial-looking base of the baroque form and created a lighter, less stable-looking object; the delicacy of the rococo style was brought into the basic shape as well as into the decoration.

These features can all be seen on three pieces made by Paul Revere (Fig. 8) in the full rococo style. Both the coffee-pot and the sugar-bowl are in the new inverted-pear shape, which the silversmiths referred to as 'double-bellied', as opposed to the single-bellied form. The lids of both pieces are doubly domed, and capped with a pine-cone finial. The repoussé ornament of the sugar-bowl is a tangle of floral motifs, C-scrolls and ruffles. The coffee-pot has a double-scrolled handle and a large cast shell applied to the base of the spout. The top of the spout has an added furl, and

the arms engraved on the side are enclosed in an asymmetrical cartouche. Gadrooning, which made its return to silver towards the end of the rococo period, has been added to the edge of the lid and to the base. The tray also epitomises rococo design in its irregular border, emphasised by its moulding, which is composed of conjoined S- and C-scrolls interrupted with alternating large and small tattered shells. The vocabulary of rococo ornament has also been enunciated in the engraving of the delicate asymmetrical cartouche of the arms.

Outstanding among American examples of rococo silver is the tea-kettle and stand made by Joseph Richardson of Philadelphia (Fig. 7). Not only is the body of the tea-kettle double-bellied, but the frame on which it rests is festooned with floral garlands and ruffles. Even the lamp under-

Fig. 6 **Marks** of Benjamin Burt (Fig. 1), Paul Revere (Fig. 8) and Myer Myers (Figs. 5, 9, 10 and 11). American silversmiths often used their whole name rather than just their initials.

6

Fig. 7 **Tea-kettle and stand** by Joseph Richardson Sr., Philadelphia, c.1760. Engraved with the arms of Plumstead. Height $14\frac{3}{4}$ ins. (M. B. Garvan Collection, Yale.)

Fig. 8 **Sugar-bowl, salver and coffee-pot** by Paul Revere (1735–1818), Boston; the coffee-pot, c.1781, height $12\frac{7}{8}$ ins., the others c.1761, heights $6\frac{3}{4}$ and $13\frac{1}{8}$ ins. (Museum of Fine Arts, Boston.)

8

9

7
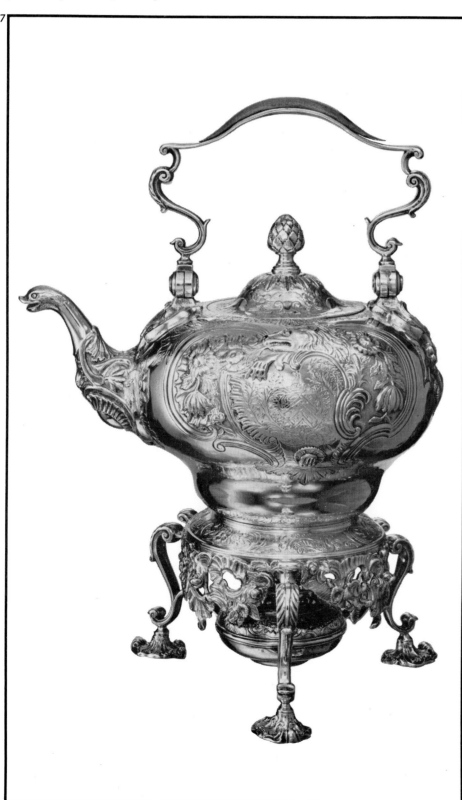

10

Fig. 9 **Cake-basket** by Myer Myers, New York, c.1765. Made for Samuel and Susan Cornell (see also Fig. 11). Length 14½ ins.
(Metropolitan Museum of Art, Morris K. Jesup Fund, purchased 1954.)

Fig. 10 **Candlestick,** one of a pair by Myer Myers, New York, c.1760–75. Engraved: 'The Gift of Peter & Sarah Vn. Brugh to Cathae: Livingston'. Height 10⅛ ins.
(M. B. Garvan Collection, Yale.)

Fig. 11 **Dish ring** by Myer Myers, New York, c.1760–70. Initialled for Samuel and Susan Cornell, marked below and to left and right of initials. Height 4⅞ ins.
(M. B. Garvan Collection, Yale.)

Fig. 12 **Pair of sauce-boats and cruet-stand** by John David (1736–98), Philadelphia, c.1765. The cruet-stand engraved 'CR' for Ringgold, height 10¾ ins., the bottle tops hallmarked in London. The sauce-boats engraved 'TSC' for Cooch, height 4¾ ins.
(Henry Francis du Pont Winterthur Museum, Winterthur, Delaware.)

Joseph Szaszfai

Museum Photo

neath is ornamented, a feature rarely found in elaborate English silver. The naturalism of the Rococo can be seen in the animal's head worked into the fantastic repoussé ornament at the top of the swirling cartouche, as well as in the bird's head which forms the lip of the spout. To achieve the fullness of the late rococo style, Richardson had to combine chasing, engraving, repoussé and cast ornament. As with all well-designed objects, the space enclosed by the raised handle is as pleasing to look at as the shape of the piece as a whole.

The same shell foot found on the Richardson tea-kettle and stand was used by John David for a cruet-stand and a pair of sauce-boats (Fig. 12). In fact, shells and C-scrolls are everywhere in these pieces. The handles of the sauce-boats are especially stylish since they are free-standing at the top and, in common with much rococo design, they give the impression of being perilously poised. The lightness and airiness are also qualities to be seen in the cruet-stand, which holds five glass containers. Reverse scrolls, which seem to be on the brink of toppling over, support the asymmetrical frame of five lobes, and ruffled rings of gadrooning contain the bottles. The handle for the frame stands high and open, surmounted by a delicate, furled shell. The piercings of the imported English castor tops give a further delicate swirling pattern to the composition.

Piercing was a form of decoration for silver which became increasingly popular in the late rococo style. A large cake-basket (Fig. 9) made by Myer Myers is an excellent example of the light, graceful and airy effects that piercing could give to an otherwise bulky piece of silver. The gothic additions to rococo design can be seen in the quatrefoil piercings and the Chinese element in the fretwork pattern of the base-band. Gadrooning decorates the undulating rim of the basket in cusped sections and lightly outlines the diamond piercing of the handle. The total effect is like lace, and the pattern cast in the shadow is ephemeral and fleeting, as was the intention behind all rococo design.

MUSEUMS AND COLLECTIONS
American silver may be seen at the following:

Boston:	Boston Museum of Fine Arts
New Haven:	Yale University Art Gallery
New York:	Metropolitan Museum of Art
Philadelphia:	Philadelphia Museum of Art
Winterthur, Del.:	Henry Francis du Pont Winterthur Museum

FURTHER READING

Early American Silver for the Cautious Collector by Martha Gandy Fales, New York, 1970.
Early American Silver by C. Louise Avery, New York, 1968.
American Silver by John Marshall Phillips, New York, 1949.
Historic Silver of the Colonies and its Makers by Francis Hill Bigelow, New York, 1948.
American Silver: A History of Style, 1650–1900, by Graham Hood, New York, 1971.
American Silver, 1655–1825, by Kathryn C. Buhler, Boston, 1972.

The American Chippendale Style

Fig. 1 *The Deming Parlour* built *for Jonathan Deming, an officer in the Continental Army and a prosperous merchant, Colchester, Connecticut, c.1778. This interior is smaller in scale than a comparable room of the later eighteenth century in England. Because the house from which it was taken was basically of timber frame construction, the original builder found it necessary to conceal one of the structural timbers in the corner behind a two-sided pilaster. A richly coloured Caucasian dragon carpet covers the floor, and the red damask curtains are hung in the contemporary manner. The contents, proceeding clockwise from the left, are as follows:*
Wing chair, Newport, Rhode Island, c.1770–75. Mahogany and other woods, the front legs stop-fluted. Height 46 ins.
Looking-glass in the 'Chinese Chippendale' manner using a favourite Chippendale device as a finial, the ho-ho bird, American, c.1770–80. Cross-banded mahogany with water-gilding. Height 45 ins.
Pembroke table, American, c.1775–80. Mahogany with pierced C-scroll cross stretchers. Height 28 ins., top when open 40 x 31½ ins.
Tassel-back chair made for the Van Rensselaer family, New York, c.1760–70. Mahogany. Height 38½ ins.
Secretary-bookcase with swan-neck broken pediment, characteristic flame finials and fan decoration, and short cabriole legs, attributed to Joseph Hastings or John Leavitt of Suffield, Connecticut, c.1755–65. Cherry. Height 8 ft. 2½ ins.
Small looking-glass labelled on the back 'John Elliott [1713–91] No. 60 South Front Street between Chestnut and Walnut Streets, Philadelphia, sells wholesale and retail looking glasses in neat mahogany frames etc.'. Walnut. Height 18 ins., width 8½ ins.
Tripod table, American, c.1780–85. Cherrywood, height 26¾ ins.
(American Museum in Britain, Claverton Manor, Bath.)

Fig. 2 *Tripod table, Philadelphia, c.1770. Mahogany, the top supported by a 'birdcage'. Height 28 ins., diameter of top 35 ins.*
(American Museum in Britain.)

2

Museum Photo

As influential in the Colonies as in England and Ireland, the Chippendale style was supremely dominant in American furniture until the coming of the Revolution

Of all the names associated with furniture and its design, that of Chippendale is the most familiar.

Thomas Chippendale was born in 1718 and died in 1779, and his son Thomas was born in 1749 and died in 1822, having run his father's firm since his death. Thus the two generations represented a total of one hundred and four years, a factor that must have played a part in the subsequent fame attached to the name; but essentially Thomas Chippendale the elder was a publicist. The extent to which he himself was responsible for the designs that appeared in his famous pattern-book, *The Gentleman and Cabinet-Maker's Director* (first edition 1754) is not certain, and he probably employed designers such as Matthias Lock to assist him.

Without doubt, however, the book was immensely significant, for it represented the fashions set by all the leading London cabinet-makers and it was to influence the design of furniture in various British colonies, not least in North America. Just as public buildings in the American colonies were influenced by James Gibbs' *The Rules for Drawing the Several Parts of Architecture* (1732) and domestic buildings by Batty Langley's *Builder's Jewel or Youth's Instructor & Workman's Remembrancer... Explaining Short & Easy... Rules for Drawing, etc.* (1754), so Chippendale's *Director* influenced colonial American furniture design in the second half of the eighteenth century.

The elite colony who lived in the English Pale in eighteenth-century Dublin evolved an elegant way of life, the background of which was a style of furniture and furnishing today known as 'Irish Chippendale'. So the phrase 'Chippendale furniture' is necessarily hazy. Suffice it to say that the term 'American Chippendale' is usually applied to furniture forms derived from England in the mid-eighteenth-century post-walnut, pre-satin-wood epoch. Though this style was derived from England in the middle of the eighteenth century, its adoption in America occurred in the latter half of that century. On the other hand, it is possible that mahogany was in general use in America before it was widely used in England. In the Van Cortland Manor House in New York there is an early eighteenth-century mahogany gate-leg table, by English standards a particularly early example of the use of solid mahogany.

Large quantities of mahogany were imported from the West Indies

Three basic types of mahogany were in use in both England and America in the second half of the eighteenth century. These were the varieties from Cuba, San Domingo and Honduras. The finest of them was the Cuban, a wood that is characterised by great weight, hardness and close-ness of grain. When it is worked, minute white flecks of a chalky character appear in the wood. Honduras is lighter in weight and colour. The mahoganies from San Domingo and Jamaica fall somewhere between Cuban and Honduras in quality. Flame mahogany refers to the character of the grain, and it is taken from the 'pair of trousers', the name given to the first branch or crotch of the tree. Another much sought-after 'figure' (meaning the character of the grain) was mottled, and often referred to as 'plum pudding' mahogany. Large quantities of these mahoganies were imported into the U.S.A., as advertisements in contemporary journals demonstrate. In the New York Gazetteer of July 1774 appeared a notice of a 'November landing from on board the brig *Content*, Captain Benjamin Stammers from Honduras Bay, and to be sold by Anthony Van Dam:

30,000 feet of Mahogany
30 tons of log wood
1,500 weight Sasparerilla
Also Molasses, West Indian Rum, Maderia Wine, Guatamala Indigo, Cocoa, etc.'.

Nevertheless, in the Chippendale period in America, cherry was more often used than mahogany by Connecticut cabinet-makers. Throughout the U.S.A. the main structure of carcase furniture was of softwood, whereas in England at this time hardwood such as oak was favoured.

Virginian walnut, known in the timber trade as 'black' walnut or 'bastard' walnut, sometimes has a reddish colour akin to mahogany. This variety of walnut was used in England in the last phase of the walnut period when English walnut was scarce and the walnut famine in France resulted in an embargo on the export of this variety to England in 1730. As a result American or Virginian walnut was used as a last resort.

Once Britain had gained mastery of the New Netherlands in 1674, British political power and subsequent socio-political influence extended from Massachusetts almost to Florida. This was a vast area whose population, whether of British descent or not, tended to adopt not only the British language but also the British way of life, and this was reflected in the furnishing and decoration of their homes. It is thus not surprising to discover that

Fig. 3 **Lowboy**, *Philadelphia,
c.1765–80. Mahogany with brass
mounts.*

*Although the maker of this fine
piece is unknown, the ornament
is closely related to that on the
trade card of the cabinet-maker
Benjamin Randolph. The
carving is of as high a standard as
is ever seen on colonial furniture.
At a later period, such quality was
only achieved by a man of the
calibre of McIntire. Although
there were some American
makers, most brass mounts were
imported.
(Karolik Collection, Museum of
Fine Arts, Boston.)*

3

Museum Photo

American furniture in the manner of Chippendale
was created by men who were not exclusively of
British descent. George Gostelowe who worked
in Philadelphia was of Swedish extraction, and
Andrew Gautier was a Huguenot. Though little
of the latter's work has been traced, it is clear
that he was working in an English manner if not
specifically in a Chippendale one.

Some of the most remarkable makers of this
sumptuous furniture were Quakers, for example the
Goddards and the Townsends of Newport, Rhode
Island, and William Savery of Philadelphia. In the
whole history of American colonial furniture the
Townsends and the Goddards (the two families
intermarried) are truly remarkable for the quality
of their work and for the number of them of different generations who made furniture, altogether
some twenty individuals from three generations.
Of the Townsends, Christopher and his sons John
and Job and his grandsons Job Junior and Edmund
were well known, while of the Goddards the best
known was John. The combined efforts of the
brothers Job and Edmund Townsend produced in
1767 'a large mahogany desk at £330' for one
Nicholas Anderese, a fee which demonstrates the
respect which they commanded in their own day.

Block-front carcase furniture (where the centre
front recedes in a shallow concave curve between
slightly convex ends) seems to have been unique to
North America. Certainly Chippendale illustrated
no furniture of this type in the first edition of *The
Director*. It is thought that the style originated in
the area of Boston, Massachusetts, in the second
quarter of the eighteenth century and, it later
assumed a Chippendale character. The first known
documented piece is a fine bureau-bookcase signed
'Job Colt 1738' now in the Henry Francis du Pont
Museum at Winterthur, Delaware. A fine block-
front bureau in the American Museum in Britain at
Bath is interesting in that the outward projections
are carved out of the solid and not made of
separate pieces of wood. The fall-front of this
bureau and the drawer fronts are thus made from
pieces of wood of considerable size (Fig. 8).

Another characteristically American furniture
form was the highboy, a type that is also occasionally block-fronted. In England the chest-on-stand
of the late seventeenth and early eighteenth
centuries was abandoned in favour of the tallboy
or chest-on-chest where the lower section is supported on low bracket feet. In contrast the highboy
is supported on high cabriole legs, the top being
surmounted by a swan-neck broken pediment
sometimes known in America as a 'bonnet top'
(Fig. 6). The centre of the pediment is usually
embellished with a cartouche, of the type illustrated
in the first edition of *The Director* except that in
America the belly (the area originally designed for
a heraldic device) of the cartouche has shrunk to
insignificance. Chippendale illustrated a few
examples of the chest-on-stand which he called the
'chest on frame'. The stand or frame is of a very
simple kind and encloses no drawers within its
frieze. In the eighteenth century the highboy was
known as a 'high chest of drawers'. These are
usually elaborately carved as it was customary for
such pieces to be exhibited in the drawing room,
despite the fact that they were designed to contain
belongings of a personal nature. John F. Watson,
the Pennsylvanian banker and historian, noted in
his *Annals* (1829) that 'every household in that day
deemed it essential to his continuance of comfort
to have an ample chest of drawers in his parlour
or sitting room in which the linen and the clothes
of the family were always of ready access. It was
no sin to rummage for them before company. These
drawers were sometimes nearly as high as the
ceiling'.

Unsophisticated techniques were used even on the smartest pieces of furniture

The lowboy, as its name implies, was composed
in effect of the lower part of the highboy, and was
elaborately embellished with carving (Fig. 3). Most
of the brass hardware that occurs on highboys and
other American furniture of this period was
imported from England, but it is known that there
were American makers. English provincial
'Chippendale' chairs often exhibit features of
Queen Anne or early Georgian character and a
strong, though very much earlier type of construction. That which was true of the English provinces
was also true of the English colonies in North
America. It is by no means unusual to see American
chairs of 'Chippendale' form with Queen Anne
back-splats or kidney-shaped seats (Figs. 4 and 5)
while dowelled-through tenons continued to be
employed in America, even in sophisticated furniture, up to the late eighteenth century (Fig. 7). In
England this feature had died out in all but country
furniture by the early eighteenth century. Of course
there are exceptions which avoid these anomalies so
that identification is dependent upon more subtle
points such as the less extreme line of the 'back-
foot' (a chair-makers' term for the back leg) as
compared with the English examples which are less
vertical. However, in America, cabriole legs tended
to be somewhat curlier than in England.

In America, as in England, chair-making was a
distinct department of furniture manufacture, its
specialist requirements demanding specialist
craftsmen. The reason for this division of labour is

6

Derek Balmer

Fig. 4 **Chair**, *Massachusetts,
c.1765–75. Mahogany in the
Chippendale manner but with a
Queen Anne style kidney-shaped
seat. Height 37½ ins.
(American Museum in Britain.)*

Fig. 5 **Chair**, *one of a pair
labelled on the back with metal
plates bearing the name Hopkins
for the original owner, John
Estaugh Hopkins of Haddenfield,
New Jersey, possibly made by
Samuel Nickle (who returned to
his birthplace, Haddenfield, in
1776 for three years), c.1776–79.
Mahogany in the Chippendale
manner but with a Queen Anne
style splat. Height 40 ins.
(American Museum in Britain.)*

Fig. 6 **Highboy**, *Philadelphia,
c.1765–75. Mahogany with
carved shell and fan motifs and
quarter-round fluted columns.
Height 7½ ft.
(American Museum in Britain.)*

Derek Balmer

Derek Balmer

7

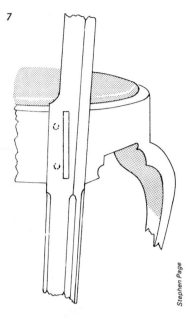

Stephen Page

simple: a chair contains few right-angles, a fact which complicates the joints and renders cramping up (holding the parts rigid while the glue dries) difficult. In particular, on curvilinear examples, especially in France, it was customary to leave projections on the component parts of a chair in order to facilitate the application of cramps when gluing up. These projections were subsequently carved off. Another method frequently employed involved the use of a long strip of flexible metal on each end of which was bolted a block of wood; the strip of metal could then be wound round in form and built up with G-cramps or sash cramps on the blocks. For this reason it is often difficult to repair chairs though in the eighteenth century tourniquets were sometimes employed in addition to the methods already mentioned. There were, on both sides of the Atlantic, craftsmen who made both chairs and case furniture but they were the exception, and it was usual for them to emphasise this fact in their trade cards as did Jonathan Gostelowe of Philadelphia whose card declared him to be a 'Cabinet and Chairmaker in Church Alley'.

Another form of furnishing that is much associated with the name of Chippendale is the

method of gilding on a gesso ground, water-gilding. John Elliott of Philadelphia, whose trade label was printed in both English and German, imported large numbers of English mirrors.

Chippendale maintained that it was possible for 'skilful workmen' to execute his designs unlike 'so many specious drawings impossible to be work'd off by any Mechanic whatsoever.' He continued: 'I will not scruple to attribute this to malice, ignorance and inability and am confident I can convince all Noblemen, Gentlemen and Others, who will favour me with their Commands, that every Design in the Book can be improved both as to beauty and enrichment in the execution of it, by their most obedient servant Thomas Chippendale'.

Records exist of 'handicraft slaves' and their relative values

Records dating from before the American War of Independence prove that there were many skilled craftsmen in the country. In Boston, for example, there were one hundred and fifty known cabinet-makers, chair-makers and carvers prior to the American War of Independence, while in Newport there were over fifty. In the South, craftsmen-slaves were able to produce good work. Thomas Elfe of Charleston, whose records for the year 1768 to 1775 have survived, wrote of many 'handi-craft slaves'; for instance, 'four sawyers valued at £1,400 and five cabinet-makers at £2,250'.

In America the influence of Chippendale drew to a close with the founding of the new republic. Thomas Jefferson's house, Monticello, was designed in a Palladian manner. The new republic demanded new furniture forms and if Palladian architecture was scarcely new, the furniture forms that emerged were certainly of a different order. Indeed Thomas Jefferson inveighed against the Chippendale period of design as 'that burden of barbarous ornament'.

8

Derek Balmer

Fig. 7 *Dowel and tenon construction, which continued in use in the Colonies as late as the end of the eighteenth century. Though very strong, this primitive method was abandoned in sophisticated English furniture early in the century.*

Fig. 8 *Block-front bureau, possibly Boston, Massachusetts, c.1770. San Domingo mahogany. Height 44½ ins. (American Museum in Britain.)*

so-called 'Chinese Chippendale' mirror-frame. As a rule, American furniture did not achieve a full flowering of 'Chinese', 'Gothick' or 'French' Chippendale though a much modified *bombé* form for chests of drawers was adopted. Generally speaking, American examples are infinitely simpler than those made in the mother country and are comparable with English provincial specimens, being of cross-banded mahogany and parcel-gilt. An example exhibited in the American Museum in Britain is surmounted by that favoured device of 'Chinese Chippendale' mirror-frames, the *ho-ho* bird. Large numbers of English mirror-frames were imported into the U.S.A., the extreme elaboration of the carving coupled with that most difficult

MUSEUMS AND COLLECTIONS
'American Chippendale' furniture may be seen at the following:

Boston:	Boston Museum of Fine Arts
New York:	Metropolitan Museum of Art
	Brooklyn Museum
Philadelphia:	Philadelphia Museum of Art
Williamsburg, Va.:	Colonial Williamsburg
Winterthur, Del.:	Henry Francis du Pont Museum

FURTHER READING
The Cabinetmakers of America by Ethel Hall Bjerkoe, assisted by John Arthur Bjerkoe, New York, 1978.

American Furniture of the Queen Anne and Chippendale Periods by Joseph Downs, New York, 1952.

Early American Rooms 1650–1858 edited by Russell Hawes Kettell, New York, 1966 reprint.

Early American Furniture Makers by Thomas Hamilton Ormsbee, New York, 1975 reprint.

Furniture Treasury, 3 vols., by Wallace Nutting.

American Furniture by Helen Comstock, 1980 reprint.

The First Years of Independence

Museum Photo

Fig. 1 *Liberty* by an anonymous American artist. c.1810. Oil on canvas, $29\frac{7}{8}$ x 20 ins.
(National Gallery of Art, Washington D.C. Gift of Edgar William and Bernice Chrysler Garbisch.)

Fig. 2 *Benjamin Franklin (1706–90), by Jean-Jacques Caffiéri (1725–92), c.1791. Whitened terracotta. Philosopher, scientist and statesman, Franklin epitomised the simplicity and enlightenment of eighteenth-century America. He founded the American Philosophical Society and was widely admired in Europe. This bust was presented to the Royal Society of Arts by a French disciple of Franklin in 1791. (Royal Society of Arts, London.)*

Fig. 3 *David Twinings' Residence by Edward Hicks (1780–1849), early nineteenth century. Oil on panel. The primitive painters of America often depicted farm life in almost photographic detail. From their work it is possible to study the costume, technology and way of life of the early settlers. (Colonial Williamsburg, Williamsburg, Virginia.)*

Against a background of growing tension and unrest, the American Colonies prepared to demonstrate their political maturity and economic self-reliance in the face of British obstinacy and ineptitude

The early eighteenth century saw Britain and France locked in a struggle for power – a struggle, however, which was no longer confined to Europe. The War of the Spanish Succession, the War of Jenkins' Ear and the Seven Years' War saw the conflict spread to India and the American colonies. Indeed, skirmishing between British and French forces had been going on in the disputed territory around the Ohio Valley for over two years before the mother countries officially declared war in 1756. The French settlements strung out loosely along the St. Lawrence needed the Ohio as a link with Louisiana; the British colonies, perched insecurely down the eastern seaboard, feared that their routes westward would be cut off. Wolfe's brilliant capture of Quebec in September 1759 ensured British victory, and the Peace of Paris in 1763 brought the Seven Years' War to a triumphant conclusion.

Fig. 4 *John Adams* (1735–1826), *early nineteenth century, attributed to Edgar Parker. Oil on canvas. Adams succeeded Washington as President of the United States in 1797. An able diplomat and an astute politician, he helped to negotiate peace with Great Britain in 1782. He was defeated by Thomas Jefferson in the election of 1800 and retired to write a cumbersome and exhaustive defence of the American Constitution. (The White House Historical Association, Washington D.C.)*

Fig. 5 *Thomas Jefferson* (1743–1826) *by T. Knight, early nineteenth century. Engraving. Jefferson was chairman of the committee that prepared the Declaration of Independence in 1776. As Governor of Virginia he set standards of administrative efficiency and humane liberalism which became part of the American political tradition.*

Museum Photo

Mansell Collection

With the expulsion of the French from North America the Colonists were no longer dependent on Britain for military aid, and looked for a return to the earlier, freer colonial system. In Britain, however, the expense of the war encouraged a movement towards tightening up the colonial system to make it more efficient. Parliament resented having to subsidise military operations in support of colonies which, in the eyes of its Members, were unable to pay their way. The Navigation Laws passed during the seventeenth and early eighteenth centuries (and designed to ensure that the Royal Navy would have a ready supply of ships and men in time of war) meant that colonial goods had to be carried in British ships to British ports, thus inhibiting colonial trade. The Colonies, forced to buy manufactured goods from the mother country and send her their raw materials – mostly navy stores and tobacco – soon ran into debt, and by the middle of the eighteenth century they had an annual deficit of over three million pounds sterling, even though they traded illegally with their neighbours in the West Indies. Financially they were in no position to face the new burdens Parliament tried to impose on them. In an effort to make the Colonies contribute towards the maintenance of garrisons and to close gaps in the existing laws, Parliament passed, in the period 1763–73, a series of measures which succeeded only in driving all shades of American opinion into the anti-British movement. The measures were hardly tyrannical – indeed, their piecemeal appearance and the general vacillation of the administration can be explained only by the political uncertainties of the period.

The first decade of George III's reign saw a succession of ministries differing in their views but alike in their ability – which was small. They were, as Walpole pointed out, 'men who were convinced of the urgent reason to do what was right, and that immediately, but were unable to decide what was right'. The unsatisfactory Molasses Act of 1764, which brought little revenue to the Crown but made matters difficult for the Colonists, was followed the next year by the controversial Stamp Act. This Act, which would reduce still further the Colonies' meagre resources of specie, was denounced even by English merchants as against Imperial commercial interests. In America it met widespread resistance.

The Stamp Act Congress, representing all the Colonies, met in New York and declared a boycott of English manufactured goods. This had such an immediate effect that Lord Rockingham's new government was forced by industrial interests to repeal the Stamp Act in 1766. Here, for the first time, the Colonies acted in unison and saw at once the effects of co-operation and when, the following year, yet another government imposed a new series of duties on English manufactures, the Colonial assemblies agreed jointly on a non-importation policy. In the face of such determined action in the Colonies and falling exports at home, Lord North, in 1770, repealed all the duties except that on tea. Despite the efforts of radicals such as Samuel Adams and Patrick Henry who continued to agitate against the British, the crisis might have subsided had not the East India Company reached a state of near-bankruptcy. In an effort to shore it up, Parliament, with little debate, granted it a virtual monopoly by permitting it to ship tea directly to America free of import duties and sell through its own agents there. At a stroke, American merchants, shippers and their agents were put out of business. Seizing their chance, the radicals (now calling themselves 'patriots') denounced this action as a threat to Colonial liberties. Agitation reached fever pitch, and when the first cargoes reached Boston in December 1773, rioters disguised as Indians boarded the ships and tossed the tea overboard.

From then on, events moved swiftly. An angry Parliament closed the port of Boston, suspended the Massachusetts Assembly and ordered British troops to all thirteen Colonies. In reply, the First Continental Congress, meeting in Philadelphia, stopped all trade with Britain until these Acts were repealed. It produced a Declaration of Rights, which was rejected by Parliament. In April 1775, attempting to seize an illegal store of arms and arrest Samuel Adams and John Hancock, the British commander in Boston ordered a party of troops to Concord. Confronted by the local militia at Lexington, they opened fire, killing several men. As the news spread to other Colonies, British officials were expelled and ordinary citizens took up arms to fight for their liberty.

The War of Independence, concluded by the Peace of Paris in 1783, brought into being a nation of loosely federated states, vast territories and almost unlimited resources. Just under four million people occupied an area greater than western Europe. They were independent, self-sufficient and, for the most part, country-dwellers. The urge for new farmland drove them steadily westwards into the Indian-occupied wilderness beyond the Appalachians. Only a very small proportion of Americans lived in the towns and cities – but they were the leaders of the country, the men of substance, wealth and influence who could help the new nation grow rich.

Puritan traditions of simplicity lost their hold very slowly

Even so, their way of life was simple in comparison with that in Europe, and the interiors of their houses, particularly those in the North, were much less elaborate than their counterparts in the Old World. The tradition of Puritan simplicity waned slowly and in Boston a man could still lose his reputation as a 'solid citizen' by wearing an extravagantly embroidered waistcoat.

But because their wealth was not obviously displayed, it does not mean that it did not exist. Merchants and shipowners – often the same man was both – had superseded the clergy as leaders of society. To mark the fact, their wives, stylishly dressed in fine imported silks and brocades, had their portraits painted by native artists such as the Hesselius father and son, and, later, John Copley and Charles Peale. Their new houses, designed by one of the rising number of American architects, were furnished and decorated with a mixture of imported and domestic goods. Not many, however, would go to the lengths of having wallpaper especially painted in London, as did a member of the Van Rensselaer family in the middle of the eighteenth century, or order their porcelain to be specially made in China, like Elias Hasket Derby of Salem.

As the demand for fine goods increased, the standard of Colonial workmanship rose until it could compete with the best in Europe. Cabinet-makers such as John Goddard, working in Newport, Rhode Island, in the 1760s and '70s, produced furniture of a much higher quality than had previously been seen in the Colonies. Silversmiths were abundant, particularly around Boston, where John and Benjamin Burt, Edward Winslow, and – most famous of all (although for an entirely different achievement) – Paul Revere, all had their workshops. Craftsmen, like William Henry Stiegel, a glass-maker of Pennsylvania during the mid-eighteenth century, were patronised by the leading citizens of New York, Boston and Philadelphia who, although ready to spend their money, frowned on ostentation and led respectable, if dull, lives.

The contrast with the South was already marked. There, life was gayer, society was noted for its charm and hospitality, and planters lived in gracious homes run by dozens of Negro slaves. Their style of living was largely influenced by two factors: first, the climate, which led people to build spacious, shady houses which would stay cool during the long, humid summers; and, second, religion, for a large proportion of the settlers in the South had been Anglican or Catholic, with a corresponding lack of influence by Puritan clergy in the early days. Generally, the Southern planter was more flamboyantly dressed than the Northern merchant, with fancy waistcoats and plenty of lace trims to his shirt, while his wife had dresses made of elaborately embroidered imported fabrics.

Even so, the interiors of their houses, recorded in paintings, seem to have been sparsely furnished and

journals which pushed an awareness of nationalism on the general public. But with victory, peace and the recession of danger state rivalries re-asserted themselves, and the weak central government set up by the Articles of Confederation in 1777 could not over-rule state legislatures jealously guarding their rights. The army threatened to impose military rule unless it was paid off; Shay's Rebellion, in 1786, composed mainly of small farmers and soldiers dispossessed of their farms or under threat of foreclosure, provided a possible foretaste of the future. It was in something of a panic that delegates from all but one of the states met in Philadelphia in May of 1787.

Fortunately for the future of the United States, the Federalists – those who supported a strong central government – were in the majority, led by such people as James Madison, later fourth President, and the brilliant Alexander Hamilton of New York. It was this congress that drew up, in the totally new concept of a written constitution, the governmental system which is still in use today, of President, Senate, House of Representatives, and Supreme Court. George Washington, once again responding to the call of duty, allowed himself to be elected the first President, and the inauguration ceremony took place in New York in 1789.

Under Washington's firm, dignified and disinterested guidance, the United States survived crises which varied from how the new President should be addressed to avoidance of involvement in the European war. In the spring of 1797, he was succeeded by his Vice-President, John Adams, who

6

7

Library Photo

quite austere in comparison with their contemporaries in Europe. Mount Vernon, Washington's home, is spacious and graceful, but the simplicity of the inhabitants' way of life is what strikes the visitor today. However, simplicity should not be confused with backwardness, and the defeated British, who dismissed their ex-Colonists as quarrelsome country bumpkins, were sadly mistaken. Men of the calibre of Washington, Jefferson, Hamilton and Franklin were well equipped to lead a new nation safely through its early years.

The thirteen Colonies, despite their many differences, had been forced by their mutual opposition to British Colonial policy to form themselves into one nation. An outburst of pride in being 'American' helped to swing popular opinion behind the Continental Congress, aided by newspapers and

had been nominated by the Federalist Party. Though one of America's great political thinkers, the intellectual Adams was tactless and highly unpopular with his fellow politicians.

He fell out with Hamilton, his chief supporter, over the Aliens and Sedition Acts, born of fear of the French but, when Hamilton and his followers called for war, Adams cut the ground from under their feet by signing a commercial treaty with France. It may have been a clever political stroke, but it was not popular, and in the elections of 1800 Adams lost badly to his rival, Thomas Jefferson. In March the following year, Jefferson took his inaugural oath in the new capital city of Washington, D.C.

This small and very muddy capital was one sign that the nation was growing. The Northwest

Fig. 6 *A View of part of the town of Boston in New England and British ships of war landing their troops* by Paul Revere II (1734–1818), 1768. Engraving. *Despite the formal cessation of hostilities in 1763, Indian tribes which had fought for the French during the Seven Years' War continued to harass the expanding frontiers of the Colonies. (I. N. Phelps Stokes Collection, Prints Division, The New York Public Library. Astor, Lenox & Tilden Foundation.)*

Fig. 7 *The History of the American Revolution in Scripture Style* published by Matthias Bartgis, Pleasant Dale Paper Mill, Frederick County, Maryland, 1823. Engraving. *America produced many popular histories of the Revolution, most hyperbolic and some ludicrous. This amusing example tells the story of Independence in the manner of the Bible with a naivety and pedantry irresistibly comic to the modern reader. (Maggs Brothers, London.)*

Fig. 8 *George Washington on a white charger* by an unknown artist, c.1830. Oil on wood panel, $38\frac{1}{8}$ x $29\frac{3}{8}$ ins. *George Washington (1732–99) became the first President of the United States on 30 April, 1789. He had a distinguished career with the British Army during the Seven Years' War and became one of the leaders of Colonial opposition to British policy in the 1770s. His military skill and prudence brought about the surrender of the British forces at Yorktown during the War of Independence. (National Gallery of Art. Gift of E. W. and B. C. Garbisch.)*

8

Museum Photo

Ordinance, in 1787, and the Public Land Act, in 1796, had made it possible for migrants to purchase land to the west of the thirteen states; those thirteen had already been supplemented by the admission to the Union of Vermont, Kentucky and Tennessee. But in 1803, Jefferson pulled off a coup which more than doubled the size of the country. Worried by the presence of French troops in Haiti and anxious to secure a permanent outlet for trade at the mouth of the Mississippi, he despatched Monroe to Paris to negotiate for the purchase of Louisiana or, at the very least, New Orleans itself.

On his arrival in New Orleans, Monroe was astonished to find that Napoleon had already made an offer to the American envoy in Paris to sell the whole of Louisiana to the United States for a mere fifteen million dollars. Not only would this dis-encumber the First Consul of unwanted territory in the New World and provide some ready cash, it would also stop Jefferson being forced into an alliance with the British. The agreement was quickly signed and Jefferson found himself in control of virtually limitless territories. He wasted little time, swiftly organising an expedition led by Captain Lewis and Lieutenant Clark to find 'the most direct and practicable water communication across this continent'. When the explorers returned two and a half years later, in September 1806, they had seen the headwaters of the Missouri, crossed the Continental Divide, surmounted the Rockies and wintered on the Pacific Coast. The limits of the country were now set, and the United States, firm in its policy of isolation, could get down to the business of filling the land with people and growing rich.

Paul Revere
Patriot
and Silversmith

Museum Photo

One of the most popular figures from the American Revolution, Paul Revere was a respected Boston citizen, competent engraver and prolific silversmith

Fig. 1 *The Bloody Massacre perpetrated in King Street Boston on March 5th 1770 by Paul Revere II (1734–1818) after a design by Henry Pelham. Coloured engraving, 9⅝ x 8⅝ ins. (British Museum, London.)*

Fig. 2 *Covered cream-jug by Paul Revere II, Boston, 1784. Silver engraved with the crest of Colonel Swan, height 6¹³⁄₁₆ ins. (The Paul Revere Life Insurance Company, Worcester, Massachusetts.)*

Fig. 3 *Cup by Paul Revere II, Boston, 1758. Silver, height 9½ ins. (Old South Church, Boston, Massachusetts.)*

Fig. 4 *Urn-shaped Sugar-dish and cover by Paul Revere II, Boston, c.1790. Silver engraved with the initials of Hephzibah Hall, height 9⅛ ins. (The Paul Revere Life Insurance Co.)*

Fig. 5 *Paul Revere II by J. S. Copley, 1768–70. Oil on canvas, 35 x 28½ ins. (Boston Museum of Fine Arts, Boston. Gift of J. W., W. B. and E. H. R. Revere.)*

Paul Revere II (1734–1818) (Fig. 5) was, for almost a century, better known as a patriot than as a silversmith, and his first claim to fame is still remembered even as his craftsmanship receives renewed appreciation. The late E. Alfred Jones' *The Old Silver of American Churches* shows him to have fashioned more church pieces than any of his contemporaries in New England, and his daybooks reveal important public and private patrons.

Like many of London's best-known goldsmiths, he was of Huguenot descent. His father, Apollos Rivoire, was born in Riaucaud, France, in November 1702, and before his thirteenth birthday he left home, arriving in Boston probably late in 1715. He was apprenticed to the best goldsmith there, John Coney.

He was still known as Paul Rivoire in 1728 when he was one of the subscribers to a life of the Reverend Cotton Mather, pastor of the Second Church; that he was buying a biography suggests careful schooling. He was Paul Revere in the record of his marriage in 1729 to Deborah Hichborn. Their second child, Paul, was born on 31 December, 1734.

The North End, where Paul grew up, was, in the words of Miss Esther Forbes (*Paul Revere and the World he Lived In*): 'a mixture of an almost London elegance of living, rubbing shoulders with poverty and vice . . . The tides of poverty washed about such islands of wealth as the Hutchinsons and their next-door neighbors the Clarks'.

In 1754 Paul Revere I died, leaving tea-sets and tankards, porringers, cans and a chafing dish, but nothing to compare with the variety or ability of John Coney's work; his son's versatility is a better reflection of his master's skill. Paul II was not yet of age to practise the craft, but in the manner of the day was permitted to carry on for his master's widow.

Revere I left another son, Thomas, of an age to begin his apprenticeship, and another, John, who became a tailor. One wonders who looked after the shop when, early in 1756, Revere II went off to fight the French at Lake George. The group came home at the end of the year and in August 1757 he was married to Sarah Orne.

In 1758 Paul was called upon to carry out the wishes of the Reverend Thomas Prince, beloved pastor of the Old South Church to which he had bequeathed 'a Piece of Plate in the Form and Height of that last presented to ye sd Church. I would have it plain and to hold a full pint'. Revere's adaptation of the recently given French chalice is seen in Figure 3.

Revere was received into St. Andrew's Lodge in 1760 when 'work was commenced under it [the charter] by receiving Paul Revere, a Goldsmith and engraver as Entered Apprentice'. It is possible that he taught himself engraving. Coney had been an excellent engraver, but there is very little embellishment on Revere I's known work and of his independent engraving nothing is known, although an unsigned book-plate is attributed to him.

On 3 January, 1761, Revere II began the first of his two preserved daybooks. From its pages, one learns of many distinguished patrons. The first debit was for a 'Freemason Medal 13/4d', and he continued to charge for Masonic jewels, medals and cross-keys in silver, and for engraving plates for summonses, certificates and notifications, both to individuals and to Masonic Lodges. The second entry was to his brother Thomas, then of age and perhaps leaving the shop. The third client was Joshua Brackett, who was to succeed in 1768 to his widowed mother's inn, and who was debited for two pairs of buckles and 'one od dito'. Not debited in the daybooks is the billhead Revere engraved for him, an example of which bears a date of 1771. The entry for his buckles is slashed with a covering 'X', as most entries are; it is assumed to mean payment. Yet the next two entries are for a credit 'by Silver received', which was more than swallowed up in its ensuing debit. Less than a page was used for 1761 accounts, which do not include the baptismal basin made for Zachariah Johonnot and dated in that year when its presentation was noted and thanks enthusiastically voted by the Hollis Street church. Equal appreciation was expressed by the same church in 1773 for the 'large and costly Silver Flaggon for the Communion Table', which the daybook records: 'Zachariah Johonnot Esq./Dr.

	oz	
To a Silver Flaggon	wt 55-15 at 7/	£19 – 10 – 3
To the Making		6 – 13 – 4
To Engraving		1 – 4 – 0'

The engraving included Johonnot's coat of arms in a scrolled and foliate cartouche and an inscription. Across the foot of the entry is written: 'Rec^d the above'.

A debit to one Williams for a 'gold necklace, gold

6

7

Museum Photo

Fig. 6 **Coffee-urn** *by Paul Revere II, Boston, 1793. Silver, height 17⅞ ins.*
This fine urn and its matching sugar-dish, teapot and stand are engraved with the initials of Burrell and Ann (Zeagers) Carnes. (Boston Museum of Fine Arts, Henry Davis Sleeper Collection.)

Fig. 7 **Two goblets** *from a set of six by Paul Revere II, Boston, 1782. Silver, the interiors gilt, heights 5⁵⁄₁₆ ins.*
The total cost of these beautiful cups was only £37 10s. The initials are of Nathaniel and Mary Tracy. (Boston Museum of Fine Arts, Pauline Revere Thayer Collection.)

lockett, odd gold button, turtle shell ring lin'd with gold, Pr of Spectical Bows and Glasses', and mending a 'Pockett Book', represent many such commissions unknown today but executed over his full career. Enamelled rings, Death's head rings, gold mourning rings, 'berring' (burying) rings and plain gold rings were recorded. His greatest number of items was probably spoons and buckles. Of the latter, few are known, although he made them for stock, neck, knees and shoes. His early entries show more imagination or time for frivolities than the later ones. They include: 'two Silver Handles to two Shells for Spoons'; 'riming a China Bowl wt Silver'; 'Turtle shell handle to a Knife'; 'a Sugar Dish out of an Ostrich egg'; and 'silver foot & rim to a shell'.

Among his clients were other silversmiths: Nathaniel Hurd (1729–77) was debited for 'a Silver frame for a Picture' and 'a Silver Indian Pipe wt. 9:6:0'. Samuel Minott (1732–1803) had 'two Silver Waiters Chased wt. 22:18 To the Making £6', and 'a large silver Salver 28 oz. Making £4'. For John Coburn (1725–1803) he did considerable engraving. The only candlesticks in the daybooks were for Zachariah Johonnot Esq., who also had a unique 'Pr of Snuffers & Snuf Dish'; he was credited with 'Silver Receiᵈ at times' to cover the bill which included a debit for 'a Counterfeit Cobb'.

Revere's earliest engraving known today is the view of the North Battery, c.1762, one of many such certificates charged throughout his daybooks. His first political cartoon, taken from an English print, was a protest against the unpopular Stamp Act of 1765, with Revere's inscription: 'The odious Stamp Act represented by the Dragon . . . from the Liberty Tree hangs the officer of the Crown'. His *View of the Colledges in Cambridge* was a joint undertaking, for half its cost was debited to Joseph Chadwick. Most of his pictorial engravings can be traced to another source: his *View of Boston and Landing of the Troops in 1768* (cut two years later) was probably the design of Christian Remick.

In 1763 Revere began making numerous charges to the artist John S. Copley (or Copely) for frames, which led early readers of the daybooks to believe

that Revere had carved the wooden frames for Copley's portraits on canvas despite the fact that all the entries, which only continue until 1767, are substantiated by the weight of gold or silver used. Other early clients bought frames, and he served doctors who had spatulas and probes in silver and 'a Sett of Surgin's instruments'. His own venture in the dental field was advertised in 1768 and his daybook reveals 'fastning teeth 2/', and 'To cleaning you teeth & one pot dentfrice 4/6d'.

His best-known silver, the Rescinders' or Sons of Liberty Bowl (Fig. 9), was fashioned in 1768, yet was one of the many pieces not recorded in his daybooks. *The Boston Gazette* of 8 August, 1768, noted: 'We hear that the Week before last was finished, by Order and for the Use of the Gentlemen belonging to the Insurance Office kept by Mr. Nathaniel Barber, at the North-End, an elegant Silver BOWL, weighing forty-five Ounces, and holding forty-five Jills. One Side is engraved within a handsome Border – To the Memory of the glorious NINETY-TWO Members of the Honourable House of Representatives of the Massachusetts-Bay, who, undaunted by the insolent Menaces of Villians in Power, and out of a strict Regard to Conscience, and the LIBERTIES of their Constituents, on the 30th of June 1768, Voted NOT TO RESCIND. – Over which is the Cap of Liberty in an Oaken Crown. On the other Side, in a Circle adorned with Flowers, &c. is No 45, WILKES AND LIBERTY, under which is General Warrants torn to Pieces. On the Top of the Cap of Liberty, and out of each Side, is a Standard, on one is MAGNA CHARTA, the other BILL OF RIGHTS – On Monday Evening last, the Gentlemen belonging to the Office made a genteel Entertainment and invited a Number of Gentlemen of Distinction in the Town, when 45 Loyal Toasts were drank, and the whole concluded with a new Song, the Chorus of which is, In Freedom we're born, and in Freedom we'll live, &c.'.

Although Revere is not mentioned as the maker, his pellet mark is on the bottom of the bowl. To meet the required capacity (45 gills) and weight (45 ounces), which were based on John Wilkes'

8

9

10

Author's Photo

Museum Photo

Museum Photo

Fig. 8 *Pitcher by Paul Revere II, Boston, 1806. Silver, height 6 ins. This pitcher was 'Presented by The Government of the Mechanic Association TO Mr SAMUEL GILBERT. As compensation for his faithful and extra services while their SECRETARY' (The Paul Revere Life Insurance Co.)*

Fig. 9 *The Sons of Liberty or Rescinders' Bowl by Paul Revere II, Boston, 1768. Silver, diameter 11 ins. The capacity (45 gills) and weight (45 oz.) of this bowl were determined by No. 45 of Wilkes' North Briton. (Boston Museum of Fine Arts. By subscription and the Francis Bartlett Fund.)*

Fig. 10 *Teapot by Paul Revere II, Boston, c.1785. Silver, height 5⅛ ins. A similar pot of 1785 is the first known by Revere to be of seamed rather than raised construction. (Sterling and Francine Clark Art Institute, Williamstown, Mass.)*

sympathetic paper (the No. 45 referred to in the quotation), he had to make a wrought rather than the customary cast foot.

Stirring events underlie his charges to Edes & Gill on 9 March, 1770:

To Engraving 5 Coffins for Massacre	6/
To Printing 200 Impressions of Massacre	5 – 0

The coffins were line-cuts for their newspaper, *The Boston Gazette*, for which he also cut mastheads. The impressions were of *A Print, containing a Representation of the late horrid Massacre in King Street* (Fig. 1). Henry Pelham, half-brother of J. S. Copley, wrote protesting that Revere had pirated his design: 'If you are insensible to the Dishonour you have brought on yourself by this Act, the World will not be so . But Pelham seems not to have been a good prophet.

On 15 February, 1770, Revere bought the house on North Square, then almost a century old, which is now maintained as a memorial to him. From its windows, on the first anniversary of the Massacre, he showed illuminations to keep its memory aflame and 'The whole was so well executed that the Spectators, which amounted to many Thousands, were struck with Solem Silence & their Countenances covered with a meloncholy Gloom. (*The Boston Gazette*.)

In 1773 Sarah died, and in September of that year Revere married Rachel Walker to mother his six surviving children and give him another eight, of whom three died in infancy or early childhood. Also in September 1773, he charged to Dr. William Paine, for his bride Lois Orne whose arms the pieces bear, the most complete service known, which lacks, strangely, a sugar-bowl. The pair of porringers, some spoons, the cream-pot and the wooden box which cost 3s. 8d., are all that are missing from this service in the Worcester Art Museum (Fig. 11). In November 1773, 'That worst of Plagues, the detested tea shipped for this port by the East India Company', sent Revere 'riding express to warn of the impending Tea Party and he was soon carrying letters to other Sons of Liberty in New York and Philadelphia.

On 1 April, 1775, the silver entries cease and no

further silver is recorded until 1781. Rent, food, and the 'use of my chaise' are intervening entries partially covering two pages. Revere was empowered to engrave and print paper currency in the five ensuing years and was sent to Philadelphia to learn how to erect a powder mill. He established one in Canton where eventually he was to have his bell and cannon foundry and copper manufactory. In April 1777 his son Joseph Warren was born, and in May his mother died; his daughter Deborah, almost twenty, was at home to help.

Revere wrote to them from Castle Island and from Rhode Island, before embarking on the disastrous Penobscot Expedition, of which he kept a careful diary, in 1779. In a post-war letter to a cousin in France, he summed up his activities: 'the year 1775 when the American Revolution began; from that time till May 1780, I have been in Government service as Lieutenant Colonel of an Artillery regiment, the time for which that was raised then expired and I thought it best to go to my business again, which I now carry on and under which I trade some to Holland. I did intend to have gone wholly into trade, but the principal part of my interest I lent to Government, which I have not been able to draw out; so must content myself till I can do better'.

His earliest coffee-pots had been single bellied; what was presumably the last of these was charged in 1772 and given three shell feet with shell attachments; the style of the coffee-pot from the Lois Paine (née Orne) service continued until the mid-1790s. One bulbous tankard by Revere is known, and a heavy one without a finial. His known pre-Revolutionary pieces are in the form of the Paine ones, but usually lack their enriched bases.

Beads, bodkins and jewellery are among many items charged in the daybooks which are not now known. 'Butter cupps' were listed at the same weights as his butter-boats which were usually tripod; three are known on a collet foot reminiscent of Bow porcelain examples. Buttons of gold, silver, stone and tortoise-shell for coat, sleeve or jacket are recorded in quantity but unidentified. Cans came usually in pairs and in sizes from half-pint to wine-quart; in the 1790s, he charged a 'hoop'd cann' which we know to be straight-sided with applied reeded bands. Casters in pairs, or single ones specifically for pepper, he produced throughout his working years. He made chains for buttons, scissors and pin-balls; a squirrel-chain made in 1772 brings to mind the portrait of Henry Pelham, *Boy with a squirrel*, which his friend Copley had exhibited in the London Society of Artists exhibition of 1765. Clasps were made for shoes, usually children's, and for cloaks; he recorded considerable 'cleaning and mending' of silver. He accepted a barrel of rum for a tankard, and a bookcase for a cream-pot. A silver chalice and an old salt went into the making of spoons in 1784, and 'Freight on some goods from France' helped pay for cans and marking spoons. He carried on a thriving harness business, much of it plated, and some silver. He riveted china dishes, put new lids to tankards and cloth bottoms to bottle stands. His porringers were often in pairs, sometimes in child's size; his handle designs varied, mainly in size. 'Large' and 'tea' were his usual designations for spoons; 'dessert-spoons' began c.1790, and he did not succumb to the familiar word 'tablespoon' until that decade.

Paul Dudley Sargent's coffee-pot, in the double-bellied form of Mrs. Paine's, is the only known surviving item from his 1781 charges. Thomas Hichborn's teapot (in drum form with a gadrooned border) and Nathaniel Tracy's goblets (Fig. 7) were debited in 1782. The names of many of his pre-Revolutionary clients recur subsequently, and some of his Loyalist ones, as soon as the Treaty of September 1783 permitted them to be so, acted as his agents in England. They sent him the hardware, fine materials, writing- and wall-paper with which he stocked the shop which, according to Miss Forbes, he opened 'opposite the Liberty Pole' in 1783. His silver accounts in the first daybook end in August that year, but he noted in the book, in 1784/5, the renting of his house on North Square to the miniaturist Joseph Dunkerly, whose credit 'By sundrys & p[e]r his Bill' may well have been for a charming portrait of Rachel Revere in what is traditionally regarded as a Revere gold

11

Barness Burstein

Fig. 11 *Silver service by Paul Revere II, Boston, 1773. Silver, the pot-handles of wood, height of tankard 9½ ins., of coffee-pot 13½ ins.*
The most complete silver service known, this one is missing only a pair of porringers, some spoons, the cream-pot and the fitted wooden box. Oddly, it never had a sugar-bowl. It was made for Dr. William Paine of Worcester, Mass. for his bride, Lois Orne, whose arms and initials the pieces bear.
(Worcester Art Museum, Worcester, Mass. Donated from four lines of descent in the Paine family.)

frame. A drawing of flattened bow sugar-tongs, eleven inches long, with a note of '1 oz. 2' is on the last page of this book.

On the first page of the second book, in the careful handwriting of his signature, there is a recipe 'to make Gold Sawder', with other less careful notations and a drawing of a finial. Three pages mostly record family debts, including those of Paul Jr. Fellow silversmiths who are recorded as clients were John Andrew, Nathaniel Austin, who put his own mark on Revere's spoons, Caleb Beal and Stephen Emery. In 1789 a page was devoted to 'Shop Dr. to Paul Revere Senior for Stock Ready made in the Cases'. Its total of forty-two pairs of silver buckles for stock, neck, hat, knee and shoes; shoe-clasps, buttons, brooches, spoons, ladles, spurs, sugar-tongs, hairpins, one gold necklace and seven gold rings contrasts with the hollow ware which comprised only three cream-pots and a pair of casters. One is reminded of his many credits 'by silver to make' a piece.

His teapots changed rapidly in form, and more of the 'engraved and fluted' ones of the 1790s are known than any others. With the exception of one set charged in 1764, no three-piece tea-set was charged until the 1790s; and then a fourth piece, a stand for the teapot, was usual. Cream-pots in the early 1780s were pyriform on a splayed foot; his covered one of 1784 (Fig. 2) he called a 'cream jug'. The so-called 'helmet-shapes' he made in a variety of styles; he recorded sugar-dishes, urns, vases and baskets; one of the last he referred to as a 'sugar-bowl'. His goblets for Tracy appear to be unique today; those made for Moses Hayes (in 1796) and Andrew Cunningham are in the form of his unmarked 'church cupps', which also date from 1796. In 1791 he made a plain 'tea urn'

for Mrs. Hannah Rowe; this had a cylinder for a heating rod similar to that with which he equipped the fluted 'coffee urn' for Burrell Carnes (Fig. 6), but Mrs. Rowe's urn was twice the weight. His tankards were given higher domed covers; the new lids he sometimes charged for could have been repairs or a means of updating an old-fashioned piece.

In 1786 he advertised his removal to Dock Square, or 50, Cornhill, where he was when the first *Boston Directory* was published three years later. In 1788 he had started his 'furnass' and in 1792 cast his first church bell; of a later one, the Reverend William Bentley was to write that they 'venture to prefer it to any imported bell & so did we but from patriotism'. His only known trade-cards are for the 'Bell & Cannon Foundrey', although he engraved many for fellow tradesmen. The second *Boston Directory* of 1796 gives: 'Revere & Son goldsmiths Ann Street'. Two years later this was 'Paul & J. W. Revere' for his son Joseph Warren, who had just come of age. The early directories give Paul Jr., who predeceased his father, on Fleet Street. 'Paul Revere, bell & cannon foundry Lynn street, house North Square' was amended in 1800 to 'house Charter Street'. In 1797, the last year of the daybooks, he fashioned his now unique 'waiter' for the great Salem merchant, Elias Hasket Derby.

The bell and cannon foundry was in the area of the shipyards, and Revere began working in copper. His seaworthy fittings were much appreciated by the shipbuilders. Late in December 1800, when he had mastered the technique of rolled copper, he established his rolling-mill in the town of Canton, using water power from the Neponset River. When the hurricane of 1804 had damaged Lynn Street, he moved his foundry there. He sheathed the dome of Bulfinch's State House, the cornerstone of which he had assisted in laying in 1795; and in 1809 provided copper for boilers for Robert Fulton's steamship. He was one of the founders and first president of the Association of Mechanics for which in 1806 he fashioned one of his famous adaptations (Fig. 8) of the Liverpool pottery pitchers, apparently his last.

In 1813, Mrs. Revere died. Revere divided his time between Canton and Charter Street until his death in 1818, when it was said of him that he was 'Cool in thought, ardent in action, he was well adapted to form plans and to carry them to execution – both for the benefit of himself and the service of others'.

MUSEUMS AND COLLECTIONS

American Silver may be seen at the following:

Boston: Boston Museum of Fine Arts
Cambridge: Fogg Art Museum
New Haven: Yale University Art Gallery
New York: Metropolitan Museum of Art
Minneapolis: Institute of Arts
Old Deerfield: Heritage Foundation Collection of Silver

FURTHER READING

Colonial Silversmiths, Masters and Apprentices by Kathryn C. Buhler, Boston, 1956.
Paul Revere & the World He Lived In by Esther Forbes, Boston, 1942.
American Silver, 1655–1825, by Kathryn C. Buhler, Boston, 1972.

SAMPLERS IN AMERICA

Fig. 1 *Sampler by Rebecca van Reed Gresamer of Reading, Pennsylvania, 1835. With bead-work, $33\frac{1}{4}$ ins. x $31\frac{1}{2}$ ins. (American Museum in Britain, Bath).*

Fig. 2 *Sampler (detail) by Hannah Taylor, Newport, R.I., 1774. (American Museum in Britain.)*

Fig. 3 *Sampler (detail) by Sarah Laurence, Concord, 1815. (John Judkyn Memorial, Bath.)*

Fig. 4 *Sampler by Lucy Symonds, Boxford, Mass., 1796. (Victoria and Albert Museum, London.)*

Fig. 5 *Sampler by Nabby Ford, Portland, New Hampshire, 1799. (American Museum in Britain.)*

Fig. 6 *Sampler by Elizabeth Lawson, 1833. (John Judkyn Memorial.)*

Fig. 7 *Sampler by Elizabeth G. Lusk, New Hartford, 1821. (John Judkyn Memorial.)*

Fig. 8 *Sampler by Charlotte Glubb, Washington City. 1813. (American Museum in Britain.)*

Samplers from the old countries of Europe provided the basis for those made in the New World

The word 'sampler' (or 'examplar') is used to describe those lovingly created or dutifully executed embroideries which were, in the sixteenth and seventeenth centuries, used primarily as a means of recording a repertoire of stitches. As such, they were usually made in childhood by girls who would need them in womanhood. It was only in the late seventeenth and early eighteenth centuries that a secondary significance assumed a prime importance, namely learning to read and write; hence the use of alphabets and moral verse.

Early European samplers consist of a series of fragments of decoration achieved by numerous stitches, whereas late eighteenth- and early nineteenth-century specimens in both Europe and America were conceived as pictorial entities.

Only two seventeenth-century American samplers survive: the Loara Standish sampler of about 1640, preserved at Pilgrim Hall, Plymouth, Massachusetts, and Ann Gover's sampler of about 1610, owned by the Essex Institute, Salem, Massachusetts. These remain fairly true to the European tradition of the examplar, though lettering also is included. Most of these early samplers are tall and narrow but, during the eighteenth century, the proportions generally became squarer. This was probably due in part to the influence of a book printed for James Boler in London in 1632, entitled: *The Needles Excellency. A New Book wherein are Divers admirable workes wrought with the needle newly invented and cut in Copper for the pleasure & profit of the industrious.* Although this book achieved twelve editions by the year 1640, it is extremely rare today. It is quite possible that copies reached America in the seventeenth century and were the basis for several

generations of American samplers. It can thus be seen that surviving American samplers appeared at a time when the examplar was falling out of favour, and alphabets and verse appear with predictable regularity. The latter variety are of particular interest not only because they are signed by the embroideress (and, if made in a school, the name of the 'Preceptress'), but also because they are frequently dated. Some of the children who made these samplers were extraordinarily young.

Among the specimens made in America, perhaps the most interesting historically are the genealogical samplers. These give not only dates of birth but sometimes the dates of death of members of the family and it is clear that these were sometimes kept up to date in much the same way in which some samplers show the date at which work commenced and the date on which work was concluded. The Olmstead sampler (Connecticut, 1774) lists as many as twelve persons and gives their dates of birth and marriage.

The alphabets that occur in samplers sometimes quite reasonably omit the 'J' (this letter not occurring in the Roman alphabet) while the numerals occur from '1' to '9' and '0'. One specimen includes three sets of alphabets, each of a different letter form, and two sets of numerals, one of which reads '1' to '9' and '0', the other '1' to '18'. This would appear in the latter instance to be for the purpose of filling up space.

The verses that appear on these samplers, though not always biblical, are usually pious. One example reads:

'*See how the Lillies flourish White and fair*
See how the Ravens fed from Heaven are
Then never distrust thy God for cloth and bread
Whilst Lillies flourish and the Ravens fed'.

In conclusion, it should be stated that a specifically American character began to appear in samplers of the 1720s while, by the early 1800s, this trend was firmly established.

Early Federal Furniture

Museum Photo

Association Photo

American Furniture

In the late eighteenth century it was observed that, as regards furniture, Americans 'will habitually prefer the useful to the beautiful, and they will require that the beautiful should be useful'

Fig. 1 **Side-chair**, *one of twenty-four made in Philadelphia, c.1796. Maple, painted black and with colours, height 38½ ins. These superb chairs in the Hepplewhite style were ordered in 1796 by Elias Hasket Derby, a wealthy merchant of Salem, Massachusetts. (Metropolitan Museum of Art, New York. Gift of Mrs. J. Insley Blair, 1947.)*

Fig. 2 **Sideboard**, *one of a pair by John Aitken, Philadelphia, c.1797. Mahogany, width 5 ft. 11 ins. Acquired by George Washington for his Banqueting Hall at Mount Vernon in 1797, this handsome piece relies on perfection of proportion and line rather than on detail for its effect. (Mount Vernon, Virginia. Courtesy of the Mount Vernon Ladies' Association of the Union.)*

Fig. 3 **Case of drawers** *by William Lemon, carved by Samuel McIntire of Salem, Massachusetts, 1796. Mahogany, height 8 ft. 6½ ins. One of the masterpieces of American craftsmanship, this chest in a style derived from Chippendale was also ordered by Elias Hasket Derby of Salem. (Boston Museum of Fine Arts, Boston. M. and M. Karolik Collection.)*

As the storm of what Americans call "The Revolution' (1775–83) subsided, the Thirteen Colonies, diverse in their economic interests and in their political cleavages, found themselves joined together in a loose Confederation of States. The English 'oppressors' had been expelled with the decisive American victory at Yorktown in 1781. Americans were no longer under the domination of the King and 'the lust of dominion or lawless ambition' of the Parliament.

But rarely does a new political freedom immediately emancipate the arts of a nation. Only after a decade of recuperation did America again begin to urge herself toward the economic and political stability necessary for a resurgence of creative energies. It was the ratification of the new American Constitution by a majority of the States by 1788 that drew the diverse American people together and brought new vitality and direction to their arts.

Since the new form of government embodied many of the democratic principles of ancient Greece and Rome, the tangible accoutrements which the new American 'senators' associated with the classical period became fashionable. From Maine to Georgia, many embraced neo-classical form, proportion, and ornamentation, either by transforming their 'plain farmer's houses' into modest domestic temples or by building entirely new ones. George Washington redesigned Mount Vernon, his plantation overlooking the Potomac River in Virginia, into what we see today; Thomas Jefferson designed Monticello freely choosing from classical precedent. To furnish these houses Americans continued, as before the Revolution, to look primarily to England for inspiration in furniture design.

In the designs illustrated in Hepplewhite's *The Cabinet-Maker and Upholsterer's Guide* (1788), *The Cabinet-Maker's London Book of Prices* (1788 and 1793), and Sheraton's *The Cabinet-Maker and Upholsterer's Drawing Book* (1793–94), Americans found a new style consistent with the ideals embodied in their new government. The style was simple, straightforward and unpretentious, without the heavy forms or elaborate ornamentation of the previous periods. The American cabinet-maker borrowed from these English sources (and from actual imported examples) and reworked their designs into what is now known as the 'Federal Period' in American furniture history as codified by Mr. Charles F. Montgomery in his authoritative pioneer study, *American Furniture: The Federal Period*. For the first time, Montgomery has revealed the conditions which surrounded the fabrication of Federal furniture, and regionalised the use of construction techniques and the preference for certain woods by American cabinet-makers between 1790 and 1825.

But it was the interpretation by each American cabinet-maker that made his own creation individual. Some craftsmen tried to be as correct as possible in classical details, following English designs. Others blended neo-classical ornamentation with traditional forms. More often, the American cabinet-maker chose freely from among the sources available, combining, for example, elements from several designs by Hepplewhite with ornamentation from Sheraton. Most often he adapted the designs to meet his own requirements or those of his patron, although there are pieces which are direct copies. He innovated and developed as he chose, limited only by his vision, his proficiency in the control of his materials, and his customer's taste and ability to pay. Thus, while there is no unified American interpretation of the English designs clearly recognisable as being American, there often seems to be a different emphasis in an American piece from that of its English counterpart.

Careful study of construction details and ornamentation used in labelled or documented examples, combined with positive identification of secondary woods which are indigenous to America, yields a distinct pattern of regional techniques which enables the identification of a larger group of furniture forms from each of the American urban design centres. Boston, Newport, New York, Philadelphia, Williamsburg and Charleston were augmented in the early years of the Republic by small, though no less important towns. Salem, Baltimore, Annapolis and Richmond rose to increased importance with the wave of new wealth mostly derived from invigorated sea trade with the Orient (for the seas were now free for American ship captains to trade wherever they pleased) and the American South and West. The new 'senators' required fashionable, or what they thought to be fashionable, furnishings for their houses. Likewise, their 'venture cargoes' sent abroad were in the latest styles. Thus, pieces of American furniture can often be found many miles, even a continent, away from their place of fabrication.

One such piece is the secretaire shown in Figure 4. On the basis of two paper labels of the Salem cabinet-maker Nehemiah Adams, a member of the co-operative enterprise which made furniture for export around 1800, the piece was sold in Capetown, South Africa, as 'a unique and charming piece made in the United States'. It remained far from home until about 1940, when it was purchased and returned to America. Though not unique as advertised (over a dozen related examples have survived), it is a distinctive interpretation seemingly inspired by Plate 52 in Sheraton's *Drawing Book*. The Massachusetts cabinet-maker has changed the design, substituting a secretary drawer in the lower section for the fall-front lid and drawers of Sheraton's upper section, and replacing the lid with glazed doors. He has simplified and extended the top into balanced sweeping S-curves similar to the design shown in Plate 3 of *The London Book of Prices* (1793), while eliminating the Adam-like ornamentation of the frieze and top and exchanging the diamond motif ornamentation for oval veneers and tracery.

The quality of, and the preference for, carved motifs on the flat surface of mahogany furniture that can be documented as the work of Samuel McIntire help to identify a larger group of objects made in Salem. McIntire was an important architect as well as a designer and maker of fashionable furniture. His hand is best identified in the carved details of baskets of fruit, swags, urns, *putti*, and

Fig. 4 *Secretaire by Nehemiah
Adams, Salem, Massachusetts,
c.1800. Mahogany,
height 7 ft. 6 ins.*
*Derived from a design by
Sheraton, this fine secretaire was
sold in Capetown, South Africa,
as 'a unique and charming
piece made in the United
States'. There it remained
until 1940, a tribute to the
expansion of American trade
throughout the world in the early
Federal period.*
*(Henry Francis du Pont
Winterthur Museum,
Winterthur, Delaware.)*

Fig. 5 *Lady's cabinet- and
writing-table made in
Baltimore, Maryland, between
1795 and 1810. Various
contrasting woods, some
indigenous to North America.*
*This delightfully graceful table
is a sophisticated combination of
details found in several plates of
Thomas Sheraton's Drawing
Book. So close is it in feeling
and detail to the drawings that
it could easily be mistaken for
one of its English counterparts.*
*(H. F. du Pont Winterthur
Museum.)*

Fig. 6 *Secretaire by John Shaw,
Annapolis, Maryland, 1796.*
*Although somewhat old-
fashioned for its date, this
refined piece demonstrates the
great ability of Shaw, who was
born in Glasgow, as a cabinet-
maker. Its original owner was
John Randall.*
*(Queen's Room, White House
Collection, Washington D.C.)*

Fig. 7 *Commode by Thomas
Seymour, Boston, 1809.
Mahogany and satinwood,
height 42½ ins.*
*Combining boldness with
delicacy, this commode was
made for Elias Hasket Derby's
daughter. A bill still exists not
only for the piece, but also
'for Painting Shels on Top'.*
*(Boston Museum of Fine Arts,
M. and M. Karolik Collection.)*

cornucopias, all masterfully executed on the 'case of drawers' made by William Lemon for Elias Hasket Derby, a wealthy Salem merchant, in 1796 (Fig. 3). It is considered one of the masterpieces of American eighteenth-century cabinet-making. The form is a survival from the Chippendale style, reiterated by Hepplewhite in Plate 54 of his *Guide*, modified by Lemon, and updated by McIntire's vigorous carved detail.

Elias Hasket Derby also imported elegant furniture from nearby Boston and distant Philadelphia. In 1809 Thomas Seymour charged Derby's daughter for the 'Large Mahogany Comode' (Fig. 7) and for 'Mr Penniman['s] Bill for Painting Shels on Top'. It is one of the most successful and sophisticated American combinations of inlaid and carved satinwood and mahogany, further ornamented with painted decoration. The elegance achieved by the carefully selected curly-maple veneered drawer-fronts contrasted with the cross-grained rosewood skirt and the carved mahogany posts of the front, is further enhanced by the contrasting segments and painted shell of the top. It is a marvellous combination of exuberance and restraint.

From Philadelphia, Derby ordered twenty-four oval-back chairs from his agent in 1796 (Fig. 1), also without doubt patterned after the *Guide* of 1788. Their success lies in the boldness of design, in the effectiveness and dexterity of the hand which painted the back and in the unexpected strength of construction which has enabled them to survive in spite of their delicacy of line.

4

Museum Photo

As Philadelphia remained the new nation's political and fashion capital until 1800, it was only natural for America's first President to buy much of his furniture for Mount Vernon there. In 1797, George Washington acquired a tambour desk with bookcase, based on Plate 69 of Hepplewhite's *Guide*, from John Aitken, a prominent Philadelphia cabinet-maker. Aitken infused his own sense of proportion by raising the height of the bookcase, adding a simple top, and altering the drawer-arrangement to develop a continuous semicircle in the apron of the base. The designs for both the top

and the tracery on the doors are again adaptations from *The London Book of Prices*, Plate 3.

For his new banqueting hall Washington's accounts record his payment for 'two side-boards' (Fig. 2). The sideboards are pure Hepplewhite (without the ornamentation). They appear to reflect the same concern that Washington expressed regarding his imported chimneypiece for the same room – that it would be 'too elegant and costly . . . for [his] own room and republican style of living'. Thus, rather than an extensive use of ornate inlays with swags and bell-flowers, Washington chose a plainer style, which he considered to be more fitting to his new way of life.

With the sideboard, Aitken has taken Hepplewhite's basic design and added a pair of doors, concealing a shelf, under the central drawer. He changed the design and the proportion; he transformed the piece into a seemingly more useful form, one which found great popularity in many American houses by the end of the eighteenth century, while retaining the movement and grace called for in the original design.

This same change occurred in other American cabinet-making centres along the Atlantic seaboard. However, it was in New York City that the American version of the sideboard was developed and refined to the highest degree with the 'deversified contour[s]' and the 'light and shade' called for by Robert Adam's aesthetic theory.

At the same time that Aitken was working on Washington's furniture in Philadelphia, John Shaw, a Scottish-born cabinet-maker of Annapolis, created the elegant secretaire (Fig. 6) now in The White House in Washington, D.C. It is generous in size, refined in proportion and distinctive in execution, though rather behind the times for 1796, the year in which it was made. The delicacy of the pierced scrolls and plinth at the top is a successfully individual refinement found on several pieces of the period. The inlaid shells and *paterae* and the carved cornice further enhance this distinguished piece. It demonstrates Shaw's ability as a cabinet-maker and the refined taste of its original owner, John Randall.

But it was in Baltimore that some of the most glorious pieces of high-style Federal furniture were created. The lady's cabinet- and writing-table (Fig. 5) is one such piece. Closely related to several plates in Sheraton's *Drawing Book*, it is one of the most sophisticated of the small group of tables to have survived; so close is it in feeling and detail that it could be mistaken for one of its English counterparts. The inclusion of the banded oval looking-glass, the mitred satinwood door-fronts with inset painted and gilt oval glass panels of biblical and mythological figures, and the overall proportions and composition are the American cabinet-maker's contribution. His choice of contrasting woods and his technical skill place this anonymous craftsman among the most proficient in America.

Thus, during the eighteenth century, the design of American furniture remained under English influence. Following the Revolution, as we have seen, the design-books of England's cabinet-makers found immediate acceptance in the new Republic. But it was the individual interpretation of these designs infused with the inherent creative energy of the American cabinet-maker, modified by the taste of his patron, which formed America's furniture of the Federal Period.

Museum Photo

6

White House Photo

7

Museum Photo

MUSEUMS AND COLLECTIONS

Early Federal furniture may be seen at the following:

Boston:	Boston Museum of Fine Arts
New York:	Metropolitan Museum of Art
	Brooklyn Museum
Washington, D.C.:	Smithsonian Institution
Winterthur,	Henry Francis du Pont
Delaware	Winterthur Museum

FURTHER READING

American Furniture: The Federal Period by Charles F. Montgomery, New York, 1966.

John and Thomas Seymour by Vernon C. Stoneman, Boston, 1959.

Furniture Treasury, 3 vols., by Wallace Nutting.

American Furniture by Helen Comstock, 1980 reprint.

American Clocks and Watches

1

Fig. 1 **Shelf clocks** by Chauncey Jerome, New Haven, Connecticut, first half of the nineteenth century. The centre four of these clocks are of the type known as 'steeple clocks' (Private Collection.)

Fig. 2 **Banjo clock** by Simon Willard, Massachusetts, c.1810. Simon Willard was interested in the balloon shape and devoted his energies to his 'patent timepiece'. This design later acquired the name of 'banjo clock'.
(Old Sturbridge Village, Sturbridge, Massachusetts.)

Fig. 3 **Girandole clock** by Lemuel Curtis (1790–1851), early nineteenth century. Height 39 ins.
This elaborate and rare form of the banjo clock was developed by Curtis. No more than twenty-five were made, and they are thought to be America's finest clocks.
The thermometer in the neck of this example is an unusual feature.
(Christie, Manson and Woods Ltd., London.)

The earliest clocks in America were imported by the first settlers; by the nineteenth century shelf clocks were being made in increasing numbers

The first mechanical clock came to North America with the first settlers, the Dutch and the English, in the early seventeenth century. The more wealthy of the English brought brass lantern clocks, the Dutch brought metal table clocks. On rare occasions in the last quarter of the century, a family travelled across the ocean with the awkward but very valuable possession of a long-case clock.

It is likely that the ownership of a clock had more prestige than practical value because most families would have spent all the daylight hours building a homestead, tilling the soil and tending livestock. Both English and Dutch communities were strongly religious, which might be relevant as accurate timekeeping had its origin in religious needs.

The few clocks owned by the earlier colonists had been imported individually, mostly from England. The earliest American-made clocks still extant are long-case, called 'tall' clocks by the colonists. The first immigrant clockmakers who practised their craft probably arrived a few years before 1700. They certainly came after Peter Stuyvesant surrendered New Amsterdam to the English, when it was renamed New York, for that was in 1664, and it was not until about 1670 that the long-case clock

with a long pendulum was invented in London.

Clockmakers – mainly English, but also Dutch, and German from the Black Forest, and even a few Swedes – followed the national styles that they had learned while apprentices, and there is nothing at first sight to distinguish the Colonial long-case clock from its progenitor in Europe.

It was not easy for a clockmaker to succeed financially by making every part of his clocks. In England, he would have depended to some extent on specialist makers of pinion wire, on brass-casters, hand-piercers, on dial-engravers, and certainly on case-makers. Clockmakers in the Colonies therefore tended to settle in areas where there were others, each gradually finding it more profitable to concentrate on his own special skill.

From quite early days, two distinct communities emerged, one centred on Philadelphia and the other on Boston. Each developed its recognisable style, although the basic designs were European. Makers of the Philadelphia School spread from New York up the Delaware Valley to Virginia and Carolina. Makers of the Boston School were scattered all over New England. In retrospect, although the two groups were probably of about the same importance at the time, Philadelphia was the home of the finer makers and finer clocks. English styles predominated, although clockmakers of German origin had some influence in the Pennsylvanian hills.

Weight-driven pendulum clocks were the main production, as they were accurate and did not demand the particular materials and skills of the spring-maker, which were essential for the portable

Museum Photo

A. C. Cooper

clock. The simplest and cheapest models were wall clocks with the weights and pendulum hanging below, generally known as 'the wag on the wall'. Better clocks were in tall cases and were sometimes grimly known as 'coffin clocks'. The name 'grandfather clock' did not appear until Henry Clay Work wrote the song of that name in 1876, very much later. The song has particular significance in the history of American clocks because of its lyric: 'My grandfather's clock was too tall for the shelf so it stood twenty years on the floor . . .'. The first truly indigenous American clock was the 'shelf clock'.

The most common style of American long-case clock was very similar to the English provincial style after 1750, with swan-neck pediments on the hoods. A cresting on the hood known locally as 'whales' tails' became typical of the clockmakers in Connecticut, however, having been developed by Thomas Harland, who moved there from Boston; makers in Massachusetts were fond of pierced fretwork cresting. These features are guides to origin.

The most famous maker of this era was David Rittenhouse of Philadelphia, who had established himself as a clock-maker in 1749 at the early age of seventeen. He later specialised in astronomical clocks, some of which worked orreries showing the motions of the planets. He was a man of great ability and far-ranging interests. As a surveyor, he was partly responsible for the Mason-Dixon Line. With John Winthrop and Benjamin Franklin (also a clockmaker and inventor of an accurate one-handed dial), he became famous as a Father of the American Revolution.

4

5

Museum Photo

Fig. 4 **Acorn clock** *by the
Forestville Manufacturing
Company, 1830. Height about
24 ins.
Managed by J. C. Brown from
1807 to 1872, the Forestville
factory made clocks in many
styles.
(British Museum, London.
Ilbert Collection.)*

Fig. 5 **Wagon-spring clock** *of the
type invented by Joseph Ives in
c.1825 and made throughout
the rest of the century. Height
over 24 ins.
Instead of being driven by a
coiled spring like most shelf
clocks, this clock uses an entirely
original design. Both the time
and the striking wheels are
powered by a leaf spring, as used
in farm wagons, in the base of the
clock. The inventor, Ives, went
bankrupt and had to be rescued
by a former employee, John
Birge, in partnership with whom
Ives later had great success.
(British Museum. Ilbert
Collection.)*

After the Declaration of Independence in 1776,
the Colonists found themselves increasingly short
of raw materials on which they had previously
depended, including copper and zinc which comprised the brass of the clock movement. Makers
therefore began to turn to wood for the plates and
the toothed wheels of clocks, in the same manner
as the clockmakers of the Black Forest of Germany
in the eighteenth century. From this time until
about 1810, almost all American clocks were made
by hand by clockmaker-carpenters.

The situation was changed largely through the
vision and ingenuity of a clockmaker named
Eli Terry, who was primarily responsible for chang-
ing the industry from a craft to a factory system.
Terry was also the main catalyst for the shift of
clockmaking to Connecticut. Having served his
apprenticeship from the age of fourteen to Daniel
Burnap, a maker from East Windsor, Connecticut,
who batch-produced clocks, Terry went to work
with Benjamin and Timothy Cheney in a nearby
village. By the age of twenty-one, he had established himself as a maker, in his own right, of wooden
clocks with brass wheels. At some time, he became
fascinated by the problem of producing clocks in
big quantities, probably inspired by the mass-
production pioneer Eli Whitney, who had accepted
what seemed to be an impossible contract to supply
100,000 government muskets in under two years.

Terry's chance came when, owing to an acute

shortage of metal because of Napoleon's blockade
of the British Isles, he was given an order for four
thousand tall clock movements to be made of wood
and delivered within three years. Terry sold his
water-mill-operated factory and bought a larger
mill. He spent a year setting up new works, then
completed the order on time. Despite the huge risk
he took, he was successful not only in producing
good clocks but in making a profit, for he retired
and sold the business to two young clockmaker-
carpenters with whom he had formed partnerships.
They were Silas Hoadley and Seth Thomas, both of
whom became famous on their own accounts.

Terry did not remain idle for long, however. He
became interested in the shelf clock that had
emerged in Massachusetts, and was an original conception. Two farmer's sons, Simon and Aaron
Willard, in Massachusetts, were at the idea's source.
Simon began making clocks while still living on the
farm. One wall clock, made about 1780, had a box
below it that concealed the pendulum and driving
weights. The clock part was in a box with a glass
front shaped and waisted in imitation of the then
popular English balloon clock inspired by the Mont-
golfier hot air balloons. Later, Willard designed
standing models of similar clocks. Copyists combined the upper and lower parts from Willard's
version and incorporated another glass below that
covering the dial, reverse painting it, and thus
creating the Massachusetts shelf clock.

6

Author's Photo

Fig. 6 *Banjo bracket clock,*
probably made in Boston,
c.1825; height about 36 ins.
This clock is an ornate example
of the type patented by Simon
Willard and accepted as one of
the most original American
designs.
(Private Collection.)

Fig. 7 *Pillar and scroll shelf*
clock, c.1816; height 30 ins.
This clock is of the type adapted
and refined by Eli Terry from the
widely used long-case and shelf
clocks.
(Private Collection.)

7

Author's Photo

Aaron Willard abandoned the long-case clocks he was specialising in and turned to shelf clocks, while Simon, more obsessed with the balloon shape, devoted his energies to what he called his 'patent timepiece'. The design later acquired the name 'banjo clock' and is accepted as one of the most original American designs (Figs. 2 and 6). The theme was followed by other makers and, in its most elaborate form – the girandole, developed by Lemuel Curtis of Concord, Massachusetts – has today become the most sought after American antique clock (Fig. 3). The girandole acquired its name from the elaborate girandole mirrors of the time, both mirror-frames and clock-cases being decorated all over with gold leaf.

The shelf clock, nevertheless, became the best-known and most typical American clock because it was taken up and developed by the infant manufacturing industry in Connecticut. Terry's first production model was in a box case with a plain glass door, on the inside of which the hour numerals and simple corner spandrel decorations were painted. The wooden movement could be seen through the glass, with an hour bell below it, a pendulum in front of it, and a weight each side. Seth Thomas also made such clocks under licence from Terry.

Well before 1820, Terry had refined the case, adding free-standing pillars at the sides, scroll decoration with three urn finials at the top and four feet and a skirt at the bottom (Fig. 7). In other words, he had taken some ideas from the hood of the long-case clock, made it rather larger but much narrower, and given it feet to stand on a shelf. A painted dial was added behind the glass front door through which the pendulum and escape wheel on the front of the movement could be seen. In the lower part of the door was another panel of glass, the back painted with decoration with a clear oval shape left in the centre through which the pendulum-bob could be seen – another simplification of a traditional long-case theme.

Shelf clocks were made in very large numbers and, as always seems to happen, the earlier delicate design became debased; later examples were cruder and heavier in form as the popularity and number of makers grew. The original Terry design, called the 'pillar and scroll', was eventually driven out of fashion by a relatively simple design by another Connecticut clockmaker,

MUSEUMS AND COLLECTIONS

American clocks may be seen at the following:

Bristol, Conn.:	American Clock and Watch Museum
New York:	New York University Museum of Clocks and Watches
	Metropolitan Museum of Art
Washington, D.C.:	Smithsonian Institution

FURTHER READING

Antique American Clocks and Watches by Richard Thomson, Princeton, 1968.

A Treasury of American Clocks by Brooks Palmer, New York, 1967.

The Complete Clock Book by Wallace Nutting, rev. ed., 1973.

Amelung and the Minor Glassworks

Founded by a German glassmaker, J. F. Amelung, the New Bremen Glassmanufactory was the last major glassworks in eighteenth-century America

After the failure of both Wistar's and Stiegel's glassworks, John Frederick Amelung, a practical glassmaker from Grünenplan, Germany, was the third outstanding figure in eighteenth-century glassmaking in America. After receiving letters of recommendation from Americans in Europe, such as Benjamin Franklin and Benjamin Crockett (a Baltimore merchant), he became convinced of the possibility of establishing a profitable glasshouse in America, and he arrived in Baltimore, Maryland, on 31 August, 1784.

In addition to his immediate family, he brought with him sixty-eight glassworkers recruited from Bohemia, Thuringia and other parts of Germany, and the essential equipment to build the glass manufactory he envisaged. With German capital he acquired 2,100 acres of land around Bennett's Creek, near the Monocacy River, about nine miles south of Frederick, Maryland. Undoubtedly his choice of land in Maryland had been influenced by Crockett. Here he established a small, self-sufficient community, which he called New Bremen, and erected a glasshouse which, by February 1785, was offering 'window glass, and green and white hollow wares' to the public. By 1787, when he published his pamphlet *Remarks on Manufactures . . .*, he had 'erected all the necessary buildings for the manufactory as well as glass ovens for bottles, window and flint glass and dwelling houses for 135 now living souls'. He also built a community house and a German and an English school for his workers, as well as a mansion house for himself, which still stands. It was Amelung's intention to supply from a domestic source the ever-growing demand for glass in the new republic. Amelung brought additional workmen from Europe and at the peak of his production employed some three hundred workmen his products show both German and English influence.

Little was known of Amelung's factory or products until the discovery in Bremen, Germany, in 1928 of a covered *pokal* (goblet), engraved with the arms of the city of Bremen and the inscription 'Old Bremen Success and the New Progress', and on the reverse, 'New Bremen Glassmanufactory–1788–North America, State of Maryland'. This documentary piece, now in the Metropolitan Museum of Art, New York, was undoubtedly a presentation piece sent by Amelung to associates in Bremen who had invested capital in his glasshouse.

From 1928 until 1962, Amelung's glass was primarily known from about two dozen or so presentation pieces, which constitute the finest glass produced in America in the eighteenth century. Among the earliest of these is a covered tumbler engraved with a vignette of the story of Tobias and the Angel (Fig. 4). It was made by Amelung as an anniversary gift to his wife in 1788 and bears the inscription 'Happy is he who is blessed with Virtuous Children. Carolina Lucia Amelung. 1788.' Other

Fig. 1 *Conjectural reconstruction of the John Frederick Amelung New Bremen Glassmanufactory, based on a comparable Bohemian factory at Breitenstein. Drawing by Richard Stinley.*
From the foundations of the original building as well as from similar factories, it has been possible to recreate Amelung's glassworks with great accuracy. The building contained two melting-furnaces, one apparently for making bottles, the other for tableware. There were also fourteen ancillary furnaces for preparing frit, annealing the glassware and probably for preheating pots. In the background is Amelung's mansion house.
(Corning Museum of Glass, Corning, New York.)

Fig. 2 Left: **Tumbler** *attributed to the New Bremen Glassmanufactory, late eighteenth century. Pattern-moulded diamond design above small flutes.*
(Dr. and Mrs. Martin Stohlman Collection.)
Centre: **Fragment of a tumbler** *excavated by the Corning Museum of Glass from the site of the New Bremen Glassmanufactory in 1963. Pattern-moulded glass.*
(Corning Museum of Glass.)
Right: **Fragment of a tumbler** *excavated in Alexandria, Virginia in 1967. Pattern-moulded glass.*
(Smithsonian Institution, Washington, D.C.)

Fig. 3 **Pokal** *(goblet), one of a pair by John F. Amelung, New Bremen, 1793. Free-blown, almost colourless glass, engraved 'George Trisler 1793' in a wreath of flowers and foliate scrolls, height 8¹¹⁄₁₆ ins.*
The pair of fine goblets was made at New Bremen as a gift for Amelung's friend George Trisler.
(Corning Museum of Glass.)

Fig. 4 **Covered tumbler** *by John F. Amelung, New Bremen, 1788. Clear glass engraved with a vignette depicting the story of Tobias and the Angel, surrounded by the legend 'Happy is he who is blessed with Virtuous Children. Carolina Lucia Amelung. 1788', height 11⅞ ins.*
(Corning Museum of Glass.)

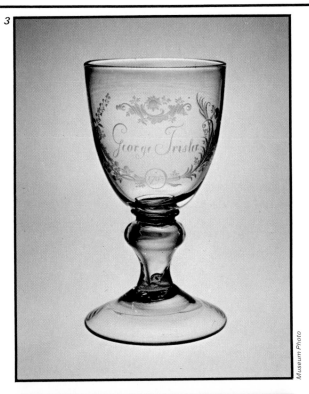

Museum Photo

presentation pieces include capacious goblets with high, domed feet and baluster stems of a style that had waned fifty years earlier in Germany (Fig. 3), a pocket-bottle (Fig. 6) and case-bottles. Most of these pieces were given to friends, merchants or persons of high standing for the purpose of gaining recognition for the New Bremen Glassmanufactory. An eyewitness account of a visit to George Washington's home, Mount Vernon, bears testimony to the fact that Amelung presented a pair of capacious goblets to General Washington, finely engraved with his coat of arms, just before he became first President of the United States. This gift may have been made, in part, in an attempt to gain government assistance and the passage of tariffs to protect the infant glass industry in America.

Except for these presentation pieces, knowledge of the production of everyday glass wares was limited, based only upon brief advertisements by Amelung and the finding of a few fragments by amateur archeologists, until 1962–63, when a professional excavation of the site was undertaken, sponsored by the Corning Museum of Glass and the Smithsonian Institution. Two seasons of excavating revealed the foundations of a factory building 112 ft. 7 ins. long by 65 ft. 7 ins. wide. The building (Fig. 1) actually contained two melting-furnaces, one apparently for making bottles, the other for tableware. It also contained fourteen ancillary furnaces for preparing frit, annealing the glassware and probably preheating pots. In addition to the foundations of the building and furnaces, thousands of fragments of glass were recovered, indicating the broad scope of Amelung's glassmaking operations.

Among the fragments found were several varieties of pattern-moulded glass, some of which confirmed the production of pocket-bottles and salts bearing a chequered diamond design (Fig. 5). Other patterns represented were simple, ribbed designs, either vertical or swirled; plain diamond designs and a small diamond design above short flutes (Fig. 2). Numerous fragments of different-sized bottles and flasks made of light green bottle-glass were found as well as many fragments of flint glass-wares, especially a wide variety of forms of wineglasses, tumblers and decanter-bases. Stoppers, fragments of rims from various vessels, handles and feet of creamers and sugar-bowls and handles of apparently large pitchers were also found. While most of these fragments were of a more or less colourless glass, a good percentage of various tones of blue and amethyst glass was found, indicating a substantial production of coloured glasswares. No fragments of fine engraved wares were found, suggesting that the engraving may have been done in a different area.

A complete analysis of the various compositions of glass made at the New Bremen Glassmanufactory has not been completed, but the excavation has revealed numerous fragments of glasswares containing lead, which, upon further study, may refute the long-held opinion that he made only non-lead glass products. It seems obvious that Amelung was constantly experimenting in his attempt to achieve a fine, colourless glass which, by his own admission in 1790, he had not fully accomplished.

Despite Amelung's practical knowledge of glassmaking and his apparent energy and intense

5

6

Museum Photo

Fig. 5 **American glass** *from the left: diamond pattern-moulded pocket-bottle, chequered diamond pattern-moulded pocket-bottle, blue glass salt, engraved goblet; the latter three pieces attributed to the New Bremen Glassmanufactory, late eighteenth century. Height of goblet 8¼ ins.*
(Isaac Delgado Museum of Art, New Orleans, Louisiana.)

Fig. 6 **Flask** *made at Amelung's New Bremen Glassmanufactory, 1792. Free-blown smoky, green-tinted glass, engraved with the name 'F. Stenger. 1792' surrounded by a floral and foliate scroll on the obverse, and with a bottle, plough and masonic emblems surrounded by a stylised wreath on the reverse, height 6¾ ins.*
(Corning Museum of Glass.)

interest in developing a successful glass factory, he met with failure after only eleven years of operation. This was possibly due in part to premature expansion of his facilities, a lesser response to his glass than he had anticipated and lack of sufficient protective tariffs, coupled with less sympathetic treatment from the government than was received by rival glasshouses in other countries.

In addition, Amelung suffered a severe financial loss when his factory was burned down on 6 May, 1790. The factory was immediately rebuilt and he resumed operations but, despite the addition of more capital, the business, although extensive, never fulfilled Amelung's anticipations. According to family diaries, Amelung suffered a stroke in 1794, which undoubtedly had some bearing on the closing of the factory in 1795. Amelung died at the home of his son-in-law, Peter Volkmann, on 21 November, 1798, aged fifty-seven.

After the closing of Amelung's New Bremen Glassmanufactory, a number of his workers migrated westwards and carried their skills and traditions with them, contributing to the development of glassmaking in the mid-West. Several of these workmen helped to establish the Gallatin Glassworks in New Geneva, Pennsylvania, in partnership with Albert Gallatin, who, in 1801, became Secretary of the Treasury. Amelung's son, John Frederick Magnus Amelung, was associated with a glass factory in Baltimore, Maryland, established in about 1798; after several years he removed to Pittsburgh, where he was associated with the Pittsburgh Glass Works established by Major Isaac Craig and General James O'Hara in 1797.

Several other glasshouses were established in the closing years of the eighteenth century. The glasshouse founded at Kensington, near Philadelphia, in 1769, operated under various managements into the twentieth century, but little is known of its eighteenth-century activities and products. On 27 February, 1775, the Philadelphia Glass Works,

as it was then called, advertised in the *Pennsylvania Packet* a wide variety of glass including tablewares, lamps, pocket-bottles, phials and chemical wares. None of these objects, unfortunately, is identifiable today. The Boston Crown Glass Manufactory was organised in 1787, but did not actually begin production until 1793, when additional German glass-workers were hired and brought to this country. From that time until the failure of the company in 1827, the glasshouse was highly successful and prosperous, its crown glass gaining a wide reputation for fine quality.

Other bottle and window glasshouses were founded in the eighteenth century in New York City, Germantown (Massachusetts), East Hartford (Connecticut) and in upper New York State, but none was on so large a scale nor, by comparison, was any as successful as the three factories established by Wistar, Stiegel and Amelung.

MUSEUMS AND COLLECTIONS

Late eighteenth-century American glass or English prototypes may be seen at the following:

Boston: Boston Museum of Fine Arts
Corning, N.Y.: Corning Museum of Glass
New York: Metropolitan Museum of Art
Philadelphia: Philadelphia Museum of Art

FURTHER READING

Chats on Old Glass by R. A. Robertson, revised with a new chapter on American glass by Kenneth M. Wilson, New York, 1969.

Two Hundred Years of American Blown Glass by George S. and Helen A. McKearin, New York, 1950.

American Glass by George S. and Helen A. McKearin, New York, 1941.

TOYS FOR THE NEW WORLD

Museum Photo

A. C. Cooper

Fig. 1 **Horse and rider,** *found in New Jersey, nineteenth century. Turned wood, height 8½ ins. This is in the style of a German toy of the period, though more crudely painted and finished. Wood was plentiful in New England and toys were made on turning-wheels that were also used for making cartwheels and full-size buckets. (Shelburne Museum, Vermont.)*

Fig. 2 **Clockwork figure on a tricycle,** *probably made by E. R. Ives, c.1890. Ives was famous for his manufacture of clockwork dolls and locomotives. Production of his toys began in the 1870s. (Christie, Manson and Woods Ltd, London.)*

The inventive genius and highly competitive spirit of the American toymakers promoted a thriving and colourful trade

The toy industry of America was brought into being during the first decades of the nineteenth century by a combination of several historical factors. After the French Revolution and the American War of Independence, America became the home of ever increasing numbers of European liberals under whose influence the rigid puritanism of earlier settlers was called into question and modified. Play, for children or adults, was no longer quite as suspect as before. Moreover, the settled conditions obtaining along the eastern seaboard brought a higher standard of living and an expanding market for luxury articles of all kinds. Toys and games equipment were in such heavy demand that foreign imports had to be supplemented by home-produced products.

The wave of patriotic feeling that swept through the land after the war against the British had been won in 1812 was also an encouragement and help to local craftsmen, and the jubilant spirit of victory and independence was expressed in advertisements proudly announcing that goods were American-made as an inducement to spending. However, little persuasion must have been needed to expand sales. Between 1800 and the early 1850s the population was to grow from some five million to twenty-three million; and though a percentage of the newcomers moved on westwards, sufficient remained to enrich anyone with enough goods to put on the market.

Many of the new emigrants came from toy-producing countries, and brought with them skills learned in Europe. Though the majority were primarily farmworkers, there was spare time, particularly in winter or during bad weather, in which to produce toys for sale in the towns. With an abundant supply of wood available, all that was

Fig. 3 **Noah's Ark,** *made in the tradition of Bavarian toys from the Erzgebirge. Hand-carved wood. Imported and provincial American toys are almost impossible to distinguish unless their provenance is known. (Shelburne Museum.)*

Fig. 4 **The Hobby-horse,** *American, c.1840, by an unknown artist. Oil on canvas, The rocking-horse was a popular toy in America, as elsewhere, though the one shown here may have been imported. (National Gallery of Art, Washington. Gift of Edgar William and Bernice Chrysler Garbisch.)*

3

Museum Photo

needed to start a home-based industry was someone with the foresight and drive to bring the craftsmen together in order to market their work.

Such a man was William S. Tower of South Hingham, Massachusetts. A carpenter by profession, he combined the manual skills usual to his trade with outstanding business acumen and a flair for organisation. He began by commissioning people he knew, in order to acquire a varied stock for sale; and then, when this proved mutually beneficial, he started a guild of toymakers.

The long-lived Tower Toy Company came into being as a fully fledged manufacturing organisation in the 1830s. An early Tower advertisement, after listing various toys, speaks of: 'Wood turning, sawing, &c., done at short notice', and gives the factory address as Wilder's Bucket Mill, which suggests the stock was mainly of wood. This is borne out by surviving examples, for the most part pieces of dolls' furniture.

Although Tower has been called 'the founder of the toy industry in America', a number of almost equally respected names were associated with him: Jacob, Wilder, Lichfield and Lincoln have all been mentioned at one time or another, and in a New England business directory of 1856 no fewer than four Herseys are listed as toy manufacturers.

In 1861 the much admired Loring Cushing joined the organisation. It is said he learned his trade from the founder; certainly his miniature chests of drawers, tables with drop sides, washstands, cradles and chairs are very fine indeed, and so meticulously finished that they give the impression sometimes of being full-scale pieces seen through a magical reducing glass. Alas, not many of them have come down to us, though Cushing continued to produce toys for about half a century.

Tower and his associates were not alone. Dozens of independent makers of wooden toys have been traced. Wherever suitable wood was plentiful, in New England, New York or Pennsylvania, turning-wheels would be set up to produce toys as part of a stock that might include full-size buckets, cart-wheels, clothes-pegs and so on. One large concern was that of a Londoner, George Hawes, who founded the Hawes Manufacturing Company in the 1830s. At one time exaggeratedly known as the largest in the world, the business thrived until the end of the century, and at its height employed over two hundred workers.

Throughout the nineteenth century, wooden toys were modelled closely on European imports. Moreover, sometimes an employee might reproduce on his lathe some trifle he had made in Bavaria or Thuringia, and the resulting novelty would be put on sale. Many an American toy is therefore indistinguishable from its folk counterpart on the other side of the Atlantic (Fig. 3).

From about 1860 onwards the toy industry began to make a bid for overseas markets. The Tower Toy Company was one of four American firms to show examples of their products in the Paris International Exhibition of 1878. Though pronounced by the judges to be satisfactory, the toys were too expensive to constitute a threat to French manufacturers.

In one sense, however, the American toy industry was more competitive than people then supposed. In the New World original materials and techniques were constantly being exploited. A typical example was the application of Charles Goodyear's vulcanising process to toy-making. Rubber balls, rattles, dolls' heads and various animals were advertised for sale in 1850, and in 1851 the first vulcanised rubber doll was produced.

For resource and inventiveness however, none could surpass the Crandalls. Of the eleven members of the two families involved in the toy trade, two men are of outstanding importance: Jesse A. Crandall and Charles M. Crandall.

Jesse Armour Crandall was born in 1833. By the time he was eleven he was working in his father's workshop, making baby-carriages and toys. It was at this relatively tender age that he first became an inventor – of a rig with evenly spaced bits which could drill ten holes at a time. In succeeding years many other practical ideas originated in his fertile brain. Around 1845, for instance, in order to overcome complaints that the firm's rocking-horses damaged nursery and parlour carpets, he devised one mounted on springs and a platform which is still being sold today. Then in 1859 he came up with an idea for a rocking toy for children too young to straddle even a small size regular horse. This consisted of two rocking-horse silhouettes cut in board with a seat fixed between. It was known as a 'Shoofly' in America, and was pirated extensively.

An incredible number of other patents were taken out by him before the end of his long life. These included velocipedes, a sand toy, jointed dolls, a folding sled, a spinning-clown top, combined hoops and jumping ropes, toy guns with special targets and many games. But probably his most lasting invention is so well known and universally used nowadays that most people imagine its origin to be of great antiquity. This was for nursery nesting-blocks in the form of five-sided boxes, all graduated in size and painted gaily with pictures or letters. They had the advantage of fitting into one another for storage, and, being containers as well as blocks, could be used for putting things into by children just reaching the stage of manipulating objects.

Jesse apparently never had any business dealings with his distant relation Charles M. Crandall; yet in many ways the lives of the two men ran in parallel. Charles was born in the same year as Jesse and he, too, entered his father's business while still a boy. Having already invented several toys, at the age of sixteen, when his father died, he took over the works and managed it alone. By 1866 he was kept busy supplying croquet-sets to satisfy a craze that had swept America shortly after the

Museum Photo

A. C. Cooper

A. C. Cooper

Fig. 5 Left: *Lion and two Monkeys*, American, 1883. Iron. This is a money-box. The two monkeys throw coins into the lion's mouth as he attempts to climb the tree after them.
Right: *Uncle Sam Bank*, American, 1886. Iron.
When a lever is pressed the carpet bag opens and a coin placed in Uncle Sam's hand falls into it; simultaneously, his whiskers move.
(Leonard W. Dunham Collection.)

Fig. 6 *Clockwork dancing figures*, made by a member of the Crandall families, 1860–70. There were eleven Crandalls in the toy trade, surpassing in inventiveness all other toy manufacturers in America in the nineteenth century. Many toys in use today are based on their models, safe rocking-horses, for example, and nursery nesting-boxes.
(Author's Collection.)

Civil War. One day he decided the boxes in which the sets were packed might better be made with tongue-and-groove joints, instead of being nailed together. A machine was installed, and in testing it short lengths of thin wood were used. To continue in his own words: 'My two infant boys were convalescing from scarlet fever, and I carried some of the blocks home for their amusement. A house, bridge, fence and other structures were built from them. In the evening our physician called, saw and admired the blocks, and ordered a small quantity for his own use . . .'.

Crandall's blocks were left as presents to the 'dusky savages' of the Congo

When put on the market, the blocks earned some ten thousand dollars for their inventor in the first year; twelve months later the sales figures were tripled. It was hardly an exaggeration when a writer in *The Inventive Age* claimed: 'His building blocks are to be found in almost every nursery in civilized nations and sets of them can today be seen in the Congo where Stanley left them as presents to the dusky savages . . .'.

One of the most popular forms of entertainment of that period was the travelling circus. In 1874 Crandall cashed in on its popularity by adapting the tongue-and-groove idea to cut-out shapes of figures and animals, the limbs of which could be put together in different ways. Crandall's *Acrobats* might be assembled in the form of a human pyramid, and his *Menagerie* was capable of being arranged in a great variety of poses and tableaux (Fig. 9). Other variant toys followed in quick

succession: *Masquerade* and *Expression Blocks*, the *Illuminated Pictorial Alphabet*, *The District School* and *John Gilpin – An Illustration of the Old English Ballad*.

During the later 1870s and '80s, Crandall's inventiveness never flagged. But it was in 1889, after he had gone into partnership with Moses Lyman, that his next best-seller appeared. *The Waverly Free Press* reported: 'The toy works are turning 8000 a day of 'Pigs in Clover' and are twenty days behind with their orders.' A craze for this puzzle swept through America. In essence it was simple enough, merely a circular, maze-like device, about six inches in diameter, along whose 'lanes' four balls or 'pigs' had to be coaxed until they reached the centre 'pen'. Why all sorts and conditions of persons should have been so enthralled by a toy of this nature is not easy to understand. Yet similar fads had been known before in history, and were to be known again.

In spite of the availability and wide use of wood, during the 1830s and '40s an increasing number of tin toys were made. Early advertisements mention several specialist firms, including one that was active for several decades, the Philadelphia Tin Toy Manufactory. Among their products was a locomotive called *The General Taylor*; pull-along toys of horses and dogs; a boat on wheels and furniture for dolls' houses.

Although the Civil War curtailed the supply of metal, it stimulated its use for making all kinds of articles when firms returned to peacetime production. Though cast-iron toys had been manufactured from the first decades of the century (there is a toy iron and trivet of about 1825 in the Museum of the City of New York), it was not until after 1865 that the material was used at all extensively.

Fig. 7 **Circus**, *made by Schoenhut and Co., c.1900. Made principally of wood and papier mâché. (Author's Collection.)*

Fig. 8 **Street-car**, *made by Converse C. Winchendon, Mass., c.1900. Pressed tin with stencil decoration. (Shelburne Museum.)*

Fig. 9 **Menagerie**, *made by Charles M. Crandall, 1870. Wood. (Mary Hillier Collection.)*

When George W. Brown & Company, specialists in tin ware, and J. & E. Stevens, who made iron toys, joined forces to form the American Toy Company, their catalogue showed more than two hundred metal playthings.

It was during the 1870s, too, that the typically American cast-iron mechanical banks were evolved (Fig. 5). The most important manufacturer of these was the same firm of J. & E. Stevens, who produced at least fifty designs. *Tammany* and *Frog* banks are probably the best known, though several other types were widely sold.

Two big names in the production of clockwork toys in the 1870s are Althof, Bergman & Company and E. R. Ives. It is from this period that their enchanting doll-and-clockwork toys come: moon-faced boys on tricycles or eccentric drivers of horse-drawn buggies (Fig. 2). Ives was also famous for his locomotives. In one of his advertisements he lays claim to being the first man in the United States to bring out a model train that ran on its own tracks; certainly he appears to have been partly responsible for the O-gauge model railway line.

As the century drew to a close there can be detected no slackening in inventive spirit. New firms came into being, like that of the German immigrant A. Schoenhut, whose toy pianos could really be played and whose *Humpty Dumpty Circus* was to be a success in the 1900s (Fig. 7). A spirit of optimism could be felt everywhere. It was almost as though American businessmen were looking forward to their biggest chance of all time – the 1914–1918 War, in which their chief rival, Germany, would, for a time, be almost eliminated. The markets of the world were soon to open wide for them.

MUSEUMS AND COLLECTIONS
American nineteenth-century toys may be seen at the following:

Hingham, Mass: The Old Ordinary
Lancaster, Pa.: Pennsylvania Farm Museum of Landis Valley
New York: Museum of the City of New York

FURTHER READING
Collecting Toys by Richard O'Brien, New York, 1982.

Antique Toys and Dolls by Constane E. King, 1980.

American Antique Toys, 1830–1900, by Bernard Barenholtz and Inez McClintock, New York, 1980.

Toys of Other Days by F. Nevill Jackson, 1968 reprint.

The Warner Collector's Guide to American Toys by William Ayres, New York, 1981.

Museum Photo

GLASS OF 'UNCOMMON BRILLIANCY'

Fig. 1 *Apple paperweight*, *New England Glass Company*, *1853–80. Blown glass, height approximately 4 ins.* *The apple rests on a cushion of clear crystal glass.* *(Corning Museum of Glass, Corning, New York.)*

Important technical developments and the skill of nineteenth-century glassmakers in America resulted in pressed, cut, patterned and coloured glass of astonishing variety and stylishness

The *Boston Daily Journal* of 26 February, 1850, carries an advertisement by the glass-merchants W. R. and A. H. Somner, promising to supply not only the latest patterns in Waterford and English glass, but also 'American glassware made to order from metal of uncommon brilliancy to match any pattern desired whether of foreign or domestic manufacture'.

Some researchers believe glassmaking to have been the earliest American industry, and we know that the first Colonists established a glasshouse at Jamestown, Virginia, in 1608. From that date, glassmaking pursued a somewhat sporadic course with a fair number of factories emerging and closing down again after brief activity or amalgamating with a more prosperous establishment. Glassworks were frequently forced to move due to circumstances either of the economics or of the natural resources of the chosen area, and often the glassworkers themselves decided upon a change and joined a new glasshouse. During the later eighteenth century such enterprising glassmakers as Henry William Stiegel and John Frederick Amelung arrived from Europe, and their work left an indelible imprint on the history of American glassmaking.

A traditional American glass design is the so-called 'South [New] Jersey' style produced in glasshouses of this region during the later eighteenth and early nineteenth centuries. It is represented by free-blown, clear glass, adapted to pleasing and well-balanced forms of cream-jugs, bowls and dishes in attractive colours – amber, aquamarine, purple, blue and green – which could be produced by varying the quantity of the natural mineral content in the raw material. The most distinctive form of applied decoration is the lily-pad motif, resembling the stem and pad of a water-lily, and apparently an entirely original conception (Fig. 2).

Applied bands and loops in glass of contrasting colours, as may be found on some specimens of the Pittsburgh Flint Glass Manufactory of Bakewell and Co., show the influence of Bristol and Nailsea. Thomas Caines, son of a Bristol glassmaker, arrived in Boston in 1812 and was instrumental in setting up the South Boston Flint Glass Works, a subsidiary of the Boston Crown Glass Manufactory. A further factory, the Phoenix Glass Works, was established by the Caines family in 1820.

By 1815, some forty glasshouses were in operation in various parts of America, but these concentrated mainly on the manufacture of bottles and window-glass by the crown technique. Prior to the Treaty of Ghent in 1814, the war of 1812 and the blockade of American ports by the British made the Americans realise that home manufacture of fine table-glass was desirable. By 1840, about thirty American glasshouses were engaged in the production of tableware.

American cutting styles were predominantly influenced by English and Irish glass, which was

Fig. 2 *Pitcher, South Jersey type, possibly Lancaster or Lockport glassworks, New York, c.1840–50. Free-blown glass, with applied lily-pad decoration, height 7⅛ ins. (Corning Museum of Glass)*

Fig. 3 *Pitcher, Dorflinger Glass Works, New York, 1852–63. Cut glass, height 12⅛ ins. (Corning Museum of Glass.)*

Fig. 4 *Candlestick, probably Pittsburgh area, c.1815–40. Purple-blue pattern-moulded glass, height 10¼ ins.· (Corning Museum of Glass.)*

Fig. 5 *Celery-vase, Bakewell, Page and Bakewell, Pittsburgh, c.1825. Cut glass, height 7½ ins. This was given by the Bakewells to Henry Clay Fry when he opened his glass factory in Pittsburgh in about 1867. (Corning Museum of Glass.)*

Fig. 6 *Oil-lamp, possibly Midwest, Pittsburgh area, c.1835–40. Blown, pressed and cut glass, height 17 ins. (Corning Museum of Glass.)*

imported in large quantities throughout the nineteenth century. By the middle of the century, Bohemian glass techniques had also made their mark upon the industry.

Bakewell's glass was highly praised for its quality, variety, beauty and brilliance

The first American glasshouse to produce cut and engraved tableware was very probably the Pittsburgh Flint Glass Manufactory, established by Benjamin Bakewell and Edward Ensell, an English glass-blower. Beginning operations in 1808, the partnership was dissolved in 1809, and the firm traded subsequently under various trade names (Fig. 5). Quality was extremely fine, with regard to both the white metal of their lead glass and the workmanship of the cutters and engravers.

It was fashionable for the stranger to Pittsburgh to pay a visit to the Bakewell glasshouse. Anne Royall in *Mrs. Royall's Pennsylvania* (Washington, 1829) writes rapturously of the quality, variety, beauty and brilliance of Bakewell's glass and assures us that it is equal, if not superior, to the Boston glass.

In his *Personal Narrative of Travel* (1817), Elias Pym Fordham wrote 'Mr. Bakewell's works are admirable. He has excellent artists, both French and English. His cut glass equals the best I have seen in England'. Henry Bradshaw Fearon in *A Narrative of a Journey* (London, 1818) expresses astonishment at finding such elegant and excellent perfection in glass on the other side of the Atlantic, although he adds that a number of specimens had been cut from a London pattern. In the absence of

a factory-mark, it is frequently impossible to be certain whether a specimen was an Anglo-Irish import or a home product.

Bakewell's produced a superb service of table-glass, made to order in 1817 for President Monroe. This is described as having been of brilliant double flint metal, engraved and cut by Mr. Jardelle, 'in which this able artist has displayed his best manner' with the arms of the United States decorating each piece. Another engraver and cutter of European extraction, William Peter Eichbaum, was employed by Bakewell's in 1810 and 'in that year cut the first crystal chandelier to have been produced in America'.

Until about 1820, the position of Bakewell's as manufacturers of fine, cut and engraved flint glass had few rivals. The factory made glass over a period of seventy-four years and finally closed down in 1882.

By 1816, the general depression had reached its height. The country was hard hit by commercial disasters, due partly to loss of foreign trade, and partly to the fact that, following the Treaty of Ghent, England swamped the American market with British wares which were heavily subsidised and prevented competitive home manufacture. For the more enterprising glass-makers transport facilities by road were poor and fraught with danger. On the other hand, the early years of the nineteenth century witnessed tremendous advances in another field of communication – water. Due to the development and expansion of the steamboat industry, hitherto unnegotiable routes began to open up, and river traffic proved a boon for the internal market.

In 1817, a group of successful Boston business-

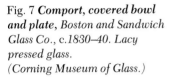

Fig. 7 **Comport, covered bowl and plate,** Boston and Sandwich Glass Co., c.1830–40. Lacy pressed glass. (Corning Museum of Glass.)

Fig. 8 Left: **Sugar-bowl with cover,** probably Providence Flint Glass Works, 1831–33, or possibly Boston and Sandwich Glass Co., c.1830–40. Lacy pressed glass.
Centre: **Lamp,** New England Glass Co., c.1830. Lacy pressed glass.
Right: **Inkstand,** Boston and Sandwich, c.1830. Lacy pressed glass.
(Corning Museum of Glass.)

grapes and other fruit, intaglio-cut landscapes and figures, faceted stems and star-cut bases were decorative devices applied to the early products of the company.

By the middle of the century, Bohemian-style cutting had become fashionable and European craftsmen, such as the German Louis Vaupel (Lewis Vaupal) at the New England Glass Company, were engaged to work for the larger American glasshouses. The resultant Bohemian-style glass could easily hold its own with the European models which had been obtained expressly for the purpose of study and copying. Cutting was frequently applied to good ruby-stained or cased glass, and, according to the recipe-book of John H. Leighton of the Boston and Sandwich Glass Company, this colour was obtained by the addition of oxide of gold to the batch. Specialists were engaged in every facet of the trade and workmen moved freely from one factory to another.

Production of cut glass was always costly and some of the executives, particularly men like Deming Jarves, encouraged production of mould-blown glass which would allow a variety of patterns, still in fine lead glass, to be manufactured more cheaply. Utilisation of the three-part mould was particularly suitable since it facilitated the lifting out of wares with complicated patterns.

A most significant development was achieved with the perfection of a practical glass-pressing machine, and once again the commercial application of this revolutionary technique is attributed to the ability and zeal of Deming Jarves, though he would not admit that this was a purely American invention. What he did maintain however was that 'America can claim the credit of great improvements in the needful machinery which has advanced the art to its present perfection'. Bakewell and Company obtained a patent for their pressed-glass furniture knobs in 1825; Enoch Robinson and Whitney of the New England Glass Company followed suit with their patent for pressed-glass knobs in 1826. A number of other glasshouses were granted patents for pressed wares, and most of these were situated along the eastern seaboard, particularly in the New England region. G. E. Pazaurek, in his unsurpassed *Gläser der Empire und Biedermeierzeit*, writes that apparently the first pressed drinking-glass with scale-cut pattern (*Schuppenschliff*) was made by Deming Jarves at Sandwich, Massachussetts, but most likely the first pressed objects were flat, such as the American so-called 'cup-plates'. These are small plates, three or four inches in diameter, in which the cup was set when the tea was poured into the saucer for cooling prior to drinking, so as to protect the table or linen from tea-stains.

When glass is blown into a mould, the inner surface of the specimen will correspond to the outside contours. In pressing, the glass mass is pressed into the mould by means of a plunger with a long handle, and consequently the interior glass surface will not follow the pattern but remain relatively smooth. It is the designer of the metal mould who must be considered as the real artist, and one of the finest craftsmen chosen by Jarves was probably Hiram Dillway, who remained with the Boston and Sandwich Glass Company all his life (d.1887).

Early American pressed ware was normally of

men purchased the defunct Boston Porcelain and Glass Company, and in February 1818 the factory commenced production as the New England Glass Company. By the act of corporation, the associates, 'their successors and assigns' were privileged to manufacture 'flint and crown glass of all kinds in the towns of Boston and Cambridge'. The company became so successful that by 1865 five hundred men and boys were employed in various parts of the large plant. In time, the company expanded and a number of branches and subsidiaries were established, generally in neighbouring areas.

The youngest and possibly most dynamic of the original partners was Deming Jarves (1790–1869), who left the New England Glass Company to establish his own glassworks at Sandwich which was incorporated in 1826 as the Boston and Sandwich Glass Company. The tireless Jarves founded a number of branch firms, for instance the Cape Cod Glass Company and the Mount Washington Glassworks (famous for its 'Burmese Glass') for members of his family, and the New England Glass Bottle Company for the exclusive manufacture of bottles. It was at Jarves' instigation that the New England Glass Company began to manufacture its own red lead (litharge) from Missouri lead, an essential ingredient of flint glass. The supply of red lead to other glasshouses proved a profitable business for the company. For the manufacture of the high-grade clay pots needed in glassmaking, Stourbridge clay was imported from England. It is therefore not surprising that the lead glass produced by the New England Glass Company was of excellent quality. Particular emphasis was given to form and outline, and fine quality lead glass, and once the piece was pressed into shape it was usually considered complete – edges and joins remained rough and unfinished. By the mid-nineteenth century three quarters of the American glass production consisted of pressed ware. The influence of this technique was enormous and revolutionised the glass industry in all parts of the world; in England, Apsley Pellat patented his process for glass-pressing techniques in 1831 and 1845.

The new 'lacy' glass had the delicate appearance of textiles or embroidery

During the early period of pressed-pattern glass (c.1825–50), a new phenomenon occurred in American pressed-glass design. This was the so-called 'lacy', now highly valued by collectors. Lacy glass patterns show a stippled background having the delicate appearance of textiles or embroidery; quite possibly the inspiration for the style came from Europe, perhaps from France, for it has decorative motifs similar in character to French designs. The actual source of the stippled background has never been fully explored; if there is a French influence, the fact that stippling represents one very specialised facet of the silversmith's craft, and that it was applied particularly to certain French and Russian work of this and earlier periods, is perhaps relevant. Early lacy glass is usually of fine quality, and patterns are so varied and numerous that to determine provenance in the absence of a factory-mark requires a great deal of study (Fig. 8).

The momentous changes and advances in the fields of politics and industry found a suitable response in a prolific output of commemorative glass objects, particularly in the cup-plates which were produced to more than six hundred different designs. Pictorial and historical pocket-flasks which were free-blown or pattern moulded appeared in large quantities and represent a study in themselves. First produced in about 1780, they continued throughout the ensuing century in numerous colour variations, and are much sought after by collectors. Among the most popular pressed objects are the delightful salt-cellars of trough-like shape and French-inspired rococo or Empire designs in both plain and coloured clear glass. Apart from the usual tableware (Fig. 7), pressed-glass whale-oil lamps came into fashion after 1820. These often consist of a pressed base and free-blown font and may incorporate cut and engraved decoration.

The earliest lacy glass has coarse stippling which becomes finer and more intricate in later ware. To exploit to the full every nuance of the delicate patterning, the glass metal had to be not only ductile, but also fluid, and this was achieved with the very high temperatures obtained by coal-fired furnaces. For these reasons, the moulds too were heated prior to being filled. The variety and richness of pattern could not conceivably have been accomplished by hand-cutting. Very much like French paperweights, American lacy glass is valued by the rarity of its design and colour.

About the middle of the century, America produced paperweights in many techniques. Floral bouquets were enclosed in the glass or miniature fruit rested on a *latticinio* bed, as

produced by Nicholas Lutz who had come to the Sandwich Glass Company from the St. Louis glassworks in French Lorraine. *Millefiori* weights made of multi-coloured glass canes enclosed in a clear glass matrix were a speciality of John L. Gilliland, who apparently worked not only for his own factory at Brooklyn, New York, but also for a number of other glasshouses. The portrait weights with sulphide enclosures in the manner of Apsley Pellat's *Cristallo-ceramie* technique were based on existing designs of coins and medals. More original are the fruit paperweights produced mainly by the New England Glass Company (Fig. 1), which were attractively coloured single fruit, nearly life-size and blown, resting on a clear glass cushion. These were mostly produced by a Frenchman, François Pierre, who had been apprenticed at the Baccarat factory. During the later half of the century, there appeared paperweights pressed into the shape of some interesting landmarks such as the Plymouth Rock, and other weights in pressed glass are found which represent books or animals, and in addition are cut or engraved.

The development in 1864 of a cheaper substitute for lead glass – the lime soda glass developed by William Leighton of the Wheeling Glass Factory in West Virginia – proved disastrous for some of the manufacturers of high quality lead glass. There followed an increase in pressed-glass production, but a lowering of quality, and a number of the New England glass factories were slow to adapt themselves to this cheaper method. Many of the glassworkers were loath to utilise an inferior substitute for their high quality metal, but, 'there was no fun in carrying on at a loss, interesting though it may be to see workmen producing beautiful glass specimens', was the comment of the stockholders.

At the close of the century, many of the finest early glasshouses had ceased operations. The New England Glass Company closed down in 1888 and the manager at that time, Edward D. Libbey, took over the charter and moved the firm to Toledo, Ohio. There it successfully recommenced glassmaking as the Libbey Glass Company.

One of the finest modern glass factories, the Corning Glassworks, grew from the amalgamation and reorganisation of a number of unsuccessful glasshouses, and was established at Corning, New York, in 1875. A new generation of enterprising glassmakers began to explore new art forms in order to revive the industry.

9

Museum Photo

Fig. 9 *Dolphin candlesticks,* *probably Boston and Sandwich, mid-nineteenth century. Pressed glass.* *(Corning Museum of Glass.)*

MUSEUMS AND COLLECTIONS

American nineteenth-century glass may be seen at the following:

Corning, N.Y.:	Corning Museum of Glass
Dearborn, Mich.:	Henry Ford Museum
New York:	Metropolitan Museum of Art
Toledo, Ohio:	Toledo Museum of Art

FURTHER READING

Early American Pressed Glass by Ruth Webb Lee, Massachusetts, 1946.

American Glass by George S. and Helen A. McKearin, New York, 1941.

Sandwich Glass by Ruth Webb Lee, Massachusetts, 1939.

Complete Guide to Pressed Glass by Bob H. Batty, 1978.

The Warner Collector's Guide to Pressed Glass by Lawrence Grow, 1982.

THE AGE OF JEFFERSON

Historical Society Photo

Fig. 1 *Fourth of July Celebration in Centre Square, Philadelphia*
by John Louis Krimmel, 1819. The domed marble waterworks in
the background was designed by B. H. Latrobe in 1800.
(Historical Society of Pennsylvania, Philadelphia.)

2

Sandak Inc.

3

Colonial Williamsburg Photo

4

Sandak Inc.

Thomas Jefferson, born on a Virginia frontier plantation, became one of the great political and philosophical leaders of the new United States

The Thirteen Colonies which became the United States did not by that act alone acquire a new national art; but the men who led them, the needs which the new state and federal governments – and business – created, the desire for self-expression of the people as individuals and as groups, all came together in the romantic neo-Classicism and eclecticism of the 'Federal' style.

Unique and overwhelming in it all was the person of Thomas Jefferson (1743–1826), Virginia landowner, author of the Declaration of Independence, Minister to France, Secretary of State, Vice-President and two-term President of the United States, founder of the University of Virginia, President of the American Philosophical Society, amateur architect, inventor, natural scientist, philosopher and farmer. Jefferson revolutionised American architecture and, through his enormous interests, studies, correspondence and involvement in all the arts, left a changed and enriched American scene, from the laying out of entire states to the planning of farms, towns and cities, from the private and public use of sculpture to the development of functional furniture and the decorative use of scientific materials and equipment.

Jefferson's vivacious and knowledgeable personality permeates the entire framework and culture of the United States from the Revolutionary period to his death in 1826. In virtually every field his life symbolises the best of that transition from a provincial British culture in the eighteenth-century Colonies to the participation in international, romantic Classicism. The contrast is suggested in the comparison of the provincial baroque town of Williamsburg, where Jefferson went to the College of William and Mary, where he first sat as a Burgess of the Colony of Virginia and where he began his term as Governor of the State of Virginia, with his Palladian/neo-classical villa of Monticello and with his design of the new Capitol of the State of Virginia at Richmond on the theme of the Roman temple at Nîmes, the Maison Carrée.

He regarded his election as President of the United States as virtually a bloodless revolution, the triumph of republican principles over the monarchist tendencies of the Federalist party. But his central role in American politics and philosophy had begun twenty-five years before his election. Just so was his influence on architecture. In 1767 he began the country house which set new standards of taste and refinement in the combination of Palladian villa principles with the decorative standards of late neo-Classicism, as well as the practicality of a truly free mind of the Enlightenment.

It was in these years that he devised the Jeffersonian modification to the Palladian plan, of having winged colonnades, with the domestic offices hidden almost entirely below ground on the garden side but exposed on the work-yard side.

In the 1780s he provided the plan for the State Capitol of Virginia, based on the Maison Carrée at

The Age of
Jefferson

Fig. 2 *View of the University of Virginia, Charlottesville & Monticello by E. Sachse and Co., 1853. Colour engraving. Charlottesville is seen here as it neared completion in 1824, from Jefferson's design. This academic village was a compilation of the neo-classical influences entering American architecture through Jefferson and those around him. Monticello, the house which Jefferson designed for himself, is visible on a hill in the background.*
(Museum of Fine Arts, University of Virginia, Charlottesville, Virginia.)

Fig. 3 *View down Duke of Gloucester Street, Williamsburg. Water-colour sketch.*
This fine view of Williamsburg's Duke of Gloucester Street shows Bruton Parish Church on the right. The scene closely resembles that so central to many periods of Jefferson's development. It reflects the continuation of the provincial Baroque into the period of America's flourishing neo-Classicism.
(College of William and Mary, Williamsburg, Virginia.)

Fig. 4 *Congress Hall: Old House of Representatives by Samuel F. B. Morse, 1822. Oil on canvas. Also known as* Lighting Up, *this marvellous painting by Morse (later inventor of the telegraph and Morse code) shows the chamber of the old House of Representatives in the Capitol as it had been finished by Latrobe. Of it, Jefferson wrote to Latrobe that it would 'remain a durable monument to your talents as an architect . . . [in] embellishing with Athenian taste the course of a nation looking far beyond the range of Athenian destinies'. The original chamber was partly destroyed when the British burned the Capitol in the War of 1812. This large canvas shows it in its second completion by Latrobe, much as it remains today in its colder, undraped use as Statuary Hall, following the completion of the new House in 1865.*
(Corcoran Gallery of Art, Washington D.C.)

Nîmes, the first use anywhere of a complete temple form for anything other than a garden temple. In his years as President he was the central figure in the group of architects and patrons, both official and private, who created the American versions of the neo-classical styles commonly called jointly the 'Federal' style.

In city planning Jefferson's hand also appears. He urged President Washington to appoint Pierre-Charles l'Enfant to design the new Federal city of Washington. Jefferson then provided L'Enfant with his collection of city plans, and thus was instrumental in the combination of grid-plan and baroque-grand-avenue plan devised by L'Enfant which had an enormous influence on the design of American cities in the nineteenth and twentieth centuries. Jefferson was involved in the laying out of the boundaries of a number of states, and after the acquisition of the eight hundred and twenty-eight thousand square miles of Louisiana Territory during his Presidency – doubling the size of the young United States – he was much involved in land division, the design of a standard grid for counties and farms within them, and of a standard grid for cities.

In sculpture Jefferson's acquaintance with the leading French neo-classicist, Jean-Antoine Houdon, led not only to Houdon's bust of Jefferson himself but also to Jefferson's arranging for him to go over to the United States to do a full-size figure of Washington from life, a great work still standing in the Capitol of Virginia. It was during Jefferson's administration that the first outdoor monument was created at Washington, the Tripoli Column erected in the Navy Yard in 1808, by the sculptor Micali of Leghorn, setting the example for neo-classical outdoor sculpture, again a feature of the American scene which has lasted into our own time. In this Jefferson was in consultation with Benjamin Henry Latrobe (1764–1820). This distinguished architect, who had studied in Germany, where he imbibed a taste for the boldest neo-Classicism, and had then worked in London, came to Washington to consult with Jefferson on plans for the Navy Yard and shortly found himself appointed Surveyor of Public Buildings. With regard to sculpture, Latrobe was employing a number of Italian sculptors at the Capitol. Together Latrobe and Franzoni created the marvellous decorations of the House of Representatives chamber, including the heroic figure of Liberty and the handsome conceit of the clock over the entrance door, rendered as the Car of History with the figure of History looking over her shoulder as her chariot moves on, its wheel rendered as the clock-face. Jefferson discussed with Latrobe the latter's creation of 'American' orders based on the maize, or Indian corn, plant (the 'corn cob capital', the Congressmen dubbed it), the tobacco plant and the cotton plant.

Jefferson's interest in sculpture included his own use of works by Houdon and Ceracchi in his rooms at Monticello. He was, it seems, the first American patron to be directly involved in the creation of new work by sculptors of the highest international repute, and he wove all this directly into his life and that of the thousands whom he influenced. Those who came to his desk during the second term of his Presidency would have seen his ink-well which was made in a sarcophagus form decorated with a miniature of the Dying Gaul; and, if they inquired, the President would almost certainly

have given a lecture on the ancient work, and perhaps on 'modern' studies of the antique past by the groups around Winckelmann and Piranesi.

Jefferson had similar interest in arranging for practitioners of other arts to come to the U.S.A., hoping to bring over the painters Richard and Maria Cosway, for instance. As early as 1778 he had written from Williamsburg to Giovanni Fabbroni about finding some artisans who might double as musicians. 'I retain for instance among my domestic servants a gardener, weaver, a cabinet maker and a stonecutter to which I would add a Vigneron. In a country where, like yours, music is cultivated and practiced by every class of men I suppose there might be found persons of those trades who could perform on the French horn, clarinet or hautboy and bassoon, so that one might have a band of two French horns, two clarinets and hautboys and a bassoon, without enlarging their domestic expenses'. Though this plan, like many another of his fertile mind, did not come to fruition, it is typical of Jefferson's open-ended channelling of artistic life from the Old World to the New.

One of the wonders of Jefferson's strong image is that it has persisted into the decades that have followed; with the rediscovery of the details of his daily life in studies of recent years, a number of inventive devices have been attributed to his ingenuity when in fact they are only his sensible use of ideas he had seen used or heard of from others. Thus the legend has grown up of the alcove-beds at Monticello being Jefferson's own devices: of course, they are simply taken from stylish French use of the time, although the one he placed in the passage between his bedroom and study so that he could step out of bed into either room, and which could be pulled up on ropes to the ceiling above to convert the two rooms into a sitting- and work-suite, is clearly an improvement on the alcove scheme.

Though foreign visitors with architectural interests quickly recognised the inventive elegance of the villa he was building at Monticello, it was the State Capitol of Virginia with which Jefferson first made a great public architectural statement. He wrote to James Madison: 'We took for our model what is called the Maison Quarée of Nîmes, one of the most beautiful if not the most beautiful and precious morsel of architecture left to us by antiquity. It was built by Caius and Lucius Caesar, and repaired by Louis XIV and has the suffrage of all the judges of architecture who have seen it, as yielding to no one of the beautiful monuments of Greece, Rome, Palmyra, and Balbec, which late travellers have communicated to us. It is very simple, but it is noble beyond expression, and [will do] . . . honor to our country [when used as the model for the Virginia Capitol] as presenting to travellers a specimen of taste in our infancy, promising much for our mature age'.

Jefferson's greatest influence was in connection with the new capital city for the United States, and its buildings, from the legislation establishing it in 1790 (when Jefferson was Secretary of State) until his appointee Latrobe resigned from the office of Surveyor of Public Buildings in 1817, long after Jefferson's own retirement to Monticello at the end of his second term as President (1809), and beyond. His degree of involvement is suggested in the surviving correspondence with Latrobe. Jefferson had, for instance, been enormously impressed with the long, segmental skylights

5

Fig. 5. *Thomas Jefferson by*
Jean-Antoine Houdon, 1789.
This fine bust was created when
Jefferson, at the age of forty-six,
was American Minister to France.
Jefferson arranged an extremely
important event in the import to
the United States of the neo-
classical style in sculpture, when
he convinced Houdon to visit
the States. There he did the
heroic figure of George
Washington which now stands
in the rotunda of the State
Capitol at Richmond, Virginia,
designed by Jefferson.
(New York Historical Society,
New York.)

Historical Society Photo

in the new Halle aux Blés which he saw in Paris in 1786, 'the most superb thing on earth', as he wrote of it. When he anonymously submitted a rotunda project in the 1791 design competition for the President's House, he showed the dome of his project with such a skylight. And when Latrobe went to work in 1807 on completing the chamber of the House of Representatives in the Capitol, Jefferson again suggested the long skylights, eliciting a long letter from Latrobe on this and other matters including the perpetually thorny problem for the neo-Classicists of how to deal with domes and cupolas with building forms which did not have them in antiquity: '. . . in respect to the panel lights,' Latrobe wrote, 'I am acting diametrically contrary to my judgement [in including them]. . . . I candidly confess that the question has suggested itself to my mind: What shall I do when the condensed vapor of the hall showers down upon the heads of the members from one hundred skylights, as it now does from the skylights of our anatomical hall, as it did from the six skylights of the Round House, as it does from the lantern of the Pennsylvania Bank, and as it does from that of our university [of Pennsylvania] – an event I believe to be certain as that cold air and cold glass will condense warm vapor?' Latrobe won this one, and the room is finished with the only external light from side windows and the cupola.

In the same letter Latrobe comments revealingly on the cupola problem and the whole matter of antique precedent and style: 'In respect to the general subject of cupolas, I do not think that they are *always*, nor even *often*, ornamental. My *principles* of good taste are rigid in Grecian architecture. I am a bigoted Greek in the condemnation of the Roman architecture of Baalbec, Palmyra, Spaletro, and of all the buildings erected subsequent to Hadrian's reign. The immense size, the bold plan and arrangements of the buildings of the Romans down almost to Constantine's arch, plundered from the triumphal arches of former emperors, I admire, however, with enthusiasm, but think their decorations and details absurd beyond tolerance from the reign of Severus downward. Wherever, therefore, the Grecian style can be copied without impropriety, I love to be a mere, I would say a slavish, copyist, but the forms and the distribution of the Roman and Greek buildings which remain are in general inapplicable to the objects and uses of our public buildings . . .'

His hand is everywhere: he suggested to President Washington the appointment of L'Enfant to lay out the city, and then was influential in its design. Though the building was designed by Washington's choice of architect, Thornton, it was revised and much of it built by Jefferson's choice, Latrobe, with Jefferson's involvement in many details, as we have seen. The dome was revised and rebuilt by Latrobe's successor Bulfinch, whose European Grand Tour itinerary was actually written out for him by Jefferson. Finally, the choice of the Lombardy poplar for the streets was entirely Jefferson's.

In addition to much communication on the Capitol building, Jefferson worked closely with Latrobe on other great projects in the city, including the large complex of the Navy Yard and, of course, the President's House itself. Latrobe completely redesigned the interior of the house and suggested reshaping the exterior with two monumental porticoes; while Jefferson added his own

variation of Palladio's wing colonnades, almost totally hidden from the main front but revealed from the garden side, a departure from his usual course. These Jeffersonian colonnades or pavilions were built, and some of Latrobe's interior changes made, but most work on the house during Jefferson's administration went to correcting structural faults, and, of course, it was all destroyed (including Latrobe's elegant 'Greek' furniture) when the British forces burned the house in 1814.

Jefferson's last great work was the University of Virginia, for which he saw to the leadership of its legislation, the design and the staffing. The compilation of neo-classical influences includes a revision of the Palladian rotunda form drawn together with Pantheon details and incorporated into a design, in this case using neo-classical geometry, so that the whole composition fits round a perfect circle. The rows of villas facing each other directly across the campus, in the French variation of Palladian dependencies, as developed, for instance, at Marly, are another wonderful Jeffersonian amalgamation, and his thought that even the buildings should teach is expressed in the villas or pavilions which were the houses of the professors, each of which was rendered in a different important order. The orders were chosen through correspondence with Latrobe, Thornton and others.

Mention of Jefferson's interchanges with Latrobe are important in making clear his involvement in architectural improvements for the U.S.A. and his role in the group of Federal period architects. He was directly in contact with so many of them: Latrobe, L'Enfant, Thornton, Hoban, Hadfield, Hallet, Bulfinch, and Latrobe's students, Mills, Graff and others. There is no other man (let alone a President) in all American architectural history, who played such a role.

Such was Jefferson the architect, the patron, the scientist and the philosopher. But it is appropriate to end with Jefferson, the romantic farmer on his mountain top at Monticello, where the picturesque quality of the natural landscape conveyed yet another new way of looking at the world and man in it. When he was still wishfully thinking that Maria Cosway might join him in returning from Paris for a visit to America, he wrote, in 1788: 'I remember you told me when we parted, you would come to see me at Monticello. Now though I believe this to be impossible, I have been planning what I would show you: a flower here, a tree there, yonder a grove, near it a fountain; on this side a hill, on that a river. Indeed, madam, I know nothing so charming as our own country. The learned say it is a new creation; and I believe them; not for their reasons, but because it is made on an improved plan. Europe is a first idea, a crude production, before the maker knew his trade, or had made up his mind as to what he wanted.'

Thomas Jefferson died on 4 July, 1826, the fiftieth anniversary of the Declaration of Independence. He had seen, and been one of those most responsible for, the movement of the group of British Colonies to one national republic, and to the creation in its peoples and in their cities and towns, their institutions and buildings, their furniture and their arts, a neo-classical spirit at once rational and romantic. Jefferson was the symbol of that spirit, which has remained an important element of American society and arts ever since.

Museum Photo

Later Federal Furniture

In the first quarter of the nineteenth century, the cabinet-makers of the United States, combining various European styles, produced furniture of quiet distinction

When building recommenced after the Revolution the old styles continued for a few years, but after 1800 the treatment of interiors tended toward the classical. The influence of Robert Adam is seen in details of doors, windows, mantels and entablatures; plain walls were favoured instead of panelling, and classical details were used in cornices, chair-rails and mouldings. They were also included in the composition ornaments that decorated Adam-style fireplaces, with their chimneypiece mirrors of gilt and tinted glass surmounted by eagles or leafy urns. Such was the setting for Federal furniture.

In the furniture itself, widespread changes in style and cabinet-making followed in the years after the establishment of the United States. During the forty years of the Federal era, American cabinet-makers took advantage of the expanding prosperity and the emergence of new markets for furniture. Thus, the neo-classical style became current almost immediately after the adoption of the Federal Constitution in 1788.

American Federal furniture includes Hepplewhite, Sheraton, American Directoire and Empire styles. The early Federal style is sometimes named after the two English furniture-designers George Hepplewhite and Thomas Sheraton. The use of antique sources was characteristic of Robert Adam, and both Hepplewhite and Sheraton were adapters of the Adam style in which the ornament was

antique but the basic style was not. Hepplewhite's designs were published in 1788, and Sheraton published a series of designs between 1791 and 1794. The name of Hepplewhite is given to the delicate inlaid and carved furniture of the late 1780s and early '90s, and that of Sheraton is used to designate furniture employing turned or reeded supports and bowed or hollowed façades, first made in America in the early 1790s. However, these names are confusing because there is an overlapping of styles. The term 'Federal' seems more appropriate since many of the pieces were carved or inlaid with the American eagle, the symbol of the Federal Union.

Early Federal design, between 1795 and 1815, emphasised colour and surface-decoration as opposed to form, which had been the dominant note in the furniture of the early eighteenth century. The proportions of furniture became light and delicate. The straight line was the basis of design and the structural lines of the furniture were rectangular, with uncomplicated semicircular or elliptical curves. The legs are straight, tapering to a narrow foot. The square-back chair with turned legs, reeded motifs and certain carved elements was introduced in the late 1790s. These forms and motifs continued to be popular until about 1815.

The Federal style brought changes in the forms of furniture. The dining-room as a separate room required furniture for storing silver and china and for serving. The sideboard, which began as a table, was supplied with drawers. The typical dining-table of the era could be dismantled into several smaller tables. Shapes vary and the legs are square or round, and sometimes fluted; late examples have a series of balusters with heavy carving. The sofa-table was long and narrow with drop leaves and legs joined by simple stretchers at each end. The lyre card-table in Sheraton style was a favourite design at the beginning of the nineteenth century; the standard

Fig. 1 **Card-table** by Charles-Honoré Lannuier (1779–1819), c.1813. Rosewood, bird's-eye maple and satinwood with gilt-brass and gesso ornament, height 31 ins.
Lannuier, a New York cabinet-maker, made some of the most elaborate furniture produced in America at this period. (Metropolitan Museum of Art, New York.)

on which the table was mounted was designed in the form of two parallel lyres and rested on carved legs. Pembroke tables became the fashionable form for tea-tables. Other innovations included the dressing-table and the lady's sewing-table. A new type of desk, the tambour, had sliding doors made up of vertical strips that moved horizontally to uncover pigeon-holes and small drawers (Fig. 5). Other desks are topped with bookcases (Fig. 3).

The earliest type of Federal chairs are the ladder-back or slat-back with Marlborough legs (straight tapered legs of square section), stretchers, three or four pierced slats and upholstered seats. From about 1790 vase- or urn-backed chairs were popular,

but five or ten years later square-backed Sheraton-type chairs with plain, upright, 'X' or gothic splats and sturdy, straight stretchers were the most popular. Settees followed similar styles and the upholstered sofa was also based on straight lines. After 1800, chair-design was based on what was known of antique classical chairs. The chair-back had a solid, thick, curving top-rail supported by thin stiles, with either a horizontal splat or a lyre, harp, or 'X'-shape to serve as a back support. An innovation of the Federal period was a type of chair that is distinctly American – the Martha Washington or 'Lolling' chair (Fig. 8). It is a tall, upholstered chair with

scrolled, open arms and legs of cylindrical or quadrangular form joined with plain stretchers.

Early in the nineteenth century a more faithfully classical style developed, based on contemporary scholarship. A design-book by Thomas Hope, *Household Furniture and Interior Decoration*, published in 1807, spread this second phase of the Federal style. London price-books also included engraved designs of furniture, which contributed to the widespread knowledge of English furniture. The late Federal style (1815–25) was also influenced by some of Thomas Sheraton's later designs, which were characterised by Greco-Roman forms – *klismos* and curule chairs – and animal supports. The presence of French craftsmen working in America in the opening years of the nineteenth century was another factor in the development of this phase of the Federal style. Furniture became increasingly heavy and bold. It absorbed the Greco-Roman and Egyptian influences of French Directoire and Empire furniture, and is referred to as 'Regency' or 'Empire', depending upon the predominance of English or French characteristics.

From the beginning of the nineteenth century, New York City was the centre of fine cabinet-making. Although New York had many accomplished cabinet-makers, the most famous was Duncan Phyfe (1768–1854), whose workmanship and interpretation of English Regency forms became a model for other cabinet-makers. Duncan Phyfe worked in New York from 1795 until his retirement in 1847. His early work reflects Sheraton's influence. The most characteristic Phyfe chair is the scroll-back chair with carved top-rail and one or more crosses in the back; reeded stiles and outflaring, reeded feet. Other Phyfe chairs have lattice-backs, ogee-scroll-, lyre- or harp-backs combined with Grecian legs. Some scroll-back chairs have carved front legs ending in paw-feet. Chairs of this type became the standard type made in New York in the mid-Federal period (1800–15).

In Salem, Massachusetts, the combination of Samuel McIntire (1757–1811), carver, and Jacob Sanderson (1757–1810), cabinet-maker, produced Hepplewhite-type chairs and Sheraton-influenced square sofas carved with festoons of drapery, fruit, flowers, *paterae*, ribbons, stalks of wheat, cornucopias, fluting and occasionally a carved eagle.

The furniture of the Boston cabinet-makers John (c.1738–1818) and Thomas (1771–1848) Seymour presented the richest interpretations of Sheraton design in the Federal period. The pieces included superb desks with tambour shutters and light wood inlays of husks, inlaid discs and string-inlaid panels.

By 1815 the French phase of the Federal style was in vogue. The French Empire bed, or sleigh-bed, made to be placed against the wall, marble-topped tables with caryatid or columnar supports and massive pier-tables were characteristic articles of furniture. The requirements for fine furniture of the later Federal era were different. The lines are usually more vigorous, the masses heavier, the scale larger and the wood darker, giving a more sober, but richer appearance. The general effect is also more dignified.

The foremost exponent of the French phase of the late Federal style was the New York cabinet-maker Charles-Honoré Lannuier (1779–1819). Lannuier made some of the most elaborate furniture produced in America (Fig. 1). His furniture is often

Museum Photo

Fig. 2 **Bed**, *Massachusetts,
1800–10. Mahogany, birch and
pine, height 8 ft. 4 ins.
This bed is exhibited in the
Franklin Room at the Museum
with other pieces probably made
in or near Boston, where, in 1706,
Benjamin Franklin, statesman,
scientist and philosopher, was
born.
(The Henry Francis du Pont
Winterthur Museum, Delaware.)*

Fig. 3 **Secretaire**, *known as the
'Sister's Cylinder Bookcase'
modelled on Sheraton's The
Cabinet Dictionary of 1803,
Baltimore or Philadelphia, c.1811,
Mahogany with satinwood
veneers and inlays, height
7 ft. 7 ins.
A straight, drop-front desk is
substituted for the cylinder roll-
top of Sheraton's design and a
graceful pediment echoes the
pyramid of the base.
(Metropolitan Museum of Art.
Gift of Mrs. Russell Sage and
other donors, 1969.)*

a skilful combination of Directoire, Consulate and Empire styles. The furniture was ornamented with gilt carvings of acanthus leaves, caryatids, dolphins and animal feet. Ormolu mounts depict classical scenes of gods and goddesses, and hand-sawn brass inlay borders in the Greek key patten were often used. Furniture of a simpler type was made by Lannuier for the New Jersey home of Napoleon's brother Joseph Bonaparte. A pair of pedestal card-tables were made with water-leaf carving, reeding and brass paw-feet. The brass inlay included a lyre, six-pointed stars and classical urns.

In Philadelphia, Joseph B. Barry made similar furniture based on Sheraton and French designs. He designed French-style pier-tables with columns resting on massive mahogany platforms and decorated with ormolu mounts.

There was a revival of interest in painted furniture towards the end of the eighteenth century. Much painted furniture was designed in England around 1790 and American furniture-makers quickly followed the style.

The finest workmanship and most elaborate in design is the painted furniture produced in Baltimore. While many Baltimore cabinet-makers may have produced this furniture, the numerous adver-

4

Museum Photo.

6

Museum Photo.

5

Museum Photo

7

Museum Photo

Fig. 4 **Grecian couch,** *Salem, Mass., 1805–15. Mahogany and cane, height 38 ins. (The Henry Francis du Pont Winterthur Museum.)*

Fig. 5 **Tambour desk,** *label of John Seymour and Son, Boston, 1794–1804. Mahogany, height 41⅝ ins. (The Henry Francis du Pont Winterthur Museum.)*

Fig. 6 **Armchair,** *attributed to John and Hugh Findlay of Baltimore, 1805. (Baltimore Museum of Art.)*

tisements for the work of John and Hugh Findlay suggest that the Findlays were the most prolific producers of this type of furniture.

The following extract from the *Federal Gazette and Commercial Daily Advertiser*, 8 November, 1805, describes this furniture: 'Elegant, Fancy Japanned Furniture . . . all colours, gilt ornamented and varnished in a style only equalled on the continent . . . with real views, Fancy landscapes, Flowers, Trophies of Music, War, Husbandry, Love, etc. . . . Window and recess seats, painted and gilt in the most fanciful manner, with and without views adjacent to this city'.

Such painted scenes were also popular on fancy chairs made in New York and New England. A set of six chairs with views of the Hudson River (New York, 1815–25) are in the Henry Francis du Pont

Winterthur Museum. Settees, card-tables and work-tables were often decorated in similar manner. In fact, the popularity of painted furniture grew rapidly and so much of it was made that after 1820 it became known as 'country furniture' and the fashion declined rapidly.

Although American Federal furniture was for the most part modelled on English furniture and followed English ideas, it was not an imitation. Many components are similar, but they are combined in different ways. One difference between American and European furniture was the wood used. Although mahogany was the primary wood used by American cabinet-makers of the Federal period, the secondary woods used were those that grew in the region where the furniture was made. A careful examination of these secondary woods not rical patterns of squares, lozenges, triangles and zig-zags. To provide points of interest, inlays of *paterae*, flowers, leaves, shells, fans, bell-flowers or eagles were used. The woods employed in stringing and inlay included holly, satinwood, boxwood, ebony and the cheaper maple and birch. Brass inlays were occasionally found on furniture made in New York and Philadelphia, and inlays were sometimes imported from England. There were also craftsmen in American cities who specialised in making inlays. Although the records of suppliers and makers of inlays are sparse, there seems little doubt that, while some cabinet-makers produced their own inlays, a large proportion of inlays used in city shops were bought ready made. This accounts for the similarity of inlays used on furniture. Patterned stringing was favoured in Boston, Salem and other centres in New England, whereas plain stringing, cross-banding and inlaid shells, eagles and flower motifs are often found on the work of cabinet-makers working in the New York area. Many three-part husks or bell-flowers, inlaid shells, eagles and flower motifs are found on Baltimore furniture and Philadelphia furniture.

Owing to the limited supply of valuable wood, the practice of veneering was used after 1790. The principal woods used in veneering American Federal furniture included bird's-eye maple, mahogany, rosewood, satinwood, sycamore, amboynawood, tulipwood and zebrawood. Figured birch was often used on the fronts of chests of drawers and on card-tables in the New England area.

Carving was another method of ornamenting Federal furniture. The finest carving is that of Samuel McIntire on Salem furniture. The carving on Duncan Phyfe furniture is also of high quality. Philadelphia carving is often scratchy and flat, and Baltimore carving varies in quality, some of it being extremely coarse. The motifs most often used were wheatsheaves, drapery, vines and baskets of fruit.

In the most famous pieces of Federal furniture, such as the Seymour tambour desks or the Massachusetts secretaire, there is an interplay of form, inlay and colour and subtle harmonies of line. The materials, workmanship and design are also so inter-related as to produce unity. These are the qualities which distinguish fine furniture, and the cabinet-makers of the Federal era produced many such pieces.

Fig. 7 *Federal room, 1800s; the mantelpiece from the house of Moses Rogers, New York, 1806; the chimney-glass, New York or Albany, c.1805; the chairs made in the shop of Duncan Phyfe (1768–1854), 1807, (The Henry Francis du Pont Winterthur Museum.)*

Fig. 8 *Federal Parlour, Massachusetts, 1790s; secretaire, Connecticut or Rhode Island, 1790–1810; Martha Washington chair, c.1800. (The Henry Francis du Pont Winterthur Museum.)*

only gives a clue to the regional origin of American furniture, but also aids in distinguishing to some extent between American and English furniture of the same style. The presence of tulip or poplar is a sign of American manufacture, and white pine is also generally regarded as proof of American origin. For less expensive furniture, birch and maple were used and often stained to resemble mahogany. Native softwoods such as pine were stained or painted; some furniture was made of bird's-eye maple and a few pieces of satinwood.

In the Federal period after 1790, veneers and ornamental inlays became one of the principal methods of ornamenting furniture. Light and dark inlaid lines and patterned stringing or banding composed of different coloured woods became a common feature. This decoration tended to be in geomet-

MUSEUMS AND COLLECTIONS

American furniture may be seen at the following:

Baltimore, Md.: Baltimore Museum of Art
Boston, Mass.: Boston Museum of Fine Arts
Dearborn, Mich.: Henry Ford Museum
New York, N.Y.: Metropolitan Museum of Art
Brooklyn Museum
Winterthur, Del.: Henry Francis du Pont Museum

FURTHER READING

Nineteenth-century America: Furniture and other Decorative Arts, Metropolitan Museum of Art, New York, exhibition catalogue, 1970.
American Furniture: The Federal Period by Charles F. Montgomery, Winterthur, 1966.
An Outline of Period Furniture by Katharine M. McClinton, New York, 1971.

Bedspreads and Quilts

Fig. 1 *The Quilting Party,*
American, c.1858. Oil on
cardboard.
This shows quilting as a central
feature of American domestic life.
Sometimes known as a 'quilting
bee', it was a traditional activity.
In the seventeenth century
Charles I had permitted the
import of quilts from China, and
in seventeenth-century Virginia
armour was made from quilted
fabric.
(Abby Aldrich Rockefeller
Folk Art Collection,
Williamsburg, Va.)

Fig. 2 *Stencilled coverlet,*
Connecticut, c.1830.
This room is from the Joshua La
Salle house, Windham. The
stencilled decoration was
probably executed by a travelling
artist in exchange for board and
lodging and a small wage.
(American Museum in Britain,
Claverton Manor, Bath.)

Fig. 3 *Quilted patchwork*
coverlet, Baltimore, c.1850.
Printed calico with diamond-
quilted background,
10ft. 6 ins. x 10 ft. 6 ins.
Quilting was functional as well
as decorative, for it was a means
of distributing evenly the filling
of a coverlet and keeping it in
place. The filling was carded
wool, cotton or down.
(American Museum in Britain.)

The quilted coverlets of America are not only finely worked objects of great beauty, but also mute witnesses to a hard, simple way of life

The chair of the chairman or the bed of the aristocrat's levee were the objects of considerable embellishment not only in Europe but also in her colonies in North America. Because of the prestigious social position of these two articles of furniture in great houses, they were treated as status symbols in lesser ones. Curtains, bedspreads and valances all formed a considerable part of such embellishment on beds. It is a curious twist of history that today the household craft of making elaborate patchwork quilts has all but died out in the Old World but persists in the countries of the New, such as Australia, Canada and the United States. For these historical reasons it is therefore not possible to discuss American patchwork quilts without some reference to Europe and, in addition, some observations upon the textile industry.

When medieval inventories allude to beds it is the hangings, the coverlets, the bolsters and the mattresses that are described in great detail, not the framework of the bed itself. This was not only due to a proper sense of the priorities of comfort, but also reflected the high cost of textiles in the age before the industrial revolution. This attitude, rooted in cost, persisted well into the eighteenth century and longer. A sale-catalogue of 1747 of the contents 'of the House and Gardens at Chelsea and all thereunto belonging to the Most Noble Robert, Earl of Orford, d'ceased' reads: 'A sacking bottom bedstead with green and straw worsted damask furniture: £2 2s. 0d., a feather bed, bolster and two pillows: £2 0s. 0d.' This contrasts noticeably with, in the same bedchamber 'A walnut tree dressing table, and an India picture: £0 10s 0d.' In view of the great value of textiles, and the feeling of opulence that they therefore imparted, it is small wonder that great ladies like Mary, Queen of Scots, and Bess of Hardwick regarded the art of crewel embroidery as an appropriately aristocratic pastime.

This, then, was the situation in Europe before industrialisation. In British America textiles were even rarer and more expensive. North America was colonised by people of many different European nationalities, including the British, French, Dutch, Spanish, Germans and Scandinavians. All were eventually to come under the political or cultural sway of England, or both.

In general it was the policy of the British government to encourage the production of raw materials but to discourage industrial development in its colonies, and this policy was as true of the textile industry as of any other (though there was little or no legislation against domestic production of textiles for personal use). Wool had long been the basis of England's wealth and in 1699 the Wool Act was passed to prevent the American colonies from competing with the mother country.

The attitude of the British government was well summed up in 1743 when the Board of Trade wrote to Governor Wentworth of New Hampshire as follows: 'It is our express Will and Pleasure that you do not upon any Pretence whatever – give your consent to a Law or Laws for setting up manufactures – which are hurtful or prejudicial to this kingdom'. On the other hand, encouragement was offered to the colonies for the production of those textiles that would not compete with the British Industry. James II, for example, encouraged Huguenots to settle in Virginia at his own expense to develop silk-weaving, and in fact the King was reputed to have worn Virginia silk on the occasion of his coronation. This political background imposed a frugal attitude, and American housewives of the eighteenth century became weavers of homespun and sewers of patchwork quilts.

Though it is true that a textile factory was established at Rowley, Massachusetts, as early as 1638, weaving remained largely a cottage industry in America not only during British rule but also after it ceased. America's industrial revolution was to need the horrors of the Civil War to provide the stimulus for manufactured goods.

American
Coverlets

Fig. 4 *Coverlet, American, mid-
eighteenth century. Crewel
embroidery on a quilted
background, 10 ft. x 10 ft. 6 ins.
Crewel embroidery was a
type of sewn decoration that
could be used with quilting.
(American Museum in Britain.)*

Fig. 5 *Quilt, made by Mrs.
Alexander Thompson, c.1821.
Trapunto, or Italian, quilting,
7 ft. 5 ins. x 8 ft. 10 ins.
The finest examples of American
quilting are often where it forms
the only decoration, as here.
Mrs. Thompson was the wife of
Lieutenant-Colonel Thompson,
whom she accompanied to the
frontier forts in Indian territory.
After his death she lobbied a
Bill through Congress to provide
pensions for the widows of army
officers.
(American Museum in Britain.)*

Fig. 6 *Reversible coverlet,
Pennsylvania, 1840. Double-
woven wool, sometimes known as
'summer and winter' weave,
7 ft. x 8 ft.
This was sold by S. Kuter of
Trexlertown, Lehigh County,
Pennsylvania, a German region.
(Mr. and Mrs. A. J. J. Ayres
Collection.)*

Fig. 7 *Coverlet, woven on a loom
using a Jacquard attachment by
Harry Tyler, of Jefferson County,
New York, first half of the
nineteenth century. Wool,
3 ft. 5½ ins. x 7 ft. 11 ins.
The Jacquard attachment,
invented in France in 1801,
meant that a loom could be
programmed with punched cards
to produce a predetermined
pattern. At this period the fabric
was woven in half widths, which
had to be stitched together.
(John Judkyn Memorial, Bath.)*

Most of the developments in the weaving industry took place in Europe, notably in France and
England. The British government of the eighteenth
century did all in its power to contain the secrets
of these developments; American agents working in
England did all in their power to smuggle these
secrets across the Atlantic, and eventually and
inevitably they were to succeed. During the first
quarter of the nineteenth century the American
textile industry was using many of these new techniques.

Simple designs woven in blue and white

Plain woven coverlets were obviously much in
use, such as the simple linsey-wolsey (coarse stuff
of linen and wool mixed, or inferior wool with
cotton). Sometimes plain woven coverlets were
embellished with stencilled or printed designs and
these were often further elaborated with quilting
(Fig. 2).

The earliest decorative weaving produced in
America appears to have been the simple four harness overshot weave. Many of these coverlet
designs, often woven in blue (from indigo grown
in the South) and white, possess delightful names,
including Bonaparte's March, Dog Tracks, Fox's
Chase, Lovers' Knot, Rose of Sharon (also known
as Indian War), Sunrise and Whig Rose (clearly of
English origin). Various checked patterns in
four harness overshot weave were also made of
two and five colours with browns and yellows pre-
dominating.

From about 1725 to 1825 the double weave, also
known as 'double face' and 'summer and winter'
weave, was popular (Fig. 6). Designs include Eight-
pointed Star, Lisbon Star, Lovers' Knot, Wheel and
Star, Snowball and Wheel of Fortune. Many of these
were surrounded by a pine-tree border. Much of
this weaving was produced in Pennsylvania and, as
this state included powerful Welsh communities,
the similarity with much weaving from the Princi-
pality may well prove to be far from fortuitous.

Unmarried girls produced thirteen patchwork quilts

Coverlets made in America and woven on looms
using a Jacquard or similar attachment were always
the work of professional weavers (Fig. 7). Jacquard,
a native of Lyon, made his invention in 1801 and
Jacquard coverlets were being woven in America by
the end of the first quarter of the nineteenth
century. The early examples, and these are rare,
were woven in two halves that were eventually
sewn together down the middle. The fly shuttle
was invented in England by John Kay of Lancashire
as early as 1733, but was not in general use in
America until the 1860s to '70s, and it was the
introduction of this and similar mechanisms that
eventually enabled these coverlets to be woven in
the full width.

It is usually held that patchwork evolved as the
result of sewing together a series of otherwise
useless pieces of material to form one 'crazy
quilt', creating a possession not only of beauty
and utility, but also one provided at little extra
cost at a time when textiles were extremely valuable,
especially in America. In England at a fairly early
date, cloth was frequently bought for the purpose of
making quilts, resulting in a greater mobility of
aesthetic choice. This threw the responsibility for
design squarely upon the needlewoman. No longer
did the conditions of frugality impose a discipline
for design, and this resulted in patchwork coverlets
of either a much higher or a much lower standard.
The perfecting of the sewing-machine in the U.S.A.
in the third quarter of the nineteenth century also
had its effect.

In America it was the custom for an unmarried
girl to produce thirteen patchwork coverlets,
often with the assistance of her family and friends.
These coverlets would eventually form part of her
dowry. The thirteenth coverlet was not usually
made until she was engaged, and the remaining
twelve were not quilted until that time. The
thirteenth quilt was expected to be the finest in the
series; it was often made in sections by different
people and then assembled to form one large quilt.

The quilting bee was an important social event

Pieced coverlets are common to both America
and Europe, though appliqué quilts are rare in
Europe. Among many examples of geometric,
pieced patchwork designs, the star is a recurrent
theme, often alluding to a particular state of the
Union. Pieced coverlets and their quilting display a
joy in geometry which is somewhat akin to the
medieval mason's similar preoccupation, as mani-
fested in tracery. This observation may sound somewhat far fetched, but it is worthy of note that the
1584 inventory of the Earl of Leicester includes 'a
faire quilte of crymson sattin vi breadths iij yards
3 quarters naile deep [a nail measuring two and
a half inches] all lozenged over with silken twists,
in the midst a cinque-foil. . . .'

In Ante-Bellum days, the 'quilting bee' was as
important socially as the 'sewing circle' was to
become during and after the American Civil War
(Fig. 1). Many letters, poems and songs have survived which point to the importance of the quilting
bee. The following reference evokes the period and
character of life with the strength of simplicity:
'Ohio, February 7th, 1841: We have had deep
snow. No teams passed for three weeks, but as
soon as the drifts could be broken through Mary
Scott sent her boy Frank around to say she was
going to have a quilting. . . .'

The different designs of American patchwork
quilts were known by rather attractive names,
although many of these names were interchangeable and some confusion has resulted. Some
evoked unpopular images and so were changed;
the Wandering Foot design was never made for a
dower chest until its name was changed to Turkey
Tracks. Other examples include: Crazy Patchwork,
Beggars' Blocks, Robbing Peter to Pay Paul, Star of
Bethlehem, Meadow Lily, Tulips, Rose of Sharon,
Death's Black Darts (yet another name for Wandering Foot), Oak Leaf, Baseballs, Cactus Rose,
Tumbling Blocks, Log Cabin, Sunburst, Cake-
stand, Lotus Flower, Dresden Plate, Princess
Feather and Geometric Snowballs.

Apart from the influence of English patchwork
design on American examples, mention should be
made of the strong significance of the German

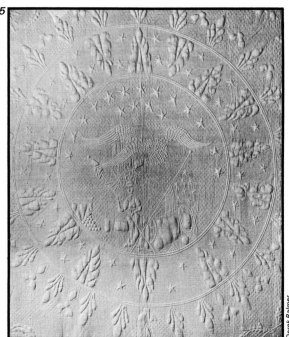

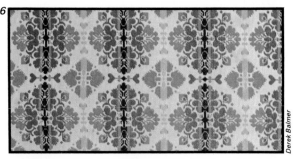

communities of Pennsylvania, known as the 'Pennsylvania Dutch'. Religion regulated the lives of these people and preserved their traditions and their domestic arts. Their designs include one of the favourite motifs of the Pennsylvania Dutch, the tulip.

Quilting was a means by which the coverlet top lining and filling (of carded wool, cotton, or sometimes down) could be kept in place, though this could also be achieved by tying. This utilitarian necessity was customarily used to decorative effect. Elaborate quilting designs were drawn with the help of templates of sized paper or textile. Princess Feather, Star and Crown, Peacock Fan, Oak Leaf, Daisy, Swirl, Acanthus, Day-Lily, Starfish, Tea-cup (overlapping circles), Running Vine, Pineapple (the pineapple is often used as a symbol of hospitality) and Spider-web are just some of the many designs used. Simpler quilting designs that did not require templates include: Crossbar, Double Crossbar and Diamonds (Fig. 3).

Sometimes quilting was used to emphasise a pieced or appliqué design but it was also used in a quite arbitrary way. The finest examples of quilting are usually to be found where quilting forms the only decoration and this Italian, or Trapunto, quilt-

ing is of the very best quality (Fig. 5).

Quilts with a cotton filling sometimes give a clue to their age. In 1793, Eli Whitney (1765–1825) invented the cotton gin which enables a worker to clean fifty pounds of cotton a day. Exports of cotton in 1795 were forty times higher because of his invention. If a quilt with a cotton filling reveals, when held to the light, a number of impurities, this would indicate an eighteenth-century specimen from before the introduction of the cotton-gin, providing the other clues as regards materials and design agree.

Quilting was known to pre-Columbian Central American cultures and in ancient China – indeed Charles I specifically permitted the importation of 'quilts of China embroidered with gold'. In seventeenth-century Jamestown, Virginia, quilted armour proved to be a sufficient protection from the slings and arrows of the stone-age natives. The use of patchwork quilts in the severe winters of North America must have been a source of comfort to many a pioneer. Coverlets employing many techniques were used in North America, some of the most beautiful being those decorated with embroidery or stencilling.

John James Audubon

Museum Photo

Fig. 1 *Virginian Partridge*
(Perdix Virginiana).
*These coloured engravings by
John James Audubon
(1785–1851) are from the series*
Birds of America *(1827–38) and,
(with the Rev. John Bachman)*
The Quadrupeds of North
America *(1841–51), reproduced
from originals in the British
Museum (Natural History),
London. The quoted passages
are Audubon's descriptions
of the animals.*

John James Audubon, considered one of the finest nature artists in history, was born on the island of Haiti in 1785, the natural son of a sea merchant and a Creole chambermaid. He spent most of his childhood in France, already showing great talent for drawing wildlife in the countryside. Before leaving for America at the age of eighteen to live on his father's plantation, he received a brief period of instruction from Napoleon's court painter, Jacques Louis David. Once in America he made several unsuccessful attempts at business, but his real interests and pleasure lay in roaming the prairies, woods and mountains, sketching any living creature or flower he came across.

It was at this point that Audubon's life work slowly started to form – his object was to produce a publication of life-size, full-colour paintings of every known species of American bird, together with appropriate backgrounds of characteristic plants and flowers. This publication, *Birds of America*, took many years to complete. Dogged by misfortune and lack of money, it was only thanks to his optimism and the staunch support of his wife that Audubon managed to persevere. One incident which nearly put a stop to his research was the discovery that two hundred of his original drawings had been destroyed by rats; it took him nearly three years to replace them.

Fig. 2 **Common American Wildcat** (Lynx rufus).
'*We once made an attempt at domesticating one of the young of this species, which we obtained when only two weeks old. It was a most spiteful, growling, snappish little wretch, and showed no disposition to improve its habits and manners under our kind tuition . . . It, one night, escaped into our library, where it made sad work among the books . . . and left the marks of its teeth on the mutilated window sashes. Finally, we fastened it with a light chain, and had a small kennel built for it in the yard.*'

Fig. 3 **Meadow Lark** (Sturnus ludovicianus).
'*This beautiful bird is dispersed over all the countries intervening between the shores of the Columbia River and the Gulf of Mexico. I found it very abundant and breeding on the Island of Galveston in the Texas, where, as in our Southern States, it is a constant resident.*'

Fig. 4 **White-headed Pigeon** (Columba leucocephala).
'*The White-headed Pigeon exhibits little of the pomposity of the common domestic species, in its amorous moments. The male, however, struts before the female with elegance, and the tones of his voice are quite sufficient to persuade her of the sincerity of his attachment. . . . The bird standing almost erect, full-plumed, and proud of his beauty, emits at first a loud croohoo, as a prelude, and then proceeds to repeat his coo − coo − coo.*'

On his travels up and down river and across the countryside, Audubon would often shoot down as many as a hundred birds in order to make as accurate a drawing as possible; he would then pay for part of his expenses by selling the bird skins. He used to ask his friends to save him any creatures such as bats, wood-rats, mice and weasels, instructing them to 'place these in common good rum and forward them to me'.

Not finding a patron in America, Audubon decided in 1826 to visit England in search of subscribers to finance his book, as well as printers. He met with almost immediate acclaim and finally chose Robert Harell, Junior, as his engraver. *Birds*

5

PLATE. XLIII.

Museum Photo

Fig. 5 **Hare Squirrel** (Sciurus leporinus).
'*Teeth, orange; whiskers, black; nose, dark brown; ears, light brown; behind the ears, a tuft of soft cotton-like, whitish fur.*'

Fig. 6 **Gray Fox, male** (Canis vulpes virginianus).
'*On a cold drizzly, sleety, rainy day, while travelling in Carolina, we observed a Gray Fox in a field of broom-grass, coursing against the wind, and hunting in the manner of the pointer dog.*'

Fig. 7 **Carolina Parrot** (Psittacus carolinensis).
'*It is easily tamed by being frequently immersed in water, and eats as soon as it is placed in confinement. . . . They are incapable of articulating words, however much care and attention may be bestowed upon their education; and their screams are so disagreeable as to render them at best very indifferent companions.*'

7

of America when completed consisted of four hundred and thirty-five individual plates, double-elephant folio size, issued in eighty-seven parts. Every illustration was accompanied by a short description written by Audubon himself. In all the publication cost $100,000 to produce.

In 1844 Audubon launched, with John Bachman, into organising another definitive work, entitled *The Quadrupeds of North America*. Audubon died in 1851, before the book was completed.

Audubon's drawings are often compared to Japanese and Chinese work for their qualities of naturalism, colour and vigour; his paintings as well as his writings always stress the action rather than the peace of the scene. Water-colour was largely employed but other media were used in combination, such as pencil, pastel and ink.

Audubon captures for us in his illustrations and text the opulence and beauty of the living wilderness of America at the beginning of the nineteenth century, a wilderness in its prime which only too soon was to start vanishing.

6

Museum Photo

THE WAR
BETWEEN THE STATES

Fig. 1 *The Great Bartholdi Statue. Liberty Enlightening the World. The Gift of France to the American People by Currier and Ives, New York, 1885. Coloured print. (American Museum in Britain, Claverton Manor, Bath.)*

2

3

A. C. Cooper

The institution of slavery in the Southern states raised moral and economic issues which led to the outbreak of war, the crushing defeat of the South and the tragic assassination of Lincoln

The political life of the United States during the 1850s was dominated by the South's 'peculiar institution' – slavery. Slave-trading had been outlawed by Congress in 1808 (and declared piracy, punishable by death, in 1820), while slavery itself had been outlawed by many Northern states even earlier. But the hopes of those who expected slavery to disappear of its own volition were disappointed. There was too much wealth and social prestige involved for plantation owners to abandon slavery without a struggle.

Increasingly hemmed in, both economically and morally, the South could see no alternative to the extension of slavery. The 1820 Missouri Compromise – a line at latitude 30°36′ dividing slave states from free – was regarded by many Southerners as only a temporary measure, although it lasted for thirty years. But the passing of the Kansas-Nebraska Act in 1854 brought out all the bitter antagonism which had lain dormant during that time. Thousands of 'border ruffians' were bribed and incited to cross into Kansas from Missouri and load the 1855 legislature elections in favour of pro-slavery candidates.

The Southerners obviously thought that the danger of prolonged lawlessness worth the risk for, as Senator Atchison of Missouri pointed out, 'if we win, we carry slavery to the Pacific Ocean'. But the abolitionists and free-staters were con-

Mansell Collection

Fig. 2 *Emancipation
Proclamation by A. A. Lamb,
c.1862. Oil on canvas,
32⅛ x 54 ins.
This thrilling allegory of the
freeing of the slaves in 1862
takes place in front of the Capitol
building in Washington D.C.
(National Gallery of Art,
Washington D.C. Gift of E. W.
and B. C. Garbisch.)*

Fig. 3 *Abraham Lincoln
(1809–65) by Daniel French
(1850–1931). Bronze, height
30 ins.
Portraying one of America's
most tragic and beloved
figures, this is a maquette for the
vast marble statue in the Lincoln
Memorial in Washington, built
in the 1920s.
(American Embassy, London.)*

Fig. 4 *Jefferson Davis
(1808–89). Steel-engraving from a
photograph by Matthew Brady.
Originally a congressman and
senator from the South, Davis
was always a conspicuous
defender of Southern interests,
notably the institution of
slavery. He was elected President
of the Confederacy in 1861, a
position which he held
throughout the Civil War
against ever increasing
opposition.*

vinced that they had God on their side, and with the new Sharps rifle in their hands they fought back. The ballot-boxes were filled with illegal votes by the slave-staters and the men thus elected pushed through a strong slave code. The free-staters, undaunted, set up a rump legislature of their own. Fighting between the two groups broke out frequently and Kansas became a miniature forerunner of the Civil War.

The elections of 1856 witnessed the emergence of the new Republican party as a force to be reckoned with. Although they lost, the strength of the Republican's vote in the North and West clearly established them as the party of the free states against the South, another indication of the harsh division within the United States.

The 1850s drew to a close amid rising passions on both sides. As the abolitionists' demands grew more pressing, so did those of Southern spokesmen; they demanded the extension of slavery to California and other free states and territories; the re-opening of the slave trade; the suppression of abolitionists in the North and stricter enforcement of the Fugitive Slave Laws.

The voices of those who advocated compromise and conciliation were lost – even Ralph Waldo Emerson failed to gain any support when he advocated emulation of the British, with financial compensation to slave-owners for losing their slaves. It was men like William Yancey of Alabama, an impassioned speaker in the Southern cause, who held public attention and guided public opinion. The Democratic convention of 1860 held in Charleston, South Carolina (a hotbed of secession), showed finally that the politicians, at least, could no longer find any common ground. Southern delegates, led by Yancey, demanded that the party declare that 'slavery was right' and this, even for the most willing of Northerners, was going too far.

The split was complete when, on 30 April, the entire Alabama delegation walked out, followed by those from South Carolina, Georgia, Florida, Louisiana and Arkansas. A second convention held in the more moderate Baltimore in June was equally futile, and resulted only in the Democratic party having two presidential candidates – one 'official' and one nominated by the seceding delegates. It was the best way to ensure a Republican victory – and with Abraham Lincoln as their presidential candidate, the Republicans swept the North, but gained not a single electoral college vote south of the Mason-Dixon line.

While the outgoing administration watched and did nothing, the cotton states started to secede. South Carolina was the first to go, swiftly followed by Mississippi, Alabama, Florida, Georgia, Louisiana and Texas. Delegates from these seven states met in Montgomery and formed, on 8 February, 1861, the Confederate States of America, with Jefferson Davis as President.

There followed a pause while politicians manoeuvred, and the people wondered what would happen: would there be war? Would the remaining Southern states secede? Abraham Lincoln, inaugurated in March, was resolved to maintain the Union but hoped to the last to do it peacefully. The uncertainty was finally shattered on 12 April, 1861, by the guns of Charleston opening fire on Fort Sumter, a Federal garrison in the harbour. On 17 April, Virginia seceded, followed by Arkansas, Tennessee and North Carolina.

The secession of Virginia was vital to the Confederacy's cause in terms of prestige, both at home and abroad. With her, many Northerners saw the last chance of re-uniting the Union go as well, and were willing to leave the Confederacy in peace. The Confederacy, showing due respect to the 'Old Commonwealth', moved its capital to Richmond, which meant that the opposing capitals were little more than a hundred miles apart – a fact which largely dominated military strategy for most of the war. Virginia, however, brought not only prestige – she brought with her two men who became legends in their own right: Robert E. Lee and Thomas 'Stonewall' Jackson, both generals in the army and both men who put their native state before all else. Lee was offered the command of the United States Army by Lincoln, but he refused and instead resigned his commission and followed Virginia.

It was inevitable that the Confederacy would lose the war, although no doubt at the time it did not appear so. Its government was confident of gaining recognition abroad (particularly from Britain and France) and hopeful that the British Government might even intervene to safeguard the raw cotton supplies needed to keep the Lancashire factories running. The people were full of confidence and determination to defend their way of life. And few of them realised that it was this very way of life which meant certain defeat.

The Southern economy was an agricultural one, based on cotton and tobacco – in 1860, the South had produced under ten per cent of the country's total manufactured goods. Their raw materials were shipped to the factories of the North, or Europe, for the most part in Northern-owned ships. The wealthy, aristocratic planters were dependent on the Yankee businessmen they despised for their income, and many of them, indeed, were mortgaged to the hilt against the following year's crop. Life in the Southern states was gracious, certainly, but it was backward looking and old fashioned.

By contrast, the North was bustling and eager to move forward, increasingly industrialised, with correspondingly fewer individual craftsmen. The great prairies of what is now called the 'Mid-West' were opening up fast, and thanks to several new inventions – the mechanical reaper, harvester and self-knotting binder – one man could now harvest more wheat than a dozen with scythes and sickles. The workers thus released from the necessity to produce food flooded into the factories of the growing new industries.

Machine-turned furniture, for example, was becoming increasingly popular, especially in the lower social strata, because of its cheapness when compared with hand-made furniture. This, along with the horsehair coverings perfected by Benjamin Gilbert, furnished the houses of a new generation. Sewing-machines put the individual seamstress virtually out of work, and, with wages at eight cents an hour, women were forced to work for one of the clothing manufacturers whose factories, under the impetus of government contracts in wartime, expanded greatly. Others of the new consumer industries benefited equally from the Civil War: tins of condensed milk were supplied to the troops, as well as canned meat from the growing meat-packing industry of Chicago and experimental tinned vegetables.

The men who were making their fortunes, however, spent them with a vulgarity and ostentation

5

6

Fig. 5 *The Battle of Gettysburg, 1863, engraved from a sketch by A. R. Waud. A major turning-point in the Civil War, the Battle of Gettysburg was a decisive defeat for the Confederate army under Robert E. Lee.*

Fig. 6 *Robert E. Lee (1807–70), engraving from a portrait. Son of the soldier and statesman 'Lighthorse Harry Lee', R. E. Lee was himself a successful soldier in the U.S. Army before the outbreak of the war between the states. He became military adviser to Jefferson Davis in 1861, commander of the Army of Northern Virginia in 1862 and, despite the disastrous defeat at Gettysburg in 1863, general-in-chief of all the Confederate armies in 1865. Only two months later, on April 9, he surrendered to Grant at Appomattox.*

hard to match. Their ornate new mansions were the backdrop for brilliant social gatherings which vied with each other for lavishness. New York's wealth was equalled only by the corruption of its administration and the poverty of its slums.

With government encouragement and the prospect of more fortunes to be made, the railways were spreading rapidly. There were over 25,000 miles of them in the North, though across the South they were few and far between, with differing gauges and a shortage of rolling stock – and what there were had been purchased from the North. The Confederacy might boast of its marksmen and its fine horses and riders, but they could not stand up to the cannon manufactured in the industrial North, nor to the overwhelming numbers of men and supplies transported on the more efficient Northern railway system. The South, in fact, was sadly lacking in the material necessities of war, such as munitions factories and depots, naval workshops, and so on – even the soldiers' uniforms (when they had them) were, for the most part, homespun. The South had acquired a few arsenals when the states took over federal possessions as they seceded, but they were not enough to keep an army in the field supplied, and in any case most of these guns were out of date. One of the most important acquisitions was the Navy Yards at Norfolk, Virginia, where they managed to raise the scuttled *USS Merrimack*, which later emerged as the terrifying Ironclad *CSS Virginia*.

With amazing ingenuity at home, and blatant looting on the battlefield, the Confederacy managed to keep its armies supplied, but it was always an uphill struggle, with never enough to meet all the demands. Finally, nothing could disguise the fact that while the South had a population of six million (plus three million slaves) they were faced by twenty million people in the North.

Lincoln, bedevilled by newspapers which raised the cry 'On to Richmond', was forced to direct the main Union effort towards Virginia. The great weight of the fighting thus fell on the Army of the Potomac, and it was against this unfortunate army that Lee – with his Army of Northern Virginia –

scored his most notable victories: The Seven Days, Fredericksburg, Chancellorsville. But though it was these battles in the East which gained publicity, it was the West where real progress was being made. Ulysses S. Grant, victor of Shiloh and the siege of Vicksburg, was recalled to Washington and given command of all the Union forces. His ruthlessness (he is credited with inventing the phrase 'unconditional surrender') paid dividends; pursuing Lee relentlessly, he inflicted a horrifying deathrate on his own army – over 6,000 men in one hour alone at Cold Harbor – but at least he could afford it. Lee could not, and at last surrendered the tattered remnants of his army at Appomattox Court House on 9 April, 1865. It was the end of whatever hopes still remained in the South.

After four years of fighting, the Union had been preserved, but at terrible cost: in the North (whose records are more accurate) the cost was put at 360,000 dead, 280,000 wounded and twenty billion dollars; in the South, apart from the 260,000 dead, the cost was a wrecked economy and the bitterness of Reconstruction.

The American Civil War is often called the 'first modern war', because it was the first time that an industrial nation had turned its resources to military ends. The transporting of armies by train, the invention and mass production of new arms, such as the machine-gun, brought a new concept to war; the ungainly Ironclads and the first attempt at a submarine marked the end of the wooden ships and brought about a revolution in naval tactics. Even photography came of age – Matthew Brady became a war photographer, abandoning posed shots in his studio to take evocative and often moving photographs of the battlefields.

The South had lost its whole way of life, but the North, too, was changed. Industrialists and financiers were supreme, and were to dominate the country, economically and politically, for many years. The legacy of bitterness and mistrust between North and South is not yet completely dissolved, and the descendants of the freed slaves have still to achieve the equality which was the reason for the war's being fought.

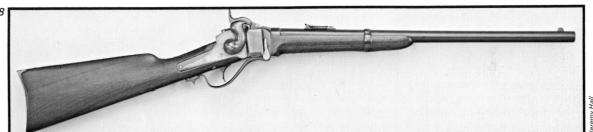

Fig. 7 *The 'New Ironsides'
and two Ericsson Batteries in
action*, contemporary engraving.
*The historic encounter between
the* Monitor *and the* Merrimack
*in 1863 prompted both sides to
experiment freely with different
forms of armoured warships.
The two most successful types
were little more than floating
batteries or floating gun-turrets.*

Fig. 8 *Sharp's New Model
1863 Cavalry Carbine. Barrel-
length 22 ins.
Some eighty thousand of these
new weapons were purchased
by the U.S. Government
during the Civil War. This
example has been converted to
centre-fire, but the only changes
in appearance are the shape of
the hammer nose and the
substitution of a firing-pin for
the percussion nipple on top of
the breech-block.
(H.M. Tower of London
Armouries.)*

Fig. 9 *Allegory of Freedom by
an unknown artist, c.1865. Oil
on canvas, 37 x 43 ins.
An event which caught the
imagination of sympathetic
Americans in the North, the
emancipation of the slaves in
1862 inspired many paintings of
this nature.
(National Gallery of Art,
Washington D.C. Gift of
E. W. and B. C. Chrysler.)*

AMERICAN HAT-BO

These decorative boxes were used in the United States during the nineteenth century for the storage and transport of clothing, hats and other personal effects. Especially popular during the 1830s, they were often covered with printed papers depicting topical and historic events and well-known sights. Similar boxes were in use in England and on the Continent for hats, but they were seldom so delightfully coloured and patterned as their American counterparts.

Fig. 1 **Bandbox**, c.1830. Still retaining colours gayer and stronger than most boxes, this delightful example bears a naive depiction of a modest brick farmhouse. The pattern is repeated three times on the sides and lid.

Fig. 2 **Bandbox**, c.1830. The faded colours of this box are enlivened by the strong patterns of the water and the sunset.

Fig. 3 **Bandbox**, c.1830. Volunteer fire-brigades were an important part of city life in nineteenth-century America. This box depicts lay firemen at work with their equipment.

Fig. 4 **Bandbox**, c.1840. More sophisticated in design than most of the earlier boxes, this fine example shows an oriental influence.

Fig. 5 **Bandbox**, c.1850. Jenny Lind, the 'Swedish Nightingale', sang at Castle Garden, shown on this box, when she toured the United States in 1850–52.

Fig. 6 **Bandbox**, c.1830. Architectural landmarks, such as the Merchant's Exchange in New York, were a favourite subject on bandboxes.

Fig. 7 **Bandbox**, c.1830. Because they were covered with paper and treated rather roughly on journeys, bandboxes are often very worn. (The boxes illustrated are made on a base of plain, thin wood and covered with specially designed and block-printed papers. They are in the American Museum in Britain, Claverton Manor, near Bath.)

MACHINE-MADE FURNITURE IN AMERICA

Derek Balmer

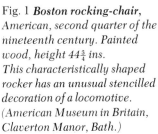

*Fig. 1 **Boston rocking-chair**, American, second quarter of the nineteenth century. Painted wood, height 44¾ ins. This characteristically shaped rocker has an unusual stencilled decoration of a locomotive. (American Museum in Britain, Claverton Manor, Bath.)*

*Fig. 2 **Slipper-chair**, attributed to John Henry Belter (1804–63), New York, mid-nineteenth century. Laminated rosewood, height 40 ins. See Figure 4. (American Museum in Britain.)*

*Fig. 3 **Side-chair** by Lambert Hitchcock (1795–1852), second quarter of the nineteenth century. Painted wood, height 34 ins. In Hitchcock's factory, men built the chairs, children applied the background colour and women the stencilled decoration. (American Museum in Britain.)*

*Fig. 4 **Back of the slipper-chair** seen in Figure 2. The overall form of Belter's chairs was created in a steam press before the carved embellishment was added. Between these two processes, the laminated rosewood was fret-cut to provide the required silhouette. The back of this chair has been left unadorned, and it demonstrates the intermediate state. (American Museum in Britain.)*

*Fig. 5 **Back of the side-chair** in Figure 3. Hitchcock's business thrived throughout the 1820s, but in 1829 he went bankrupt; he later re-started it with Arba Alford Jr. (American Museum in Britain.)*

The introduction of new machines and technical processes, and limited funds, gave an important boost to the high-grade mass-produced furniture of men such as Hitchcock and Belter

The introduction of machinery in the second half of the eighteenth century, especially in England, furthered an already recognisable trend towards specialisation in furniture production. At the same time, new materials and new means of employing old ones were being evolved. In the Colonial years, America had developed its natural resources to only a small extent; due to the legislation of the mother country, manufactured goods were largely imported from Britain. After Independence, indigenous American industry emerged and was, indeed, encouraged to do so. In the early nineteenth century, Britain attempted to reassert her previous colonial power over the newly independent states in North America, but the war of 1812 established their freedom beyond dispute.

Lambert Hitchcock (1795–1852) was one of the first makers to mass-produce furniture in America; indeed, he must be regarded as a pioneer of industrial methods at a universal level. In High Wycombe, England, groups of craftsmen specialised in making chair parts which were sold in bulk to the 'chair-makers' in the district. Likewise, Lambert Hitchcock, in 1818, established a workshop specialising in chair parts at Barkhamsted, in western Connecticut. The manufactory prospered and became the leading industry in the town, shipping the parts to the South and as far west as Chicago.

In about 1825, Hitchcock ceased making chair parts for others to construct and, instead, made complete chairs himself. This new departure was so successful that by 1826 he had built another three-storey building, where more than one hundred men, women and children were employed. A community grew up in the vicinity to house these workers and this settlement was named Hitchcocksville (now Riverton).

Because Hitchcock's chairs were mass produced, they retailed at about one dollar fifty cents, which was relatively cheap for Americans, whose wages tended to be higher on average than wages in England. The frames of these chairs were usually of birch or maple, although identification is often difficult as the earlier examples were always painted to simulate rosewood, and the later ones to imitate ebony. Lemon yellow was also sometimes used for chairs which were often embellished with multi-coloured stencilled decoration. Stencils were used extensively, cut from paper which was sized to give greater durability. Chairs of simulated rosewood or ebony were stencilled in gold, which must have set off to advantage the inlaid brass so popular in late Regency or Federal furniture. Vases of flowers and bowls of fruit were popular motifs for ornamenting these (Fig. 3), together with linking areas of abstract pattern picked out in gold. Gilding also occurred on the ring turnings of legs and stretchers. Children applied the background colour and women the decoration, while the basic structure was worked by the men in the factory.

Boston and Cape Cod rockers were a speciality

This efficient breakdown of the labour force not only resulted in quick production, but also enabled a variety of chair forms to be created; in addition to the simple side-chair with split-cane seat, Hitchcock's factory also produced Boston rockers with a roll seat (Fig. 1) and Cape Cod rockers. Hitchcock rockers with very high stick-backs are rare. In England, stick-backed Windsor chairs were made of ash or yew, woods that possess enormous tensile strength. In America these chairs were often of hickory, a wood with even greater tensile strength; pick-shafts are today made of this material.

Hitchcock's business thrived until 1828, but in 1829 he was forced into bankruptcy with liabilities of $21,525.31. The trustees of the business employed Hitchcock as their agent. Later in 1829, Hitchcock's fortunes revived and he took into partnership a man whom he had employed from the founding of the business, Arba Alford, Jr. Chairs made by the factory after that date are stencilled as follows: 'Hitchcock, Alford & Co., Hitchcocksville,

Conn.; Warranted'. The warrant was Hitchcock's guarantee of their quality and the care that he took over the selection of wood (Fig. 5).

In 1843 Hitchcock opened an independent factory at Unionville, producing identical furniture. Specimens made at the new works were marked 'Lambert Hitchcock, Unionville, Conn.' At the same time, Arba Alford took his brother Alfred into partnership and their furniture is simply marked 'Alford & Co.' However, the two Alford brothers added a retailing general store within the confines of the factory and by 1846 had ceased to produce furniture. Hitchcock, on the other hand, extended his furniture-producing ventures and, during the years 1838 to 1840, bought up the company of Holmes & Roberts, of Colebrook. Lambert Hitchcock died in 1852, naming his former partner, Arba Alford, as an executor of his estate.

The free forms of some contemporary furniture are made possible by the use of materials such as plastics. In the mid-nineteenth century, such free forms were made possible by the use of papier

of two layers of wood, one of which had the grain running vertically, while in the other the grain ran horizontally. The two layers were then glued and placed in cramps, the jaws of which were shaped to achieve approximately the desired section. This process was then repeated seven times or more, each stave of 'two ply' stuck on to the back of its predecessor, each placed round a heated core (or cawl) further to shape the lamination and with each stave placed in such a way that the joints between the staves overlapped. The whole 'barrel' was then compressed between the core and the outer mould under heat and left to dry for at least twenty-four hours. The resulting 'barrel' was cut vertically into four sections to provide backs for four chairs. The interior layers of wood were of oak or black walnut (American walnut), while for the outer layers Belter recommended rosewood. He himself said of this process: 'This work is more graceful in appearance and better adapted in form to its intended use than ordinary pressed work, and is much stronger and stiffer. The dishing form in effect adds to the thick-

6

7

Figs. 6 and 7 *Piano-bed, American, c.1870. The nineteenth century in America, as in England, was a time when new techniqes in furniture-making were abundant. In addition to the processes of mass production used by Hitchcock and Belter, new methods were applied to the many ingenious mechanical devices which were received with delight on both sides of the Atlantic. This curious example is a cabinet which bears a strong resemblance to a piano, and which opens out to form a bed. (Miss Elinor Merrell Collection.)*

Paul Hamlyn Ltd.

mâché. There was, however, a second method that achieved these results, namely that of using laminated wood. John Henry Belter refined this method by using the steam press to create the basic shapes of his designs as seen, for example, in the generous and voluptuous curves of his chair-backs (Figs. 2 and 4). Born in South Germany in 1804, Belter served his apprenticeship in Württemberg and emigrated to America in about 1840. Just as Hitchcock was designing in the weakening tradition of a classical revival, so Belter's furniture was a supreme example of the Victorian Rococo Revival.

While Hitchcock developed a good breakdown of labour, Belter evolved important industrial methods involving two patents, one of which, dated 23 February, 1858, was for the 'improvement in the method of the manufacture of furniture'. The patent involved two major innovations. The first provided a means of pressing chair-backs into curves on two planes – this is known as a 'curve on curve', and hitherto only a curve on plan or a curve on elevation had been possible; the second aspect involved the means by which several such chair-backs could be produced simultaneously.

The process is explained in the patent as a series of staves, as in a barrel. Each stave was composed

ness of the material'.

An earlier patent, dated 31 July, 1847, describes 'machinery for sawing arabesque chairs'. This was a form of fret-cutting using something like a jig-saw, a machine fret-saw. Once the general silhouette of the decoration had been achieved, the carving was created by hand; most of Belter's carvers came over to America from the Black Forest region of Germany. Where extra relief was required, additional pieces of rosewood were glued on. This resulted in some lack of control over the design as the relief carving ceased to conform to the disciplining effect of a common plane.

As a footnote to Belter, it should be remembered that after about 1820, the Austrian Biedermeier craftsmen used 'pressed work', but they achieved only a curve on one plane as opposed to a curve on curve. In about 1830 Michael Thonet began making bentwood chairs in Boppard, on the Rhine, and a table constructed in this way was exhibited at the Great Exhibition at the Crystal Palace in 1851. If the description that appears in the catalogue is correct, it is possible that Thonet's chairs antedate those of Belter. It is more likely that Thonet and Belter grew out of the same tradition: that their particular region of Germany (Boppard/Stuttgart)

Derek Balmer

Fig. 8 **The New Orleans Bedroom** *in the American Museum in Britain. Prudence Mallard of New Orleans, Louisiana, was one of the giants of American furniture design and manufacture of the mid-nineteenth century, along with Hitchcock and Belter. This fine example of a Southern bedroom has a typical Mallard bed hung with the mosquito net which was an essential feature of all beds in the Mississippi Delta. The dense lushness of the overall effect is a particularly Southern adaptation of the Victorian taste.*

developed methods of construction now forgotten.

John Henry Belter was successful as an inventor and as a setter of taste, for the products of his factory were fashionable in New York City from about 1844 to 1867. Belter died in 1862, but his company continued in operation until 1867, when the firm went bankrupt, probably partly because the methods he had pioneered enabled others to develop really large-scale mass production.

There were, of course, other aspects of American furniture manufacture in the nineteenth century, notable among them being the production of clocks in the Boston area. It is not without significance that mass-produced clocks formed a large proportion of the United States stand in the Great Exhibition of 1851. As the contemporary catalogue so rightly summed up: 'There were two causes which gave to the production of American industry displayed in the Great Exhibition a character totally distinct from that which is found in those of many other countries. In the first place, whole districts are solely devoted to the pursuit of agriculture, disregarding mining, trades and manufactures; and secondly, in the United States, it is rare to find wealth so accumulated as to favour the expenditure of large sums upon articles of luxury'.

MUSEUMS AND COLLECTIONS

Examples of mass-made American furniture of the nineteenth century may be seen at the following:

Boston: Boston Museum of Fine Arts
New York: Metropolitan Museum of Art
                Brooklyn Museum

FURTHER READING

The Cabinetmakers of America by Ethel Hall Bjerkoe, New York, 1978 reprint.

American Furniture of the Nineteenth Century, 1840–1880, by Eileen Dubrow, 1982.

Victorian Furniture, Our American Heritage, by Kathryn McNerney, 1981.

A Selection of Nineteenth-Century American Chairs by Joseph S. Van Why and Anne S. MacFarland, New York, 1973.

Angelo Hornak

Museum Photo

CLOCKS & WATCHES FROM 1830

Fig. 1 **Columned clock** by Seth Thomas, Thomaston, c.1860. Rosewood case with ringed gilt columns, panel of flowers and a game bird. This rare, double-decker, striking wall clock has an eight-day lyre movement and dead beat escapement. (Strike One, London N.1.)

Fig. 2 **Eight-day shelf calendar clock** by the Ithaca Clock Company, Ithaca, New York, c.1870. From about 1860, this was the most favoured type of domestic clock in America. (Henry Ford Museum, Dearborn, Michigan.)

4

Angelo Hornak

Museum Photo

Fig. 3 **American square clock** by Jerome and Company, c.1860. Finely figured walnut veneer case.
Like many of Jerome's famous brass clocks, this eight-day wall clock is fitted into an ogee case. These cases, which had returned to favour in about 1844, had simple picture-frame mouldings.
(Strike One.)

Fig. 4 **Ogee shelf clock** with alarm movement, by the · Waterbury Clock Company. Waterbury, Connecticut, c.1870.
(Henry Ford Museum.)

Fig. 5 **Drop octagon wall clock,** with Whiting wagon spring movement, by Atkins, c.1865.
The steeple clock was the most popular form of shelf clock at this period, but the octagon wall clock, such as this example, the hour-glass and the skeleton clock were also made.
(Henry Ford Museum.)

Pillar-and-scroll clocks, ogee clocks, steeple, American square, gothic, beehive, novelty and ticket clocks – these were some of the types which made America unrivalled in the nineteenth-century production of clocks

The 1830s saw great changes in the American clock industry, which began mass producing and exporting brass clocks in such numbers that the pattern of world production was radically altered. During the same period a new kind of watch industry emerged, based on principles that every watch-manufacturer anywhere subsequently had to adopt.

The pillar-and-scroll shelf clock, Connecticut's most important contribution to American clock design, reached the peak of its popularity a few years before 1830, when it was challenged by a smaller and cheaper version that still had a wooden movement, since cast brass was expensive and used only for eight-day clocks.

The most successful challenge to the pillar-and-scroll design was devised by Chauncey Jerome. It was a shelf clock with a single door and bronzed looking-glass instead of a painted glass panel in the lower part of the door. The Jerome design was heavier than the earlier ones and the top cresting very basic. It was truly a debasement of, rather than an improvement in, design. It appealed to the public, though, with the result that many other makers followed the style, some reverting to scenic panels instead of using mirrors, and introducing thick, carved pillars at the sides and heavily carved cresting in the Empire style on the top.

By the 1830s, a heavy case with a flat top and thick, plain pillars at the sides was in greatest favour. From about 1844, there was a reversion to the simpler case with an undecorated moulding all round, rather like a picture-frame. Such clocks are known as 'ogee', after the ogee form of moulding

Museum Photo

6

7

Wallace Heaton Photo

Fig. 6 **Briggs Rotary Pendulum Clock**, Bristol, Connecticut, c.1870.
Under a glass dome instead of in a wooden or other case, this strange novelty clock has a pendulum which swings in a small circle rather than oscillating.
(Wallace Heaton Collection.)

Fig. 7 **Ormolu clock** by the Ansonia Clock Company, Ansonia, New York, c.1890, inspired by a mid-eighteenth-century French clock.
Towards the end of the century, makers had to devise many sorts of novelty clocks and cases in order to stay in business.
(Henry Ford Museum.)

which shows in section a double continuous curve: concave passing into convex.

The great depression of 1837 forced most makers of wooden clock movements into bankruptcy and almost destroyed the industry. Chauncey Jerome was one of those seriously affected. His customers would not pay bills, so he decided to set out himself on a debt-collecting trip. One night in Richmond, Virginia, lying awake in bed (as he wrote later), it suddenly struck him that all the American brass clocks had been eight-day clocks and that there should be a market for thirty-hour brass clocks. The high quality image of the brass clock should ensure sales at a low price, and, at the same time, trouble through dampness and the fragility of the wooden clock movement would be avoided.

Jerome designed a clock movement out of the factory-made, rolled brass that had recently become available, instead of cast brass. It was small, spring-driven and to be wound daily, and he set up a factory to make it in large quantities. Spring-driven clocks were still a relative novelty. Elisha Brewster was the first to make springs of tempered brass for American clocks. They were superseded in about 1830, when imported steel springs became available.

Jerome's cheap, brass clocks were fitted into simple, wooden cases of gothic form; this was the time of the Gothic Revival in Europe. With his brother he made so many cheap clocks from about 1838 that he nearly forced the Connecticut mass-production pioneers, Terry and Co., out of business. Seth Thomas, the other big manufacturer of wooden clock movements, quickly assessed the future and converted his own factory to the production of brass clocks, and the handful of other Connecticut clockmakers who had survived the recession followed suit.

In the 1840s the Jerome and Seth Thomas production was so vast that they were selling clocks in the traditional clock-producing countries of Europe at such low prices that they caused severe damage to the English industry, which recovered only temporarily by concentrating on better quality, and to the German Black Forest industry, which, by adopting American methods, recovered completely in the 1850s.

Many of Jerome's brass clocks were fitted into ogee cases and were known in this form as 'American square' clocks (Fig. 3). Chauncey Jerome did not succeed financially, despite his brilliance. He went into partnership with the famous showman P. T. Barnum, and lost everything in a spectacular bankruptcy. The Seth Thomas company became one of the world's biggest companies, incorporated today in the General Time Corporation which still manufactures under his name (Fig. 1).

Gothic influences on style persisted for many years. Shelf clocks were made with tops of inverted V form and conical steeples at each side, and in this form they became known as 'steeple clocks'. The gothic arch form, favoured by clockmakers in many countries and called the 'lancet', was named the 'beehive' in America. It appeared in the late 1840s in a form about eighteen inches high, and it persisted into this century. Jerome even offered for sale a version which incorporated his cherished mirror panel.

The most extraordinary spring-clock was invented by Joseph Ives; for its motive power it had a leaf-spring identical to those used on carts and wagons. The spring was mounted in the base: one end operated the timekeeping mechanism, the other the striking mechanism. The first was made in about 1825 and most were produced after 1850, the best known being by Birge and Fuller in the steeple style. There were, however, other forms of shelf clock: the octagon wall clock (Fig. 5), the

Fig. 8 *Shelf clock by the
Forestville Manufacturing
Company, Bristol, Connecticut,
c.1840.*
*This rounded gothic shape is
more unusual than the steeple
shelf clock.*
(Henry Ford Museum.)

Museum Photo

hour-glass and the skeleton-clock forms. Most went for eight days, and a few for thirty days.

From about 1860, one of the most favoured domestic clocks had a second dial below, about the same size as, or even larger than, the clock dial. This indicated the date by a hand, and often the day of the week and the month (Fig. 2). There were many standing and wall models, some later ones combining the clock and calendar dials.

As the nineteenth century ran on, many makers had to find novelties to stay in business. Some turned their attention to the Augsburg 'blinking-eye' clocks of the seventeenth century for inspiration and made cast-iron clocks in the shape of dogs and lions, the eyes of which moved with the beat of the pendulum. One novelty clock of brightly-coloured cast iron in the form of Black Sambo reflects a social attitude of the period.

The Ansonia Clock Company was very active at this time and devised many strange shapes of clock. Some were taken from earlier European ideas, such as a pendulum in the form of a child on a swing, patented in the 1880s. The same company made quite accurate copies of French ormolu cases that were themselves copies of French eighteenth-century cases (Fig. 7).

A more important American contribution that became more than just a novelty was the ticket clock, showing the time in numbers – digitally – instead of by hands. The first version was known as the 'Plato time indicator' and was patented in 1902. Within about four years, the Ansonia Company had made forty thousand of them.

Electric battery clocks were new in the very early twentieth century. One produced in New York, the 'Tiffany Never-wind', had a torsion pendulum that oscillated slowly beneath the dial and was under a glass dome instead of in a case. A mechanical clock of about the same time was similarly cased and had a more unusual time-base, a conical pendulum that was mounted in front of the dial and swung in a small circle (Fig. 6).

Towards the end of the nineteenth century, alarm and domestic clocks became more and more like their European equivalents, the two streams continuing to merge until today, when designs are almost universal.

The infant American watch industry first tried to make English-style verge watches in quantity but, despite an embargo on the import of English watches, without much success. In the 1830s the embargo was lifted, for by then the English were producing the new and much more accurate lever pocket-watch, which became so popular that it put an end to early watchmaking efforts in America.

Success eventually came partly through the efforts of a clockmaker named Edward Howard, who had been apprenticed to Aaron Willard at The Neck in Boston. Howard learned the technique of mass production from Aaron Willard and developed the banjo clock, invented by Simon Willard, in a style of his own; the lower part of the clock was round, like the dial, instead of rectangular. It was made in Boston from about 1842.

With his partner, Davis, Howard also made banjo clocks with rectangular bases, but with convex instead of flat sides. These clocks were offered in five standard sizes and were, at the time, favourite railroad station timekeepers, competing with the Seth Thomas regulators. Later, he set up as E. Howard and Co. He was the last of the famous

Boston School, and the company he formed still exists, making public tower clocks. His was one of the most original and inventive minds of the time; he designed steam-engines and fire-engines as well as timepieces.

Howard's contribution to watchmaking was that he joined Aaron Dennison and Samuel Curtis, both from Boston, in buying a business which had been started by four brothers named Pitkin, and which had made the first serious attempt to mass-produce watches. The first watch was made in 1834. It was a lever watch with a going barrel like today's watches, instead of the English fusee and chain drive. Unfortunately the brothers quarrelled and finally one of them, after losing his mind and destroying many watches, committed suicide in 1846. About eight hundred watches were made, of which only about three hundred were sold.

Aaron Dennison – 'Father of the American Watch Industry'

Dennison was the driving force in the group of three and the final achievement that founded the industry was due to him. Curiously, Dennison, although known as the 'Father of the American Watch Industry', was largely unsuccessful in his financial affairs. He set up the American Horloge Company, which eventually became the Waltham Watch Company and spawned most of the other American watchmaking companies.

Dennison himself emigrated to England in order to set up a watch factory. That failed, but in 1874 he founded a company for the manufacture of watch-cases that survived until 1967.

For many years collectors had not bothered much about American watches, but now they are considered important as examples of pioneer methods of mass production. Probably the most interesting are the rotary watches, made sometime after 1876, and the Waterbury 'Long Wind', both of which had movements that revolved in the case to reduce timekeeping positional errors. The Waterbury had a mainspring that was eight feet long or more, and there were many contemporary jokes based on the time the owner took to wind the watch. 🕮

MUSEUMS AND COLLECTIONS

American clocks and watches of the nineteenth century may be seen at the following:

Bristol, Conn.: American Clock and Watch Museum

New York, N.Y.: New York University Museum of Clocks and Watches
Metropolitan Museum of Art

Washington, D.C.: Smithsonian Institution

FURTHER READING

Antique American Clocks and Watches by Richard Thomson, Princeton, 1968.
A Treasury of American Clocks by Brooks Palmer, New York, 1967.
The Complete Clock Book by Wallace Nutting, rev. ed., 1973.

Currier & Ives Prints

Fig. 1 *Loading cotton on the Mississippi, Currier and Ives, 115 Nassau Street, New York, 1870. Coloured lithograph. (American Museum in Britain, Claverton Manor, near Bath.)*

Fig. 2 *New York Ferry Boat, Currier and Ives, 125 Nassau Street, New York, second half of the nineteenth century. Coloured lithograph. (American Museum in Britain.)*

Fig. 3 *Midnight race on the Mississippi, Currier and Ives, New York, 1875. Coloured lithograph. (American Museum in Britain.)*

The American way of life in the nineteenth century was depicted in the colourful lithographs of Currier and Ives which went out from the presses in New York to every corner of the U.S.A.

On the evening of 13th January, 1840, the steamboat *Lexington* caught fire and sank in the Long Island Sound, one hundred and twenty-three lives being lost and only four saved. The *Sun* newspaper in New York published an extra edition giving details of the 'melancholy occurrence'. This broadsheet, headed by a luridly coloured picture of the sinking ship in flames, was printed by the firm of N. Currier, New York. Despite – or perhaps in part due to – its subject, this lithograph had enormous success and established, overnight, Currier's reputation.

Currier and Ives provided the public with prints of important events and personalities of the day

Nathaniel Currier (1813–88) had started his lithographic printing business in 1834. The first experiments in lithography in the U.S.A. had been made by the artist Bass Otis in 1819, and the first commercial press had been established by William S. and John Pendleton at Boston in 1824. In 1828 Currier had entered the Pendletons' employ as their first apprentice, and it was from John Pendleton that he and his partner Stodart bought a press in New York, at 137 Broadway, in 1834.

The partnership of Currier and Stodart was not successful, and in 1835 Currier established his own press at 1 Wall Street, moving the next year to Nassau Street. Until his success with the *Lexington* print of 1840, he seems to have carried out commissioned work such as architectural plans and portraits.

In 1840 Currier became publisher as well as printer, choosing his subjects for their popular appeal as well as for their topicality. James Merritt Ives (1824–95) was taken on as a book-keeper in 1852, was made a member of the firm in 1857 and a partner in 1865. The firm of Currier and Ives, which continued until 1907, was born.

The success which the prints, first of Nathaniel

Currier and then of Currier and Ives, enjoyed was due largely to three factors: the selection of subjects which had the greatest popular appeal; extensive advertising and distribution of the prints and the highly efficient organisation of production.

The selection of subjects for publication was often made by Currier and Ives themselves from the many suggestions of the artists they employed. Prints showing current events were strong sellers: there were no illustrated daily newspapers, and Currier and Ives provided the public with prints of the important events and personalities of the day. Then, as now, Presidential elections received a great deal of pictorial coverage. Apart from topical events, themes which were treated in the lithographs were those which most readily gratified the popular taste of the nineteenth century. A covering letter sent out with the Currier and Ives catalogue in the 1870s listed: 'Juvenile, Domestic, Love Scenes, Kittens and Puppies, Ladies Heads, Catholic Religions, Patriotic, Landscapes, Vessels, Comic, School Rewards and Drawing Studies, Flowers and Fruits, Motto Cards, Horses, Family Registers, Memory Pieces and Miscellaneous in great variety, and all elegant and salable Pictures'. Not mentioned in this list, but providing a large number of titles, were sport, hunting and life in the West. Currier and Ives emphasised the universal appeal of their prints; their trade-cards bore such legends as 'Publishers of Cheap and Popular Pictures' and 'Coloured Engravings for the People'. Altogether there are well over four thousand titles known to collectors.

Push-cart pedlars sold the prints in the streets of New York

Ives was an astute businessman and it is possibly to him that the efficiency of publicity and distribution should be ascribed. There was the retail store in Nassau Street but this provided the means of disposing of only a small fraction of the firm's output. Push-cart pedlars would collect a stock from Nassau Street and sell the prints round New York, working on a sale or return basis.

The frontier was ever moving west. New towns, villages and settlements were springing up daily. This made the travelling merchants an integral part of any large sales operation, and Currier and Ives made certain these salesmen carried good stocks of their prints to be hung, or simply pinned, on the

walls of frontier cabins and saloons. As a settlement became permanent and grew to the proportions of a town, Currier and Ives ensured that the general store carried a selection of their lithographs. In the larger cities such as Chicago they appointed agents to collect orders. They also opened an office in London from which they operated an extensive campaign in Europe.

To all their stockists delivery was as prompt as the mail services permitted. Payment was always in advance; six dollars secured one hundred prints, sixty dollars a thousand. This price applied to all 'stock' prints, which were the smaller ones. The larger 'folio' prints were more lavishly produced and cost up to as much as four dollars each.

Ives had a flair for making the prints appeal to popular taste

Currier and Ives prints were manufactured with an efficiency which, although adding little to the self-esteem of the artists, delivered the goods in large quantities at low cost. Many of the surviving sketches, from which the lithographs were drawn, bear instructions such as 'move figures into fore-ground among horses' and 'put more tail on Mac'.

4

These instructions are often in the handwriting of Ives, who in this way exercised his flair for making the prints appeal to popular taste. He was a self-taught artist and designed a few of the firm's prints himself.

Many designs were co-operative efforts, with one artist drawing the background and another the figures. Fanny Palmer (1812–76), who emigrated from England in the early 1840s, specialised in landscapes and atmospheric effects. Arthur Tait (1819–1905), also from England, did many of the hunting and camping scenes which, among the vast

Currier and Ives production, are notable for their quality. Other artists of distinction were Louis Maurer, who created the *Life of a Fireman* series, and Thomas Worth, responsible for the large and very successful group known as *Darktown Comics*. From the huge pool of immigrant and insolvent artists in New York during the nineteenth century, Currier and Ives picked each draughtsman for his speciality: horses, boats, figures or architecture.

All the prints were hand coloured; it was cheaper to pay the young women and girls who did the colouring than to buy the extra stones required for

Fig. 4 *The Tree of Life*, *Currier and Ives,* *115 Nassau Street, New York, 1870.* *Coloured lithograph. The inscription under* *the title of this unusual allegorical print* *reads: 'On either side of the river was there* *the Tree of Life which bare twelve manner* *of fruits.' Revelation, Chap. XXII, 2.* *(David Walston Collection.)*

Fig. 5 *The Bay of Annapolis, Nova Scotia,* *Currier and Ives, 125 Nassau Street, New* *York, c.1880. Coloured lithograph.* *(Baynton-Williams, Old Maps and Prints,* *London.)*

K. Hoddle

Derek Balmer

Fig. 6 *The Independent Gold Hunter on his* *way to California* *by N. Currier, c.1845.* *Coloured lithograph.* *Born in Massachusetts, Nathaniel Currier* *(1813–88) set up a printing business in New* *York in 1834. Here he made numerous* *lithographs on his own until 1865, when he* *took into partnership J. Merritt Ives (1824–* *95). This charming example of Currier's* *work before his partnership with Ives bears* *the legend 'I neither borrow nor lend'.* *(American Museum in Britain.)*

Fig. 7 *Crossing the Rockies,* *Currier and* *Ives, New York, second half of the* *nineteenth century. Coloured lithograph.* *(American Museum in Britain.)*

Derek Balmer

chromolithography. The colourists worked from a 'model' which, like the original designs, had been vetted. If a 'rush print' of a topical subject was being made, extra colourists were called in and stencils were cut.

Currier and Ives, whose careful selection of subject, efficient methods of production, intense advertising and large-scale distribution presaged the growth of the mass media which have supplanted their prints, created a panoramic view of the American people which does much today to enliven our knowledge of life in the nineteenth century.

MUSEUMS AND COLLECTIONS
Currier and Ives prints may be seen in most museums in the United States.

FURTHER READING
Currier and Ives' America by Colin Simkin, New York, 1952.
American Lithographs by Helen Comstock, New York, 1950.
Currier and Ives: Printmakers to the American People by Harry T. Peters, New York, 1976 reprint.

COLT REVOLVERS

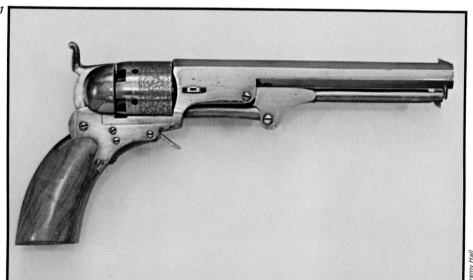

Jeremy Hall

Jeremy Hall

Inextricably linked with the opening up of the West and the romantic heroes of that era, Colt revolvers have been produced continuously from 1836 to the present day

A revolver is a repeating pistol in which the ammunition revolves in a chambered cylinder for successive discharge through a fixed barrel; it may be described as 'single-action', when it must be cocked by the thumb before firing, 'self-cocking' where trigger-pressure alone operates the firing, or 'double-action' where it permits either means of discharge.

Samuel Colt, whose name is central to the history of such weapons, was born at Hartford, Connecticut, in 1814 and died there on 10 January, 1862. Although his family had no background in the small-arms industry, he was sufficiently interested to invest in the manufacture of a working-model revolver by Anson Chase, of Hartford, and then to secure English and American patents protecting the design of it.

By September 1836, Colt had secured financial backing and had licensed his U.S. patent to the Patent Arms Manufacturing Company, of Paterson, N.J., which produced about two thousand Colt revolving arms during its short life. All were muzzle-loading, percussion weapons; the rammed-down gunpowder and lead bullet in each chamber were fired when a small percussion-cap was struck by the hammer of the weapon. Single-action revolvers of the type shown in Figure 1 predominated, although rifles, shotguns and carbines, some self-cocking, were also made: those weapons are now rare and

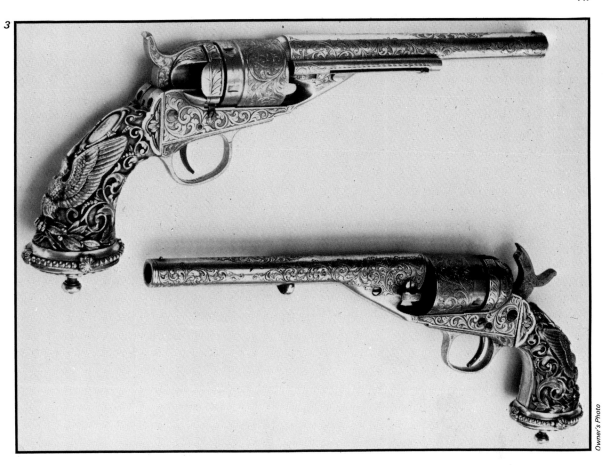

Fig. 1 *Paterson-type percussion revolver, similar to those made by the Patent Arms Manufacturing Company, Paterson, New Jersey, 1836–42. Five-shot, single-action, ·28 calibre, barrel-length 4¼ ins. (H.M. Tower of London Armouries.)*

Fig. 2 *Colt percussion revolver, the design credited to Elisha K. Root (Factory Superintendent and later President of Colt's company), introduced in 1857. Five-shot, single-action, ·265 calibre, barrel-length 4¼ ins. These weapons were the first Colt revolvers to have solid frames in place of barrel/frame assemblies held together by transverse wedges. (H.M. Tower of London Armouries.)*

Fig. 3 *Pair of Colt revolvers, 1869–72. Five-shot, single-action, breech-loading, ·38 centre-fire calibre; silver plated, engraved barrels, butts and frames; gilt cylinders, trigger-guards and hammers; cast-bronze butts; barrel-lengths 6½ ins. Known to modern collectors as 'small-frame conversions', these started as muzzle-loading percussion arms. (Messrs. Wallis and Wallis, Lewes.)*

extremely valuable. In 1842 the Paterson Company failed and Colt recovered little more than his U.S. patent rights from the venture, for these arms had been too complicated and expensive to arouse the interest of the U.S. Army, although some field-tests were carried out in the Seminole War and in Texas. Without official approval, stockholders were unwilling to increase, or even sustain, their investment. Two years later, however, the outbreak of the U.S. War with Mexico brought a demand for revolvers from men who certainly recognised defects in the Paterson design, but had used Colt pistols in more private disputes and acknowledged the value of the repeating principle in the kind of fighting with which they were now faced. Ironically, the inventor had not even a specimen revolver to show when U.S. Army enquiries reached him, but, with that energy which so characterised his activities, an order for a thousand improved arms was secured and their manufacture sub-contracted to the factory of Eli Whitney at Whitneyville, Connecticut.

By 1848, Samuel Colt had his own factory in Pearl Street, Hartford, Connecticut

The resultant arm, which is rare and valuable today, embodied features of design suggested by Captain Samuel S. Walker of the Texas Militia. It was a huge, four-pound nine-ounce, single-action, percussion revolver, six-chambered, in ·44 calibre and with a 9 ins. barrel. Known to modern collectors as the Walker, Whitneyville-Walker or Model 1847 revolver, this weapon was similar to the pistol in Figure 7 (above), and differed from its predecessors by using fewer lock-mechanism components, a trigger-guard and a powerful, hinged loading-lever, or rammer.

By 1848, Colt had his own factory in Pearl Street, Hartford, but in 1855 he transferred it to a site on the Connecticut River. While he lived, only single-action percussion revolvers were made there, most of them based on the successful Model 1847 design:

1848 A six-shot Dragoon, or Old Model Army, revolver (Fig. 7, above) in ·44 calibre, but now with a 7½ ins. barrel.

1848 A five-shot pocket revolver, without a rammer, in ·31 calibre and with 3 ins., 4 ins., 5 ins. or 6 ins. octagonal barrel at choice.

1849 A pocket revolver with the lever-rammer; five- and six-shot versions were made and in a choice of barrel-lengths.

1851 A six-shot belt, or Navy, revolver in ·36 calibre and with 7½ ins. octagonal barrel (Fig. 7, below), followed by a pocket version with a shorter barrel and lighter cylinder.

1857 A variant pocket design with solid frame (Fig. 2), which was also used in rifles, carbines and shotguns.

1860 Another six-shot Army revolver in ·44 calibre, with an 8 ins. round barrel and a new ratchet rammer.

1861 Another Navy six-shot, ·36 calibre revolver, similar in appearance to the new Army pistol, but with 7½ ins. round barrel.

1862 A similar five-shot New Police revolver.

By the time of Colt's death, large quantities of these models had been manufactured by the Colt's Patent Fire Arms Manufacturing Company: 118,000 Navy Model 1851 revolvers, 197,000 Pocket Model Arms and nearly 100,000 others. With revolver prices at between U.S.$9 and U.S.$21, this was a big business to have built up in fifteen years, and there has always been considerable interest in how the task was accomplished.

Demonstrably, Samuel Colt was born at the right time and in the right place. In America alone, between 1847 and his death in 1862, he had the markets

4

Mansell Collection

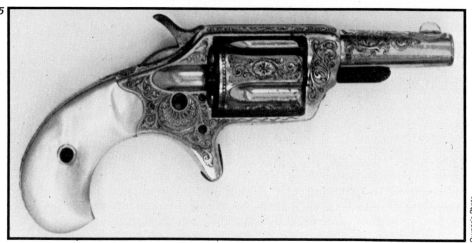

5

Owner's Photo

6

Owner's Photo

created by the Mexican War, the California gold-rush, 'Abolitionist' disturbances in Kansas, secession rearmament and the outbreak of the Civil War. Further, Colt's important ability to supply arms with interchangeable parts was made possible by the emergence of machine-tool designers such as E. K. Root, his Factory Superintendent, and F. W. Howe, whose milling, forging and drilling equipment, even in unskilled hands, regularly met requirements for manufacturing tolerances that craftsmanship alone could not accomplish. He also had a work-force capable of almost infinite expansion or contraction to meet his needs, since his factory was largely operated by self-employed workmen, who contracted to supply his revolver components at negotiated prices using his machines and factory facilities.

Finally, Colt had, through his own foresight and tenacity, an American monopoly to manufacture revolvers in which the cylinder was rotated mechanically. This position in America was based on his U.S. patent of 1836 and established only after bitter litigation. Because Colt had no real competitors prior to 1851, the monopoly can be said to have been of value only between 1852 and 1857, but the advantage was real. Needless to say, Colt turned his attention to markets overseas, to attempts at licensed manufacture in Belgium, England and Russia. Little is known of the actual use made of his manufacturing techniques in the Tula arsenal near Moscow, but an English factory, off Bessborough Place, London, operated from January 1853 until December 1856, with local labour, American superintendents and machinery.

The short operational life of Colt's London factory, which made about 39,000 Navy Model 1851 and 10,000 pocket arms, has been blamed on the British gun-trade, poor labour relations and the British Army's adoption of a competing British revolver. In fact, the venture appears to have been largely a window-dressing operation with which Colt backed the claim he made, before a Parliamentary Committee, that his manufacturing techniques produced arms with fully interchangeable parts. The market he sought was for single-shot infantry rifles and, since the new Hartford factory was capable of meeting all European civilian demands, the London plant was closed as soon as it became obvious that no rifle contracts would be forthcoming from H.M. Board of Ordnance.

In Belgium, under the patent law, Colt had to arrange local manufacture or lose his patent. Since Liège had so large a gun-making industry, success must have appeared easy when such reputable houses as Pirlot Frères, Gilon or Ancion & Cie. were among Colt's licensees, but quality-control proved elusive and, although many 'Colt Brevete' revolvers were made, their finish never approached the standards of London or Hartford.

After the Civil War, competition for the reduced American market was keen, and several revolver-manufacturers went out of business. Such demand as there was for revolvers was for breech-loading arms, but the Colt Company, with other U.S. manufacturers, was prevented from producing such arms by the fact that Smith & Wesson, of Springfield, Massachusetts, controlled a U.S. master-patent for the necessary bored-through revolver chamber – an ironic situation in view of Colt's equivalent monopoly in an earlier decade.

The Colt Company toyed with a U.S. patent of Alexander Thuer, an employee, by which muzzle-

Copyright reserved

Jeremy Hall

Colt Revolvers

Fig. 4 *Revolt of the last Redskins by H. Meyer, late nineteenth century. Engraving. This contemporary conception of the famous scout Buffalo Bill Cody (1846–1917) is characteristic of the romanticised and inaccurate view of the opening up of the West which was current until very recently. In this picture, the revolver carried by Buffalo Bill bears little relation to Colt's products and is merely a generalisation based on weapons of the period.*

Fig. 5 **Colt New Line revolver** *of a type introduced in 1874. Five-shot, single-action, breech-loading, mother of pearl grip, engraved, plated frame; ·32 rim-fire calibre, barrel-length 2¼ ins., overall length 6¼ ins. These revolvers were intended for the cheaper end of the market. (Messrs. Wallis and Wallis.)*

Fig. 6 **Colt Model 1878 revolver**, *available until after 1900. Six-shot, double-action, breech-loading, ·45 centre-fire calibre, barrel-length 5½ ins. This gun has a low serial number (1659) and the London depot address of 14 Pall Mall on it. Although a slightly better weapon than the Lightning revolver (Fig. 8), its lock-mechanism was still too frail for serious use. (Messrs. Wallis and Wallis.)*

Fig. 7 Above: **Dragoon percussion revolver,** *Colt model 1848. Presentation-engraved, six-shot, single-action, serial number 9628, ·44 calibre, barrel-length 7½ ins., weight 4 lbs. unloaded.*
Below: **Navy percussion revolver,** *Colt model 1851. Presentation-engraved, six-shot, single-action, ·36 calibre, barrel-length 7½ ins. (By gracious permission of H.M. the Queen.)*

Fig. 8 **Colt Lightning revolver.** *Six-shot, double-action, breech-loading, ·38 centre-fire calibre, barrel-length 4¼ ins. (with a rod ejector). (H.M. Tower of London Armouries.)*

7

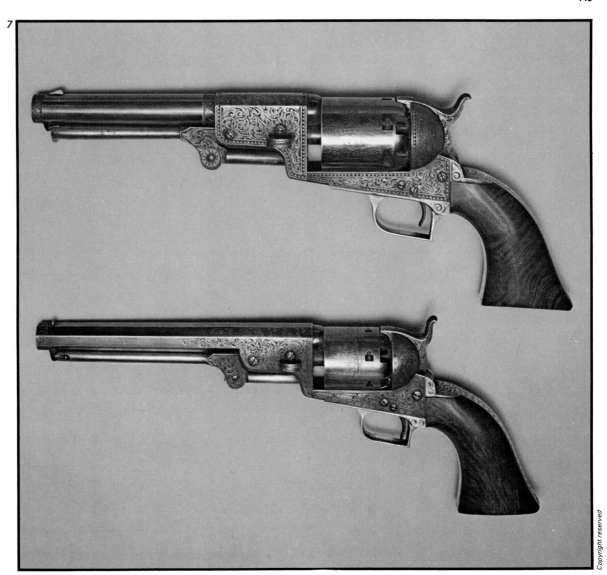

8

9

10

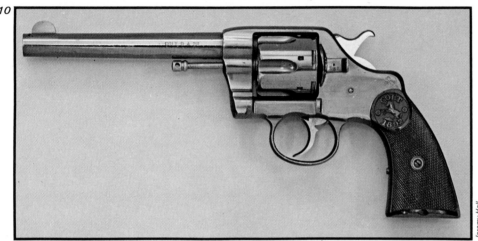

Fig. 9 *Peace-maker Colt Model 1873 revolver. Six-shot, single-action, breech-loading; ivory grips, rod ejector, barrel-length 7½ ins.*
Also known as the 'Frontier Six-Shooter' or the 'Single-Action Army', this was undoubtedly the best-known Colt revolver, by virtue of its association with the American West and many real or imaginary incidents there. Manufacture ran from 1873 to 1940, and was resumed in 1957. They were sold in twenty different calibres and five barrel-lengths.
(H.M. Tower of London Armouries.)

Fig. 10 *New Double-Action Army revolver, Colt model 1892. Six-shot, double-action, ·38 centre-fire calibre, barrel-length 6 ins.*
These weapons had the swing-out cylinder introduced by the Colt company in 1889, and were the first of such arms to be issued to the United States Army. Their combat performance in the Philippino uprising of 1899–1901 was disappointing.
(H.M. Tower of London Armouries.)

loading revolvers would be converted to use curious, front-loading, rimless, centre-fire metallic cartridges. Effectively, however, they had to await expiry of the Smith & Wesson patent in 1869 before entering the new market. When entry did occur, the relevant Colt revolvers were merely adapted muzzle-loading designs, made from forgings and components designed a decade or more earlier (Fig. 3). However, in about 1874 the Colt Company introduced a novel line of breech-loading revolvers including the various House, New House, New Line or New Police pocket-weapons illustrated in Figure 5. Predominantly rim-fire arms (in calibres ·22, ·30, ·32, ·38 and ·41), no trigger-guards were fitted, and a solid frame was used for the first time since the Model 1857 revolver. Retailing for around $10 in plain finish, these little pistols were popular and still widely used at the turn of the century.

In 1873 a Colt revolver appeared which more than any other model has identified the Colt name with handguns. Known variously as the 'Frontier Six-Shooter', the 'Peacemaker', the 'Single-Action Army' or the 'Model 1873' revolver, this was another single-action, six-shot, gate-loaded revolver (still with the separable butt and trigger-guard common to the muzzle-loading arms) with a sturdy solid frame (Fig. 9). These were sold in twenty different calibres – between ·22 and ·476 – and five barrel-lengths. Despite production to this day (with a short break in the 1950s), interest is keen and values relatively high.

Around 1878, the Company added two double-action, solid-framed, gate-loading revolvers to its range of models. The first, a so-called 'Lightning' model, shown in Figure 8, had the separately attached butt and trigger-guard of earlier arms; the Model 1878, or Double-Action Army & Frontier

model, illustrated in Figure 6, has the frame and butt forged as one component. Although offered until after 1900 in a range of calibres and barrel-lengths, and pursued by enthusiasts today, these were poor weapons by reason of their over-delicate lock-mechanism.

Finally, in 1889, the Colt Company developed a new design, and introduced, as the Navy Model of 1889, a six-shot, double-action revolver with a solid frame from which the cylinder could be swung outwards on a crane; manual operation of an ejector-rod protruding from the front of the cylinder then ejected all the cartridges simultaneously. The lock-mechanism, although far from perfect, was a great improvement upon that used in the Lightning or Model 1878 arms, and the U.S. Army supplemented its stock of elderly Model 1873 pistols with purchases of a New Double-Action Army model in 1892 (Fig. 10).

This weapon was improved in 1894, 1895 and 1896, and had a deserved success; a version much sought after by collectors was adopted by the U.S. Marine Corps in 1905. However, the design had its defects, notably in the lock-mechanism, and steps were taken to eliminate them as early as 1895.

In that year Colt introduced the New Pocket Revolver, visually similar to the existing swing-out cylinder models but in ·32 calibre. This model was shortly afterwards followed by New Police (·32 calibre) and New Service (·45 calibre) models, to which many collectors are turning their attention today. These three new models were primarily distinguished by their double-action lock-mechanism, now a well-tried European design, the use of which overcame those objections levelled at the earlier arms. Too long regarded as modern revolvers by many collectors, these early Colt swing-out cylinder arms are difficult to find in good condition, and surprisingly expensive when found.

MUSEUMS AND COLLECTIONS

Examples of Colt revolvers may be seen at the following:

Hartford, Conn.:   Wadsworth Atheneum

FURTHER READING

Colt Firearms from 1836 by J. E. Serven, 1979 reprint.

The Gun Collector's Handbook of Values by C. E. Chapel, New York, 1979.

The Peace-Maker and its Rivals by J. E. Parsons, New York, 1950.

Fig. 1 **American Eagle** *from the stern of an American ship, nineteenth century. Carved, painted and gilt fir, width 51 ins. Ship-carvings – figureheads, sternboards and other embellishments – were often produced in the shipyards. (Arthur and James Ayres Collection.)*

AMERICAN FOLK ART

'Flat likenesses without shade or shadow' was the idiom in which many of America's folk artists – men and women – worked, and calligraphy and woodcarving shared their naive freshness

'Folk', 'popular', 'naive' and 'primitive' are only a few of the many terms that have been used to describe an aspect of the visual arts not easily defined but readily identifiable. Some examples of folk art are the work of professionals, usually men with a highly developed technique harnessed to a naive outlook; others were by sophisticated amateurs, often women. The materials employed were varied, among them wood, ceramics, glass, paint and textiles.

The artists of pioneer America worked within a craft tradition rather than following academic standards. Some carpenters graduated to become woodcarvers. Some began as house-painters; others as signwriters progressing through inn-signs to easel painting. These journeymen craftsmen travelled in the summer, mostly adding the faces of their clients to pictures that had been prepared speculatively during the winter months. Portraits of this kind are charmingly wooden in appearance, except where the demands of a particular sitter reveal observation from life. In addition to the faces, it should be noted that portraits of women often included symbols of leisure, such as embroidery, that conformed to middle-class ideals if not to the actual social situation of the sitter, while those of their husbands sometimes included reference to their professions – soldiers, sailors, lawyers or doctors. Children are often portrayed with favourite toys.

Some of these artists were capable of painting in a more academic style. William Matthew Prior (1806–73) was one such artist, and he advertised some of his work as 'flat likenesses without shade or shadow' for between $5 and $20, while for his more sophisticated products he charged his Bostonian clients about $25. Prior, as with other artists in this genre, painted all manner of subjects in addition to portraits.

In considering the artistic customs of America, it is crucial to remember that the medieval traditions of northern Europe lingered on unconsciously in the immigrants' work. The Renaissance of the Mediterranean that was later patronised by Northern courtiers and tutored by Northern academies meant nothing to the labourer, artisan or yeoman who had, for the most part, colonised America. Before Independence, the American artist often strove beyond the means of his accomplishment and aped the sophisticated styles of Europe through the 'mezzotint-eye view'. Some, like Benjamin West (1738–1820), went over to Europe and accepted her standards with meteoric success. Nevertheless, it was Independence that permitted America's true character to emerge, and the first half of the nineteenth century saw a blossoming of American folk art.

The boundaries of this epoch are delineated on the one side by Independence and on the other by the full emergence of the camera at the time of the

Fig. 2 Mourning-picture,
American, nineteenth century.
Water-colour, 22 ins. x 26 ins.
Mourning-pictures hung in
almost every home. After the
national mourning following the
death of Washington in 1799,
the stock elements of tomb,
weeping willow, church and
mourners were usually present.
The inscription on this example
was left blank to cover future
contingencies.
(American Museum in Britain,
Claverton Manor, near Bath.)

Fig. 3 Theorem painting,
American, nineteenth century.
Stencilled on velvet, 21 ins. x
25 ins.
Still-life compositions of fruit
were highly popular, their bright
colour contrasting attractively
with the cotton velvet
background.
(American Museum in Britain.)

Fig. 4 Whirligig, American,
nineteenth century. Carved and
painted wood, height 12 ins.
These whirligigs were frequently
designed as soldiers and, with
their paddle-arms and revolving
bodies, were popular as wind
indicators on smaller buildings.
(American Museum in Britain.)

Fig. 5 Cigar-Store Indian,
American, nineteenth century.
Carved and painted wood, height
5 ft. 10 ins.
Inspired by the Indians who
were first observed smoking
tobacco, these figures were
designed as signs to advertise the
tobacco-shop. This example was
very probably carved by one of
the group of craftsmen who made
figureheads, sternboards and
figures for carousels and circus
wagons.
(American Museum in Britain.)

Fig. 6 Horses, *signed by*
A. C. Fuller, American,
mid-nineteenth century. Pen
and ink 19¾ ins. x 26 ins.
The introduction of the flexible
steel nib, with ability to produce
varying thicknesses, made
calligraphy a desirable and
ladylike accomplishment.
(John Judkyn Memorial,
Freshford Manor, near Bath.)

American Civil War, when it was often used for journalistic purposes by such great photographers as Matthew Brady and Timothy O'Sullivan.

One of America's most remarkable folk artists, and certainly her most famous, falls within this period. Edward Hicks was born at Attleboro (now Langhorne) in Bucks County, Pennsylvania, in 1780, and for most of his life he lived and worked in Newtown, Pennsylvania. By trade, he was a sign- and coach-painter, by conviction a Quaker preacher. As a painter, a Quaker and a native of Pennsylvania, his favourite subject was Penn's treaty with the Indians.

It would appear that for those subjects further from home, Hicks specialised in peopled landscapes, re-interpreting the work of others. For example, *The Falls of Niagara* in the Chrysler Garbisch Collection is dated 1825, and is clearly derived from a vignette with precisely the same title that occurs in *A Map of North America constructed to the latest information by H. S. Tanner,* 'entered according to the State of Pennsylvania – printed by W. Duffee – engraved by H. S. Tanner'. Although Hick's painting is virtually identical, item for item, with the Tanner engraving, the overall

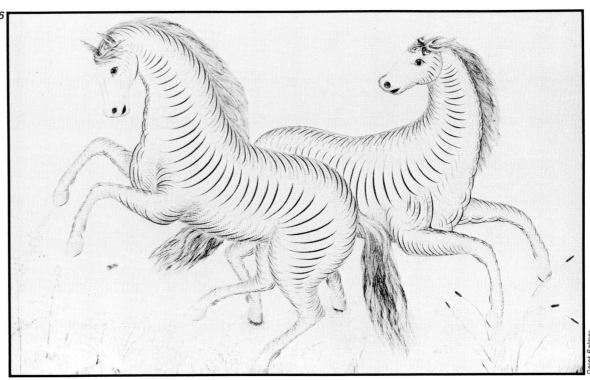

6

character of each is totally different.

The German communities of Pennsylvania, which even today maintain many of their traditions in language, religion and agriculture, produced folk art of a high order. The rose and tulip decoration of dower-chests and the calligraphy, or *fraktur* (fractured) writing, of their birth, baptismal and marriage certificates are characteristic examples of their work.

The *fraktur* writing was mainly the work of itinerant scribes, or of schoolmasters who were expected to have a good hand. Baptismal certificates were favoured by the Lutheran and Reformed Churches, but not by Sectarians such as the Mennonites and others who did not believe in infant baptism. These documents were popular in the eighteenth century and the standard was maintained into the nineteenth century, especially at the Ephrata cloisters, where there was a revival – as

it were – of this survival of the medieval illuminated manuscript. Eventually their quality was debased by printed examples and their use was discontinued.

Painting in water-colours was considered as much an appropriate pastime and accomplishment for ladies as embroidery, and the early nineteenth-century mourning-pictures are examples of their work. Stencil-painting on furniture and on velvet for more elegant effect was also popular, the latter sometimes being described as theorem painting. Calligraphy was also considered a ladylike accomplishment. The introduction of the steel nib resulted in calligraphic exercises of amazing complexity made possible, if not easy, by the flexibility of the steel nib which could produce a line of many thicknesses.

Carved decoy ducks are still made today and it is thought their use is derived from an American Indian method of hunting; they provide a uniquely American contribution to the history of folk art.

Ship-carvings – figureheads, sternboards and other features – were usually produced by men who worked in the shipyards. When the war of 1812 had drawn to a close in 1815, it was a time for economy and William Bainbridge, a distinguished

American naval officer in the first third of the nineteenth century, urged that ships were to have no more decoration than could 'give them relief'. Nevertheless, by 1828, a naval officer named J. D. Henley was able to write to John Rodgers, President of the Naval Board, recommending that Laben S. Beecher of Boston be brought to Portsmouth, New Hampshire, to carve the stem and stern of the *Concord* as there were no carvers there who could do the work.

Beecher was descended from an illustrious Connecticut family and he moved to Boston to begin his apprenticeship in 1822, at the age of nineteen. His career as a woodcarver was short for, soon after he had completed his work on the *Constitution* in 1834, Beecher became interested in the timber business and moved west to Wisconsin, where he became a prominent landowner. John Mason eventually took over from Beecher as

Fig. 7 *The Falls of Niagara* by
Edward Hicks (1780–1849),
1825. Oil on canvas, 31½ ins. x
38 ins.
*One of the most remarkable and
most famous folk artists of this
era, Hicks was a Quaker preacher
as well as a sign- and coach-
painter. He specialised in
paintings of Penn's treaty with
the Indians and, it is thought, in
re-interpretations of the work of
others. A good example of this
latter talent is his well-known
Niagara Falls picture which is
virtually identical with the
Tanner engraving illustrated in
Figure 8, although the overall
character is totally different.
(Metropolitan Museum of Art,
New York. Gift of E. W. and
B. C. Garbisch, 1962.)*

Fig. 8 *Falls of Niagara,* detail
from 'A Map of North America,
Constructed According to the
Latest Information: by H. S.
Tanner', engraved and published
in Philadelphia, 1822.
*Typical of the vignettes used to
illustrate maps throughout the
nineteenth century, this scene
was the inspiration for Hicks'
painting in Figure 7. To the left
of this vignette on the same
map is a further scene entitled
'Natural Bridge in Virginia'
which appears to be the source
of Hicks' picture* Peaceable
Kingdom of the Branch, *an oil on
wood panel of c.1825, now in the
collection of the Yale University
Art Gallery.
(John Judkyn Memorial.)*

Fig. 9 *Portrait of Mary L.
Hansman aged 12 Years,* signed
by H. K. Grausman (?) and dated
1849 (?).
*Oil on canvas, 20¾ ins. x 23½ ins.
Primitive portraits were often
painted by adding the face of the
client to the body which had been
speculatively prepared by the
artist during the winter months.
(John Judkyn Memorial.)*

7

Above, below, where'er the astonished eye
Turns to behold, new opening wonders lie,

The Falls

of Niagara

With uproar hideous first the *Falls* appear,
The stunning tumult thundering on the ear.

This great o'erwhelming work of awful Time
In all its dread magnificence sublime,

Rises on our view, amid a crashing roar
That bids us kneel, and Time's great God adore.

18   25

8

Derek Balmer

Derek Balmer

11

Derek Balmer

Fig. 10 *Carousel figure,*
American, nineteenth century.
Carved and painted wood,
height 5 ft.
Early roundabouts at circuses,
such as that of Barnum and Bailey
(founded in 1881), provided rides
on wooden birds and animals,
both real and imaginary. Later it
was found that children preferred
horses, especially dapple-grey
ones, and animals like this fine
giraffe disappeared.
(American Museum in Britain.)

Fig. 11 *Fraktur, or Family*
Record, American, eighteenth
century. Water-colour and ink on
paper, 13½ ins. x 11½ ins.
The keeping of birth, marriage
and death records was an
important family obligation
before the establishment of
public records. Even after the
introduction of official records,
the tradition persisted. Great care
and attention was lavished on
many of them, as on this fine New
England example.
(American Museum in Britain.)

a carver.

William Rush, born in 1756, is sometimes described as the first native American sculptor for, in addition to the figureheads that he carved, he created sculpture for his home town of Philadelphia and was a founder of the Pennsylvania Academy of Fine Arts, the earliest organisation of its kind in the United States. Among the numerous figureheads he carved, the most famous is *The Spirit of Schuylkill.*

Samuel Robb, of New York, also renowned for his figureheads, is known to have worked for the Sebastian Wagon Company which specialised in circus and menagerie wagons and their carved embellishments. The first recorded travelling circus in America is said to date from 1824, when John Robinson took three wagons, five horses and a tent across the Allegheny Mountains. This was a form of entertainment that by the end of the century had culminated in 'The Greatest Show on Earth' of Barnum and Bailey.

The names of Barnum and Bailey are virtually synonymous with the circus and the fairground. Phineas Taylor Barnum and James A. Bailey formed the Barnum and Bailey Circus in New York in 1881 and sold over eighty-two million tickets for their exhibitions. The 'Big Parade' of the circus, menagerie or fair that heralded the arrival of the circus in town demanded flamboyant carved decoration for the purposes of publicity. The sales talk was equally florid: 'Dazzling, dancing scene in the Magical, Mighty, wordless play, combining the weird wizardry of India and Arabia,

in opulent, oriental grandeur'. Much of this work was done in the Midwest in Milwaukee and Baraboo, Wisconsin, which were for many years the traditional winter quarters for circuses. The early roundabouts or carousels provided rides on many wooden birds and animals, both real and legendary. It was soon discovered, however, that children preferred horses, especially dapple-grey ones, and by the end of the century roundabouts had become veritable hippodromes. Some of the finest specimens were made at Gustav Augustus Dentzel's Carousel factory in Germantown, Pennsylvania, during the 1890s.

American folk painting and sculpture, unlike their British equivalent, have the advantage of having been assembled in collections that are large enough to be studied seriously. Furthermore, American naive art of the nineteenth century is not so rare as much of the folk art of England, no doubt because the elegance of the Court, based upon the wealth of the British Empire both territorial and industrial, desired and possessed the material wealth to achieve a greater level of sophistication in art at all levels. Furthermore, in Britain shop-signs were prohibited by Act of Parliament in 1762 and, although this Act was not particularly effective, it certainly discouraged their widespread use.

In America, on the other hand, the cigar-store Indian became virtually the symbol of a new and short-lived independent urban peasantry, whose art we admire today, though in a spirit other than that in which it was created.

Museum Photo

Museum Photo

ART GLASS IN AMERICA

Fig. 1 ***The Morgan Vase,***
Hobbs-Brockunier & Company,
Wheeling, West Virginia,
c.1890. Coral, or Wheeling
Peach Blow, glass, height $9\frac{7}{8}$ ins.
The form, and to a large extent
the colour, of this piece emulates
a Chinese ceramic vase purchased
by Mrs. Pierpont Morgan for
$18,000. The event created a
great stir of public interest.
(Corning Museum of Glass,
Corning, New York.)

Fig. 2 ***Berry-bowl and stand,***
Mount Washington Glass
Company, New Bedford,
Massachusetts, 1880–90.
Etched cameo glass, the stand of
silver plate, width 8 ins.
(Corning Museum of Glass. Lola
Kincaid Ford Collection.)

Fig. 3 ***Covered goblet and***
pitcher, *attributed to the Boston*
and Sandwich Glass Company,
Sandwich, Massachusetts,
1870–88. Clear glass with
mechanically threaded
decoration, height of goblet 9 ins.
(Sandwich Glass Museum,
Sandwich, Massachusetts.)

In the last thirty years of the
nineteenth century American
manufacturers produced several
new types of decorative – sometimes frivolous – glass, using
sophisticated chemical processes

The making of 'art glass', as it was called in its
heyday – about 1875 to 1900 – and as it is still called
by collectors today, was due to the combination of
social and technological factors: the fondness of
late Victorians for highly ornate and colourful
decoration and developments in the chemistry of
colouring glass. These factors led to the production
of many types of glass which often looked like other
substances and which were sometimes novel,
frivolous and by today's standards in bad taste.
Nevertheless, art glass epitomises, probably more
than any one other product, the late Victorian era.

Art glass was, at least in the Western world, an
international style, with centres in England,
Bohemia and other central European areas. It is difficult to ascertain whether it was developed first in
Bohemia or in England. Both areas, but in particular
England, had a strong influence on its development
in America.

Silvered, or mercury, glass, along with opal-
decorated glasses, may be considered the first type
of art glass. A patent for the first commercially practical method for producing silvered glass was
granted to Hale Thomson in London in about 1851.
In America, William Leighton, an Englishman who
became superintendent of the New England Glass
Works, was granted a patent on 16 January, 1855,
for silvered-glass door-knobs, which he claimed were
superior to silver articles.

It is interesting to note, in view of this patent date,
that listed among the wide variety of glass exhibited
by the New England Glass Company at the New
York Crystal Palace Exposition in 1853 were 'Two-
hundred glass door-knobs, silvered' and 'One large
silvered-glass bowl on foot, very richly engraved'.

'Opal-decorated' wares, as opaque-white or
'milk' glass was called by glassmakers, were produced in large quantities by numerous American
glasshouses from the middle of the 1850s.
English firms such as W. H. B. & J. Richardson, with
their opal-decorated products, undoubtedly had a
marked influence on American production of these
wares. For example, William L. Smith and his two
sons, Alfred and Harry, decorators, emigrated to
America and began working for the Boston and
Sandwich Glass Company in about 1855. In 1871
the Smith brothers were employed by William
Libbey to operate the large decorating shop he
established at the Mount Washington Glass Works.
Three years later they leased this shop and
apparently before 1876 moved their business to
28 and 30 William Street, New Bedford.

Vases called by the generic terms 'ring' or 'Smith

Museum Photo

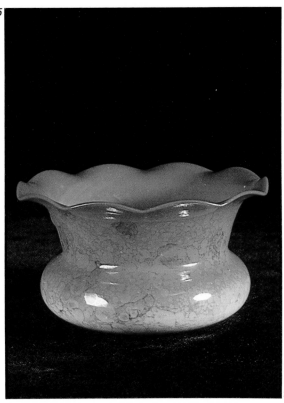

Museum Photo

Fig. 4 **Wild Rose vase**, *New England Glass Company, 1885–88. Height 8¼ ins. (Corning Museum of Glass.)*

Fig. 5 **Agata bowl**, *New England Glass Company, 1887–88. Diameter 5¼ ins. (Corning Museum of Glass. L. K. Ford Collection.)*

Fig. 6 **Plated Amberina vase**, *New England Glass Company. Height 8¼ ins. (Corning Museum of Glass. Mr. and Mrs. Richard Greger Collection.)*

Corning Museum Photo

7

Museum Photo

8

Museum Photo

9

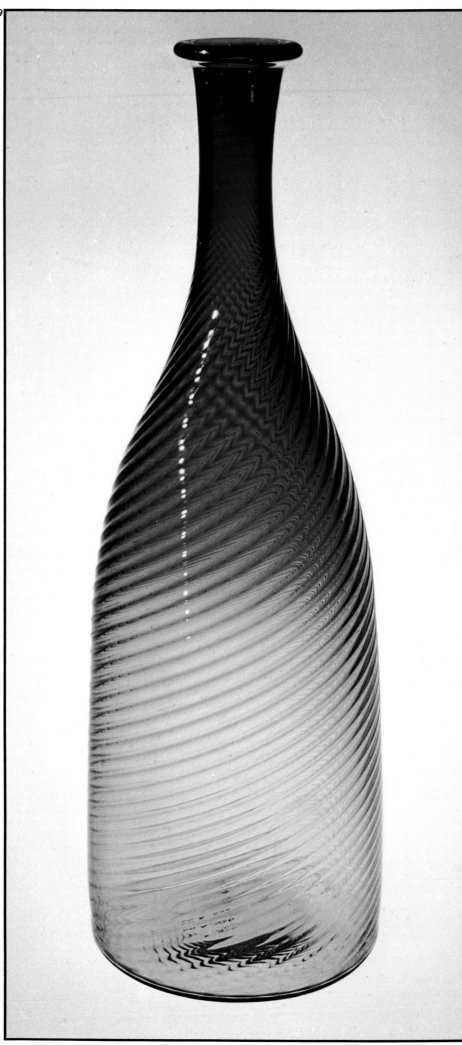

Fig. 7 *Burmese candleholder*,
*Mount Washington Glass
Company, 1885–95. 'Burmese'
glass, height 7½ ins.
A contemporary price-list shows
that these candleholders were
sold for $15 a dozen.
(Corning Museum of Glass.)*

Fig. 8 *Royal Flemish bottle*,
*Mount Washington Glass
Company, c.1890. Colourless
glass decorated with light stains
and raised gilding, height 13 ins.
This firm was called the
'Headquarters in America for
Art Glass'.
(Corning Museum of Glass.
L. K. Ford Collection.)*

Fig. 9 *Amberina glass bottle*,
*New England Glass Company,
1883–88. Pattern-moulded
bi-partite glass, height 9⅞ ins.
This was the earliest sort of
shaded art glass to achieve
success, and it attracted many
imitators.
(Corning Museum of Glass.)*

Fig. 10 *Vase, Hobbs-
Brockunier & Company,
1886–91.
Ruby-opalescent glass pressed in
a mould with hobnails, height
6½ ins.
A paper label on the base reads
'Patented June 1, 1886.'
(Corning Museum of Glass.)*

Brothers', became popular and continued to be decorated by them after they left the Sandwich firm, but they were also made and decorated by other firms. Many of the blanks decorated by the Smith brothers were made in Europe, probably in Germany or Bohemia, although some were obtained from the Mount Washington Glass Company. A photograph of the Smith Brothers' display at an unidentified trade show illustrates the wide variety of opal lamp-shades decorated by them. It probably dates from about 1880. A stereoscopic view of the New England Glass Company's showroom, taken in about 1875, indicates that that firm was also a major producer of this type of ware, as was the Mount Washington Glass Company, which constantly advertised 'opal decorated wares' among its products. Frederick S. Shirley, an Englishman with consummate glassmaking knowledge and considerable business acumen, became the agent of the latter company in 1874, and under his direction it developed into the 'Headquarters in America for Art Glass Wares'.

The first bi-partite, or shaded, art glass to achieve success was Amberina (Fig. 9); it was patented on 24 July, 1883, by Joseph Locke, another Englishman, who had emigrated to work for the New England Glass Company located in East Cambridge, near Boston, Massachusetts. This glass shaded gradually from an amber colour near the base to a deep ruby or fuchsia red at the top.

Pages from Locke's sketch-book, and the relatively large number of pieces still extant, indicate the wide variety of forms and the extensive production of Amberina. Its success was so great that it was copied by the Mount Washington Glass Company, which, after being threatened with a lawsuit by the New England Glass Company, agreed to call its product 'Rose Amber', although their advertisements frequently used the terms 'Rose Amberina' and 'Amberina'.

The development of other shaded art glasswares followed rapidly. On 15 December, 1885, Shirley, of the Mount Washington Glass Company, was granted a patent for Burmese glass (Fig. 7), an opaque glass containing gold and uranium oxides which produced a glass gradually shading from a delicate pale yellow to a plushy pink colour. This glass, too, caught the public's fancy and was a great commercial success. A price-list indicates that it was made in about two hundred and fifty different forms which were available in their natural glossy, or plush, finish, called 'satin glass' by today's collectors. A number of the forms were decorated.

Shirley's business acumen and salesmanship undoubtedly helped to make Burmese the success it was. He sent as a gift to his former queen, Victoria, a tea-set decorated with what he termed the 'Queen's Burmese' pattern (Fig. 12). He subsequently received an order from the Queen for more Burmese, and Thomas Webb & Sons of Stourbridge, England, were licensed by the Mount Washington Glass Company in 1886 to produce this glass; each piece was marked on the base: 'Thos. Webb & Sons, Queen's Burmese Ware, Patented'.

Peach Blow was another parti-coloured glassware produced by the Mount Washington Glass Company. It shaded from a slightly bluish white to a pink colour, and although very attractive, appears not to have been so commercially successful as Burmese. Nevertheless, it was emulated by the New England Glass Company, whose Wild Rose

shaded from white to a deep pink colour. Both firms produced these wares in natural and plush finishes, and both decorated some of them (Fig. 4).

The most popular of the Peach Blow glasses was that made by the Hobbs-Brockunier Company, of Wheeling, West Virginia, which they termed 'Coral'. It was a cased, or plated, glass, consisting of an opaque-white interior covered with a thin layer of transparent glass shading from a pale yellowish colour at the base to a deep orange-red at the top (Fig. 1).

Very much like Coral, or Wheeling Peach Blow, except in colour is the New England Glass Company's Plated Amberina, for which a patent was issued to Edward D. Libbey on 15 June, 1886. It is apparently Amberina encasing an opaque-white glass, and is almost always pattern-moulded (Fig. 6). It was seemingly produced in limited quantities, and is much sought after by collectors.

Joseph Locke, of the New England Glass Company, was granted a patent on 18 January, 1887, for Agata glassware (Fig. 5), which was simply Wild Rose glass which had been decorated by brownish and purplish stains, usually applied in a random splotched pattern. This was achieved by partially or wholly covering an article with a metallic stain or mineral colour and then spattering it with a volatile liquid such as alcohol, benzene or naphtha. This produced a mottled effect which became permanent when fired. Agata, which is usually found in the same forms as Wild Rose, was not commercially successful, and it is rare today.

Popular satin glass was widely produced

Probably, Pearl Satin Ware, or 'satin glass', as it is most frequently called today, was one of the most popular types of art glass, and it was widely produced. Frederick Shirley was granted a trademark for Pearl Satin Ware on 29 June, 1886. Undoubtedly his glasshouse produced quantities of the ware, the satin-like finish of which was achieved by either exposing the glass to the fumes of hydrofluoric acid, or dipping it in a bath of this acid, for a few minutes. Thomas Webb & Sons was licensed in 1886 by the Mount Washington Glass Company to produce Pearl Satin Ware.

Hobbs-Brockunier & Company is one of the best-known to collectors for its art glass. A pink and white satin-ware vase decorated with an invitation to President Cleveland to visit Wheeling and the Hobbs-Brockunier factory, now in the Oglebay Museum, Wheeling, is an example of this firm's production of this type of ware. This company also produced a wide variety of art glasses bearing applied decoration, as well as a variety of novelty forms – some mould-blown, others pressed – and many coloured glasses.

In 1883 William Leighton Jr. originated a spangled glass, which was made by picking up flakes of mica on an initial gather of glass, then covering them over with a glass of another colour. Figure 10 illustrates a ruby-opalescent vase bearing a label reading: 'Patented June 1, 1886'. In February 1886, the New England Glass Company licensed this firm to manufacture pressed Amberina.

Two other types of art glass utilising applied glass for decorative effects were mechanically threaded glass (Fig. 3) and 'overshot', or 'ice', glass. The

Fig. 11 *Page from a catalogue of the Pairpoint Manufacturing Company, New Bedford, Massachusetts, c.1894.*
One of the best customers of the Mount Washington Glass Company was the Pairpoint Manufacturing Company which made silver-plated mounts for art glass. It was established next door to the glassworks in 1880, and later took over the glassmaking operation.
(Corning Museum of Glass.)

Boston & Sandwich Glass Company, established in Sandwich, Cape Cod, Massachusetts, in 1825 and noted for its production of 'lacy' pressed glass in its earlier years, made both types of glasses. Often these mechanically threaded pieces were engraved above the threading with marshland scenes or foliate forms.

Numerous companies produced art glass, but obviously the Mount Washington Glass Company was justified in describing itself as 'Headquarters in America for Art Glass'. In addition to the art glasses noted above, this firm produced a wide variety of 'rich decorated' ware. This included opal-decorated glass, Albertine, Crown Milano, Napoli and Royal Flemish (Fig. 8). Except for the last, which was a colourless glass decorated with thin stains and raised gilding, all these glasses were

cameo glassmaking enjoyed a revival after John Northwood sucessfully copied the Portland vase in 1876, little true cameo glass was made in America. But acid-etched cameo glass was another product of the Mount Washington Glass Company. Although produced largely in the form of bowls, often intended for use in silver-plated holders, this type of glass was also used in lamps. These 'cameos' are found in translucent pink, light blue and yellow glasses cased over opal or opaque-white glass. The designs usually consist of classical or pseudo-classical motifs (Fig. 2).

The production of art glass declined as the century drew to a close and ceased by 1900. Its place was largely taken by glass in the Art Nouveau style, an entirely different artistic expression and another chapter in the history of glass.

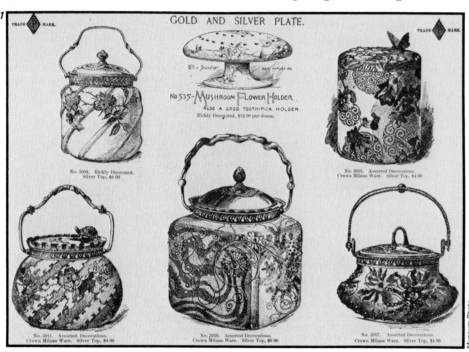

Fig. 12 *Burmese lamp, Mount Washington Glass Company, 1885–95. Decorated with the Queen's Burmese pattern, height about 20 ins.*
A shrewd businessman, Shirley of the Mount Washington Glass Company assured the success of his Burmese glass by sending to Queen Victoria a tea-set decorated with this pattern. He subsequently received an order for more Burmese, and Thomas Webb and Sons of Stourbridge, England, were licensed to produce the glass in large quantities.
(Mr. and Mrs. Samuel Feld Collection.)

opaque white, richly enamelled and gilded. Many examples of Crown Milano and Royal Flemish glass are exotic in form and decoration.

A number of these art glasses were used in silver-plated stands or holders, and silver-plating companies purchased a considerable portion of the output of art glass. One of the best customers of the Mount Washington Glass Company was the Pairpoint Manufacturing Company. This firm was established in 1880 in New Bedford, Massachusetts, next door to the glassworks. Some of its officers were also associated with the glassworks and in 1894 the latter became part of the Pairpoint Manufacturing Company, but it retained its own name for many years afterwards. Many types of glass made by this glassworks are illustrated in catalogues of the Pairpoint Manufacturing Company (Fig. 11). It is evident from these catalogues that the same type of glass was called by more than one name.

Novelty wares of decorated opal glass were also part of this company's production. They included decorated eggs and tomato-forms to be used as salt- and pepper-shakers, sugar-sifters and containers for marmalade, sugar, sweetmeats or rose-leaves. The Smith Brothers' firm also decorated some eggs which were made to stand at an angle, to circumvent the Mount Washington Glass Company's patent for the upright egg.

In contrast to England, where the ancient art of

MUSEUMS AND COLLECTIONS

American art glass may be seen at the following:

Corning, N.Y.:	Corning Museum of Glass
Milan, Ohio:	Milan Historical Museum
New York:	Metropolitan Museum of Art
Norfolk, Va.:	Walter Chrysler Museum
Toledo, Ohio:	Toledo Museum of Art

FURTHER READING

Art Glass Nouveau by Ray and Lee Grover, Rutland, Vermont, 1967.
Nineteenth Century Glass, its Genesis and Development by Albert C. Revi, New York, 1971.
Nineteenth Century Art Glass by Ruth Webb Lee, New York, 1952.
Pairpoint Glass by Leonard Padgett, 1978.
American Art Nouveau Glass by Albert C. Revi, 1981.

SHAKER FURNITURE

Shaker furniture, with its ingenuity, simple design and excellent workmanship, is admired throughout the world as a fine example of functional art

Shaker furniture is a physical manifestation of the discipline and moral values of a religious group which created the austere style that is so admired today. It is as if the precepts of modern designers were conceived and executed in the early nineteenth century long before the modern concept of functionalism was mentioned.

The Shakers were a religious sect founded by Mother Ann Lee in England during the eighteenth century. In 1758, when Ann was twenty-two years old, she became a Quaker; she later married and had four children. It was religion that gave her the power to become a leader during a period when women did not normally have such rights. In prison, where she was sent in 1770 for profaning the Sabbath, she meditated and began to believe that she was the daughter of Christ.

Mother Ann, her husband and a few of her sect left England for the Colonies in 1774. The group, with the exception of Ann's husband who left her for another woman, founded a settlement in Watervliet, New York, where they could farm, garden, prosper and practise the many rules of their religion.

The history of the growth of the Shaker families is remarkable, for Mother Ann decreed celibacy and it was only through conversion that new Shakers could join. The rules of each settlement were strict. Hard work was required, and frivolity was unknown; only the 'dancing' at their religious services offered any respite. The Shaker religion was at its height in 1860 when eighteen settlements with 6,000 members were located in the United States – in New England, New York, Ohio and Kentucky. What is also remarkable is that such a small group should have been so original in their thinking and arts while remaining so rigid in their social behaviour. Their inventions were many and included the flat broom, the automatic spring, the

Derek Balmer

Fig. 1 *Room in the style of the early nineteenth century. (American Museum in Britain, Claverton Manor, near Bath.)*

2

Fig. 2 **Ladder-back chair** from
Pleasant Hill, Kentucky, first
quarter of the nineteenth
century. Cherry or walnut painted
red, with the original seat-tapes.
These seat-tapes were a popular
Shaker product and were sold to
surrounding communities.
(Shakertown, Pleasant Hill,
Kentucky.)

Fig. 3 **Round stand** from New
Lebannon, c.1820. Cherry,
height 27 ins.
Evolved from the early
candlestand, these round stands
were made for the retiring-room.
They were very important to the
Shakers, whose rules stated that
'one or two stands should be
provided for the occupants of
every retiring-room'. Other types
were used for such purposes as
washing and sewing.
(American Museum in Britain.)

clothes-peg, metal pen-point, a chair-leg that tilted,
the threshing machine, pea-sheller, apple-corer,
static electricity machine and the circular saw.

Mother Ann said: 'Do all your work as though you
had a thousand years to live, and as you would know
you must die tomorrow'. If a Shaker baked a pie or
made a chair, the result was to be as close to perfection as possible. Perhaps it was this philosophy,
together with the prohibition on unnecessary
decoration, that led to the Shaker style.

Shaker furniture is an extension of the religious
beliefs of the group and, in order to appreciate the
design and ingenuity of the Shaker craftsman, the
ideology must be considered. Some Shakers
believed that the furniture designs were originated
in heaven and transmitted to the craftsman through
angels. The quality of workmanship was always
high and the wood carefully selected for suitability
and well seasoned. Old-growth pine, maple, cherry,
pear, apple and walnut were all favoured.

Designs had to conform to religious principles

Many of the Shakers came from rural areas and
were familiar with the work of the country craftsman; provincial styles influenced all the work done
in the Shaker villages. When a convert joined a
Shaker community, he brought with him his
family, his money and his humble possessions.

It was the country furniture of the times that
furnished the Shaker homes – Windsor chairs,
banister-back, slat-back and Dutch-style chairs,
stretcher-tables, chests of drawers, cottage beds and
candlestands. The need was so great that all
furniture was accepted and used even though the
pieces might have been ornate.

The communal groups began to build their own
houses and meeting-places by 1788. Converts were
often very poor and could not afford to buy
furniture. The first chair-factory, blacksmith's shop
and tannery were in use in New Lebannon (Mount
Lebonannan), New York, by 1789. In a few years,
the Shakers were also making bricks, whips, felt
hats, silk, nails, medicine, shoes and woollens. They
made almost everything that was needed for the
community except satin and glass.

The furniture-makers were, however, faced with
a problem of design. They had to follow the teachings of Mother Ann, who said: 'Whatever is
fashioned, [let] it be plain and simple . . . unembel-
lished by any superfluities which add nothing to its
goodness or durability'. Some designs, such as the
highboy, the canopy-bed and elaborate chairs, were
not only difficult to make, but also too ornate for
the religious teaching. Some plain forms such as
candlestands, trestle-tables, slat-back chairs and
low-post beds were acceptable, but the cabinet-
makers adapted the designs to conform with their
materials, needs and religious views. No carving,
inlays or veneers were used. Turnings were used
only in a functional way, with no excess permitted.
The designs became more and more restrained until
even the bulk of wood was diminished to the
absolute minimum. Chair-posts were sometimes as
small as half an inch in thickness and were rarely
over an inch in diameter. 'Sinful' mishandling of
the furniture was never permitted in Shaker
dwellings and many of the lighter pieces have
survived.

There are a few design characteristics that can be
noted in all Shaker pieces which are a result of the
drive toward simplicity and usefulness. Rod-shaped
and slightly tapered turnings on the furniture legs
can be found; they often have almost no foot. Metal
mounts are omitted, only simple, turned pegs being
used for drawer-handles. Exposed dovetailing has a
decorative value, but was only included for structural reasons. Large chests and counters had
sharply angled bracket feet designed to hold great
weights. Beds had large wooden castors for ease of
movement. Extra drawers or drop-leaves added to
the usefulness of many tables and stands. Many
chairs, tables and stands were designed very low by
today's standards. The finish used on all pieces was
similar: red, yellow and green stain and a light
varnish or oil were used on the furniture made in all
the settlements.

The backs of pieces of furniture were as perfectly
finished as the fronts. No Shaker pieces are found
with poor finishing, sloppy paint-work or uneven
measurements.

That some new forms were developed seems
consistent with the inventive nature of the Shaker.
The sewing-desk was a form which differed from
society to society. Combination pieces were made
for dual purpose. One type of chair had an extra
top-rail to hold the folded bedspread. Pegboards
for the walls, swivel stools and wall clocks seem to
be unique to the Shakers.

The earliest cabinet-makers among the Shakers
started with chairs. The craftsman kept refining the
ladder-back chair until the characteristic design
appeared. The first factory-made chairs appeared in
1789 and they were evidently sold to surrounding
areas the following year. From this time until about
1860, the three-slat side-chair was made. This chair
had turned front and back uprights, the rear
uprights ending in acorn-shaped finials. The slats
were slightly concave, to adjust to the shape of the
user's back, and were about twelve inches long and
two and a half inches wide. The arms were shaped,
slightly flared and held to the front upright by
sockets. Two box-stretchers on the legs helped to
give the chair structural soundness. The legs were
made of plain turnings.

The rocking-chair was popular among the Shakers

The seat was of rush, splint or a colourful and
popular woven tape that was made by Shaker
women and sold to surrounding communities
(Fig. 2). Most chairs were made of maple. Some
were made of birch, cherry or butternut, with pine,
ash or hickory for specialised parts.

The dining-chair was a special Shaker form. It
was made so low that it could be pushed under the
table when not in use. The chair usually had one slat
across the back and was twenty-five inches high,
with the seat set only sixteen inches from the floor.
The seat was wider in the front than in the back, for
added comfort. There was a two-slat version of the
low dining-chair, but the design seemed to be a
regional one. A one-slat chair appears in Massachusetts, and in later years, the two-slat variety
appeared in New York and New Hampshire.

The rocking-chair was one of the most important
Shaker designs and was popular with the many
elderly people who lived in the Shaker communi-

Derek Balmer

4

Derek Balmer

Fig. 4 *Tailoress' counter from
Watervliet, New York, 1820–30.
Pine and curly maple.*
*The first Shaker settlement was
founded in 1774 by Mother Ann
at Watervliet, the origin of this
beautiful piece. Note the fine
grain of the wood, discreet
moulding along the drawers,
simple turned knobs and delicate
but sturdy tapered legs.*
(American Museum in Britain.)

Fig. 5 *Press, nineteenth century.
By the middle of the nineteenth
century, the influence of the
'worldly' people could be seen in
some Shaker furniture, especially
that from Kentucky. Note here
the decorative turning on the legs
which would certainly not have
been found on an early press, but
which does nothing to negate the
pure functionalism of the piece.
(Shaker Museum, Auburn,
Kentucky.)*

ties. The chair was very similar to the side-chair,
but had four slats and arms in several different
styles. Five types of rocker were made; the scroll-
arm, rolled-arm, front upright with mushroom end
(Fig. 1), cross-rail and armless sewing-rocker are
the types now recognised. Each one was named
for its most obvious design feature. Some rockers
were made with drawers which held sewing-equip-
ment, with special tray-like arms and with other
refinements. The male Shakers, like most men,
could not resist tipping back their side-chairs, so
an inventive member of the sect developed a tilting-
chair. A ball-and-socket device was made to fit the
back legs so that they remained vertical when the
chair was tipped.

Shaker chairs were so well made and so cheap
that thousands were sold outside the Shaker settlements. In 1807 the chairs were sold for seventy-five
cents each. By 1828 a rocker cost two dollars and
fifty cents. The chairs were advertised in newspapers, and sales brochures were distributed.
Marked examples are occasionally found with a
'No. 3', or another number ranging from one to
eight, according to size, on the label. The chair was
larger, wider and higher, and made to suit the
physique of the buyer.

The Shakers ate in communal dining-rooms; the
brothers at one sitting and the sisters at another.
The dining-table was of a trestle type with a shoe
foot, and had two or three boards in the top. The
rectangular top was up to twenty-eight inches wide
and up to eight feet long. One very large communal
dining-table that still exists is twenty feet long.
A characteristic underbracing is seen on most of the
tables and benches. The parts were joined with
mortice and tenon joints. Early tables and benches
were stained dark red, but later a light stain and
varnish were used that allowed the grain of the
wood to show.

Shaker beds were cots only three feet wide

Shaker chests were made with simple, moulded
edges and turned wooden knobs (Fig. 4), and were
often built into the room as a permanent part of its
design (Fig. 6). Mushroom-shaped turnings as
knobs were preferred at some settlements. The
cupboard doors were narrow, held closed with
wrought-iron catches. Each member of the society
had a limited number of drawers and cupboards for

Shaker Furniture

Kalman Papp

personal use.

The free-standing chests were of two types: a high chest slightly over five feet tall, made of maple, birch or butternut, and a small chest that was under three feet high. The high chest had four full-width drawers topped by four half-width drawers in two tiers. The low chest had one row of half-width drawers and three full-width drawers.

Shaker beds were simple cots, about three feet wide (Fig. 7). The bed had a short headboard and a shorter footboard. Almost all of the beds were painted green. Each bed had rollers or castors so that it could be moved for easier cleaning. The bed was made with lightweight slats that could 'give' with the body – a great improvement over the ropes that were used on 'worldly' beds.

The Shaker stands were numerous. The rules of the Shakers stated: 'One or two stands should be provided for the occupants of every retiring-room'. The sewing-shops had stands for one or two workers. The washstand, of course, was important for cleanliness; it often had a tapered shaft sup-

turning or curve of the leg is seen on a press or stand (Fig. 5); even a shaped apron on a chest might be rarely found in Ohio. The character of the design, the simplicity of the approach and the obvious attention to excellence that marks all Shaker furniture remained in even the less pure examples dating from the 1860s.

Today, there are only four living Shakers, all women, who reside in a Shaker community in Maine. Mother Ann predicted that one day there would be too few Shakers remaining to bury the dead, but she also had another vision; that when the Shakers numbered less than seven, there would be a great revival. Although the religious views of celibacy and perfect order seem to have little appeal to the masses today, it is interesting that the culture of the Shakers, their architecture and furniture has been of increasing interest to the United States. The old Shaker villages are being preserved and restored and the furnishings of the Shakers are known throughout the world as fine examples of functional design.

Author's Photo

Fig. 6 **Shaker storeroom.**
Cupboards were often built into a room as a permanent part of the architecture in Shaker houses. Here, a typical Shaker chair hangs from a pegboard, as was the custom when the floors were being cleaned.
(Henry Francis du Pont Winterthur Museum, Winterthur, Delaware.)

Fig. 7 **Shaker bedroom,** *with a Pleasant Hill walnut bed and a cherry washstand, both made in the first quarter of the nineteenth century.*
Shaker beds were simple cots with lightweight slats instead of the rope bases, common then. Almost all were painted green.
(Center Family House, Shakertown, Pleasant Hill.)

ported by three rod-like feet. Round-topped stands that were evolved from the early candlestand were made for the retiring-room (Fig. 3); square-topped sewing-stands with small, underslung drawers were used for sisters in the workrooms.

The Shakers made almost every type of furniture needed for the settlements. Clocks, boxes, box desks, baskets, work-tables, stoves, standing-racks to hold bedding, racks of shelves to hold dishes, bookcases, wood-boxes, blanket-chests and small hanging-cupboards are still to be seen.

Although Shaker furniture was supposedly made by closely following the designs passed on to the craftsmen by angels and the rules of Mother Ann, by the 1850s the influence of the 'worldly' people could also be seen in some pieces. The change was particularly apparent in the furniture of the Kentucky Shakers. Slat-back chairs, with flattened back stiles, and bentwood chairs were made. Tables, stands, and desks were often heavier in construction and lost some of the characteristic Shaker delicacy.

Furniture produced in the East was often made of maple, cherry, butternut and other similar woods, but in Ohio and Kentucky, poplar (whitewood) and black walnut were favoured. Sometimes, an extra

MUSEUMS AND COLLECTIONS

Shaker furniture may be seen at the following:

Boston:	Boston Museum of Fine Arts
Philadelphia:	Philadelphia Museum of Art
Shaker Heights, Ohio:	Shaker Historical Society
Winterthur, Del.:	Henry Francis Du Pont Winterthur Museum

FURTHER READING

The American Shakers and Their Furniture by John G. Shea, New York, 1971.
Religion in Wood, a Book of Shaker Furniture by E. D. and F. Andrews, Bloomington, Indiana, 1966.
American Country Furniture 1780–1875 by Ralph and Terry Kovel, New York, 1965.
The Shakers: Their Arts and Crafts, Philadelphia Museum of Art, Philadelphia, 1980.
Shaker Furniture by E. D. and Faith Andrews, New Haven, 1937.
Illustrated Guide to Shaker Furniture by Robert Meader, New York, 1972.

American Art Pottery

Fig. 1 **Vase**, *Grueby Faience and Tile Company, early twentieth century. Lustreless dark green matt glaze and decoration suggestive of plant forms, modelled in low relief, height 11⅝ ins.*
(All the pottery illustrated is from the collection of the Smithsonian Institution, Washington, D.C.)

Fig. 2 **Weller Sicardo plaque**, *Samuel A. Weller factory, Zanesville, Ohio, early twentieth century. Iridescent purple ground almost entirely covered with metallic lustre, signed 'Sicard', 13 ins. x 16 ins. The most significant contribution of the Weller firm was Sicardo, created by the French potter Jacques Sicard. A similar ware using metallic lustres was made some years later under the name of Weller 'Lasa'.*

Inspired by oriental ware shown at the Centennial Exhibition in Philadelphia, commercial firms and amateurs turned to the production of artistic pottery

With the exception of the Robertsons' Chelsea Keramic Art Works, started at Chelsea, Massachusetts, in 1866, art pottery as such did not exist in the United States prior to 1879.

The early potters, such as Norton & Fenton, the United States Pottery Co., at Bennington, Vermont, and others, were primarily commercial. Although they did turn out highly artistic wares much prized by collectors, they were not art potters.

True art pottery, where emphasis was on decoration rather than utility, did not arouse much interest until after the Centennial Celebration in 1876. Then Cincinnati, Ohio, became the focal point for this emerging art industry and, within the decade 1879 to 1889, no less than six art potteries were founded in that city: the T. J. Wheatley Pottery; the Cincinnati Art Pottery; the Matt Morgan Art Pottery; the pottery of M. Louise McLaughlin, produced under the name 'Losanti'; the Avon Pottery; and the Rookwood Pottery. Five of the six had discontinued production by 1890, however, and only Rookwood survived to make its influence felt in later years.

That five of the six failed so quickly is surprising in view of the expanding wealth of the country. The ranks of the rich were being swelled by those who founded fortunes on inventions and new ventures; scars left by the Civil War were largely overlooked in this period of expanding trade and frontiers, and growing population.

This was the economic situation when William A. Long organised the Lonhuda Pottery at Steubenville, Ohio, in 1892 and hired Laura Fry, an experienced Rookwood decorator, to help initiate the production of Lonhuda art pottery.

Samuel A. Weller, owner of a commercial pottery in Zanesville, Ohio, was attracted by Lonhuda's exhibit at the Chicago World's Fair the following year and negotiated with Long to acquire the

Pottery. Under Long's direction, operations were transferred to Weller's plant in Zanesville and the Lonhuda style of art pottery continued under the new name of 'Louwelsa' Weller. Minor variations were introduced under the names 'Aurelian' and 'Eocean'. All three styles were decorated with pictures of flowers, fruits, animals and American Indians, slip-painted on a dark ground under a high glaze, and they closely resembled the Rookwood Standard wares of the period.

New styles were developed rapidly, however. Dickensware, usually decorated with drawings of characters or scenes from the works of Charles Dickens, became popular (Fig. 6). Sicardo, the most significant contribution of the Weller firm to art pottery's development, was the creation of Jacques Sicard, a French potter employed by Weller. It was characterised by designs in metallic lustres over iridescent grounds of dark purples, greens and browns (Figs. 2 and 7). A similar ware, decorated with landscape scenes, was made some years later under the name Weller 'Lasa'.

Weller continued to expand the production of art pottery by adding two or more new styles to his repertoire each year and, in 1910, advertised the firm as 'the largest pottery in the world . . .'. It may have been; certainly the amount of Weller available today would indicate that the operation was quite extensive.

Mr. Long, a key figure in involving Weller in art pottery in 1895, did not remain with that organisation. Before the year was out, Long transferred his interests to another Zanesville firm, the J. B. Owens Pottery Company.

Owens' was a successful commercial pottery, and when Long took his knowledge of slip decoration and glaze formulas there in 1896, the organisation began the production of an art pottery closely resembling Weller's Louwelsa, under the name of Owens 'Utopian'. Additional styles were added rapidly, however, and in 1904, when the Owens firm published a forty-page catalogue, it listed eight hundred items in a dozen different lines. Although each line was given a name descriptive of the ware, these were not marked on the ware, only the Owens name being used. Most of the Owens production was of a high grade, but none of the new styles merited special acclaim. Owens, at the height of his art pottery production, employed a

Fig. 3 *Roseville Pottery Company wares*, Zanesville, Ohio. From left to right: *White Rose vase, matt painted on a cast shape, height* $4\frac{1}{2}$ *ins*; *Rozane Royal vase, c.1905, light ground, height 8 ins*; *Rozane Egypto candlestick, matt dark green, height* $3\frac{3}{4}$ *ins*; *Rozane Royal vase, c.1901, dark ground, height* $5\frac{1}{4}$ *ins.*

Fig. 4 *Newcomb Pottery vases*, New Orleans. Left: *Matt-glazed, signed by Henrietta Bailey, after 1910, height* $8\frac{1}{4}$ *ins.* Right: *High-glazed, attributed to Mazie T. Ryan, 1897–1910, height* $11\frac{3}{4}$ *ins.*

Fig. 5 *Van Briggle Pottery Company vases*, Colorado Springs, *typical designs, height of tallest vase 15 ins.*

Fig. 6 *Weller Dickensware vases*, c.1902. Left: *Matt painted, height* $8\frac{3}{4}$ *ins.* Right: *More unusual high glaze, height* $10\frac{1}{2}$ *ins.*

staff of forty artists to decorate his wares. He may have become over-extended, however, for he did not survive the depression of 1907.

A third Zanesville firm classed as a commercial art pottery was the Roseville Pottery Company, which started in business in Roseville, Ohio, in 1892. By 1900 the Company had acquired a plant in Zanesville, and George F. Young, the general manager, attracted by the apparent success of Weller and Owens, commenced the manufacture of art pottery (Fig. 3).

The initial Roseville line was named 'Rozane'. Slip-painted on a dark ground and finished with a high glaze, it too, closely resembled the initial production of Weller and Owens. The name 'Rozane' was usually incised on the ware, frequently accompanied by the letters 'R P CO' (for Roseville Pottery Company). This first line, renamed 'Rozane Royal' to distinguish it from other styles introduced under the Rozane label, was continued for many years. In an effort to match its local competition, however, Roseville brought out new styles with increasing frequency. These tended more and more in the direction of modelled designs in matt-glaze colours. What Roseville lacked in artistic quality, it endeavoured to offset by the great variety of new designs which it continued to bring out. Later wares carried the name 'Roseville' impressed or embossed, and are found in considerable abundance today.

While mass-produced art pottery was being exploited by makers in Zanesville, more important developments were taking place in other sections of the country.

In New Orleans, Louisiana, the Newcomb Pottery was organised in 1897 as an adjunct to the art department of the Sophie Newcomb Memorial College for Women. Professor Woodward, head of the department, believed that a pottery operated as part of the college curriculum would offer practical training in art and design as well as actual experience in a field open to women artists. He engaged Miss Mary Sheerer, a graduate of the Cincinnati Art Academy, to direct the operation.

As the Cincinnati Art Academy and the Rookwood Pottery maintained close ties, Miss Sheerer was undoubtedly acquainted with the styles and the artists of that pottery, if not its methods and

Museum Photo

Museum Photo

techniques. It was her first intention at Newcomb to develop a pottery patterned after Rookwood's rich dark colours and under-glaze slip decoration, which was then becoming a national style. Fortunately, her attempts in this direction met with failure. In its place, an alternative was developed that distinguished Newcomb in a way that would never have happened if the pottery had relied on imitating Rookwood.

The ware that brought prominence to the southern college pottery was a carved style employing motifs indigenous to its locality – rice, cotton, magnolia and other plants – executed schematically. Miss Sheerer designed the shapes; the pots were thrown and then decorated by the students. Designs were carved or incised and then delicately sponged, exposing on the body surface a fine sand which served to produce a misty effect beneath the glaze (Fig. 4).

Shortly after 1910, a new style was developed. This also was based on local flora but the carved or incised decoration was executed in a more naturalistic manner, and the ware was finished in a matt glaze. Use of the earlier gloss glazes was gradually phased out until the matt glazes were exclusively employed on the later Newcomb pieces.

At East Boston, Massachusetts, William H. Grueby formed the Grueby Faience and Tile Company to exploit a matt glaze which he perfected after seeing the dull glazes used by the French potter Delaherche on ware exhibited at the Chicago World's Fair. The appearance of Grueby's matt glaze – actually an opaque enamel – attracted tremendous interest in the American ceramic industry, and it was soon imitated by virtually every pottery in the country. Grueby's products were characterised by heavy potting, modelled designs based on plant forms in low relief and a monochrome finish most often seen in a dark green (Fig. 1). All pots were thrown, individually decorated and usually signed by the artist, but not all were permanently marked with the Grueby name as some wares were sold with only a paper label for identification. Other colours were also used – yellows, browns, blues, purples – but the Grueby green seemed best suited to the plant forms.

Grueby's work was widely copied by the other potteries – the stylised plant forms as well as the glaze. It is ironic that this imitation by far less qualified producers forced Grueby to suspend production when he found that he could not compete with the inferior, cheaper copies. The Grueby Faience Company, as it was then called, ceased production of art pottery in 1910. It continued to manufacture architectural tiles until a disastrous fire ended its existence in 1912.

At Colorado Springs, Colorado, Artus van Briggle, who had been one of the foremost decorators at the Rookwood Pottery until ill health forced him to seek a change in climate, established a pottery under his own name in 1901. During the next three years, Van Briggle created pottery which reflected his belief that decoration should be an integral part of each shape and not merely an addition to it. This belief is reflected in the flowing forms of the Art Nouveau style characteristic of the work of the Van Briggle Pottery (Fig. 5). An early exponent of matt glaze (Van Briggle initiated interest in matt glaze at Rookwood in 1896), he produced a wide range of beautiful colours in a softly glowing matt finish. Artus van Briggle died in 1904,

American
Art Pottery

Fig. 7 *Weller Sicardo vase signed by Sicard, c.1903. Metallic lustre over iridescent green, height 26⅛ ins.*

Fig. 8 *Dedham ware, Dedham Pottery, Massachusetts, after 1895. Left to right: Jug in the Morning and Night pattern (owl on reverse represents Night), height 5 ins; Sugar-bowl in Rabbit pattern, diameter 4 ins; Plate with fleur-de-lis border, diameter 8½ ins; Knife-rest, height 2½ ins.*

tion, Robertson produced a crackle glaze on a heavy stoneware attractively decorated with borders of bird and animal designs. 'Dedham Ware', as it was promptly called, was made in forty-eight patterns and proved very popular. It is recognised today as a distinctive American pottery style (Fig. 8).

A number of other art potteries operated in the United States during this period. The seven described here, in addition to the Rookwood Pottery of Cincinnati, exerted the greatest influence on the development of ceramic art in America.

7

8

Fig. 9 *Marks on American art pottery from 1879.*

9

but the pottery was carried on under the able direction of his artist wife. Mrs. van Briggle continued to turn out ceramic pieces designed to comply to the basic concepts created by her husband. Early wares are marked with the name and sometimes dated; later productions carry the name of the pottery and an abbreviation for Colorado Springs.

At the Chelsea Keramic Art Works at Chelsea, Massachusetts, the craftsmanship of the Robertsons, father and two sons, produced a wide variety of ceramic art ranging from unglazed redware to the most intricately moulded articles finished in metallic glazes. The early items carry the name of the pottery or the initials 'C/KA/W' impressed in the ware, and they reveal a mastery of the details of the potter's art scarcely equalled elsewhere in the country at the time.

Following the Centennial Celebration (1876), Hugh Robertson, who succeeded his father as the master-potter, set out to duplicate some of the oriental glazes first seen at that exhibition. He reproduced the rich red of the Chinese *sang de boeuf* (oxblood), but it proved too costly to be of practical use. He also duplicated the crackle effect of the Japanese glazes, and this development turned into a commercial success. In 1895 the pottery was moved to Dedham, Massachusetts, and the name changed to the Dedham Pottery. At the new loca-

MUSEUMS AND COLLECTIONS

American art pottery may be seen at the following:

Chicago:	Art Institute of Chicago
Cincinnati:	Cincinnati Museum of Art
Newark, N.J.:	Newark Museum
New York:	Brooklyn Museum
	Metropolitan Museum of Art
Philadelphia:	Philadelphia Museum of Art
St. Louis:	City Art Museum of St. Louis
Washington, D.C.:	Smithsonian Institution
Worcester, Mass.:	Worcester Art Museum

FURTHER READING

Marks of American Potters by Edwin Atlee Barber, 1976 reprint.

American Art Pottery by Lucile Henzke, Camden, N.J., 1970.

The Van Briggle Story by Dorothy McGraw Bogue, Colorado Springs, 1969.

The Dedham Pottery by Lloyd E. Hawes, Dedham, Massachusetts, 1969.

Zanesville Art Pottery in Color by L. and E. Purviance and N. F. Schneider, Leon, Iowa, 1969.

DOLLS IN THE U.S.A.

1

Museum Photo

Fig. 1 *Ramshackle Inn,*
American, nineteenth century.
This Victorian dolls' house was a
gift to Mrs. J. Watson Webb,
founder with her husband of the
Shelburne Museum, from her
life-long friend Miss Zazu Pitts,
the famous comedienne. The hall
is furnished in miniature after the
set used in the stage-production
of the play Ramshackle Inn, *in*
which Miss Pitts starred.
(Shelburne Museum, Shelburne,
Vermont.)

American dolls, some of them walking and some even singing, enjoyed great popularity and affection in the second half of the nineteenth century

Until the growth of the toy-making industry in the nineteenth century, American dolls were somewhat primitive in appearance being largely dependent on the availability of local materials, and the influence of toys imported from Europe. From the middle of the century, however, they began to acquire that rather distinctive homespun character common to so much Americana, and the industry no longer relied so completely on its European counterpart. Doll-making centres in such places as Philadelphia, New England, Cincinnati and New York acquired a national reputation, with the last growing in pre-eminence and gaining an international reputation with the increased demand for American-made dolls after the First World War.

The first notable American-made dolls seem to be the rag dolls of Izannah Walker of Central Falls, Rhode Island, which her great-niece states were made as early as 1855. This is unlikely since she did not take out a patent until 1873, and, according to

patent law, it would have been illegal for her to have made these dolls before her application date which was June 1873. Her dolls are characterised by their hair, often with the then fashionable corkscrew-type curls painted in oil colours, and their delicate definition of ears, fingers and other details. They were made by several layers of stockinet material being treated with a stiffening agent and compressed into moulds; the hardened shells were then sewn together and stuffed. Surviving dolls in good condition are not only very attractive, but also unique, representing a breakthrough in doll-making at this time.

The earliest known patent issued to an American doll-maker was issued in 1858 for the papier-mâché doll's head made by Ludwig Greiner of Philadelphia. Greiner, a German by birth, had presumably been apprenticed to a doll-maker prior to emigrating to America in the 1830s, and his patent was an improvement on the papier-mâché dolls' heads currently being imported from his own country. He was not, however, as skilful as his fellow countrymen in the insertion of glass eyes, and these are seldom found. Brown painted eyes are a common characteristic as is also moulded hair with a centre parting.

Greiner heads are often found on Lacmann bodies, Jacob Lacmann being another Philadelphia doll-maker. His bodies of heavy cotton material

2

3

Museum Photo

4

Museum Photo

Fig. 2 **Doll** *by Bru Jne et Cie.,*
Paris and Montreuil-sous-Bois,
1866–99. Bisque head and
forearms, kid body, height 13 ins.
The company of Bru made dolls
dressed in the latest fashion with
luxurious materials until after
1925. Although intended for the
American market, the dolls were
also available in France.
(Shelburne Museum.)

Fig. 3 **Doll**, *American. Wood*
with glass eyes and stuffed body,
height 20 ins.
A convenient and inexpensive
material, wood has been used for
dolls throughout history. Many
were made in America by the
Co-operative Manufacturing
Company, which showed
examples at the Vienna
Exhibition of 1873.
(Shelburne Museum.)

Fig. 4 **Doll** *with twin babies in*
rocking-chair, pine with jointed
limbs held together with wooden
pegs. Height of large doll 10 ins.
(Shelburne Museum.)

Fig. 5 *Autoperipateti doll,*
American, 1862. Porcelain head,
kid arms and mechanical
walking-mechanism.
(Kay Desmonde Antiques,
London.)

provided appropriate mounts for the delicate but
rather primitive Greiner heads with their hollow
shoulders to which the stuffed bodies were
attached.

Another outstanding doll-maker working in
Philadelphia was Mary Steuber who, in 1878,
patented a commercial doll's leg, which obviated
the need for individually made feet and legs, and
thus separate stockings and boots.

Although much of the expertise and knowledge
shown by American doll-makers can be directly
traced to their European counterparts, the productions of the Jointed Doll Company in Springfield,
Vermont, and the Co-operative Doll Company
are distinctly individual and interesting. The
group of dolls originating from Springfield were
presumably invented by Joel Ellis, who took out a
patent for a jointed wooden doll in 1873. These
elegant and highly stylised dolls were made from
rock maplewood, with metal hands and feet and
heads moulded under hydraulic pressure. The wood
from which these dolls are made is supremely
durable and so they have survived well, although
their painted heads often suffer from chips and
flaking. The Ellis doll was copied and improved by
other Springfield manufacturers.

A number of delightful dolls were also made in
the mid-century, following the same lines as
German china dolls, but using such local materials
as leather, gutta-percha and rubber. Franklin
Darrow, of Bristol, Connecticut, took out a patent
in 1866 for making dolls' heads of rawhide leather,
the heads being pressed into shape and hand-
painted. Unfortunately rats and mice, having a
taste for animal skin, have deprived the would-be
collector of a number of fine examples.

Charles Goodyear, of the Goodyear Rubber

Company, was the inventor of vulcanised soft
rubber for dolls, and in 1851 his brother, Nelson,
invented hard rubber. They took out a U.S. patent
in 1853, and a British patent in 1855, and continued
to manufacture attractive rubber dolls until 1890,
or probably later.

Several types of mechanical doll were made in
America, one of the earliest being the Auto-
peripatetikos walking doll (Fig. 5), which was
patented in 1862 by Enoch Morrison, of New York
City, and was subsequently manufactured by several
other doll-makers in accordance with his patent.
The heads are found in various materials such as
untinted bisque, china, rag and papier mâché, the
first two showing an obvious confidence on the part
of the makers in the reliability of the walking
mechanism.

Another highly popular automated doll was the
Webber Singing Doll for which William Webber
was granted a patent in 1882. In the same year it
was reported that although large quantities of these
dolls were ready for the holiday trade, supplies were
exhausted by early December. The doll was described as 'of the finest French make, with wax head,
real hair and finest eyes, and is no different in
appearance from the best of imported dolls; but
within its body is a most ingenious machine which
when it is lightly pressed causes the dolls to sing one
of the following airs: "Home, Sweet Home",
"Glenville", "I want to be an Angel", "There is a
Happy Land", etc.'

An equally ingenious talking doll was the Edison
phonographic doll. A patent was taken out for these
in 1878. The earliest was described by *Harper's*
Young People in 1891 as bearing 'as little resemblance to the doll that he now manufactures as the
wood doll of the cave-dwellers bore to the dainty

6

Miki Slingsby

Miki Slingsby

Fig. 6 *Martha Chase stockinet doll*, c.1910. *Stockinet material stretched over a mark, coated with glue and hand painted; ears and thumbs applied separately. (Kay Desmonde Antiques.)*

Fig. 7 *Kewpie doll*, c.1920, *designed by Ernesto Peruggi and copyrighted by the Manhattan Toy and Doll Manufacturing Company. Rubber. (Kay Desmonde Antiques.)*

7

creature of the French court. Mr. Edison knew much more about phonographs than he did about nurseries.' By 1890 about five hundred people were engaged in the manufacture of the Edison doll producing an equivalent number of dolls each day. It took eighteen women alone to recite the nursery rhymes 'in a childish voice' for the cylinders that went into the dolls.

These are only a few of the manufacturers who founded a national doll industry which eventually relieved the necessity for importing from the Continent. Indeed in the twentieth century, many of the doll's heads manufactured in Germany were designed in America and within America, German imports decreased and home products increasingly crowded the market.

MUSEUMS AND COLLECTIONS

New York: Museum of the City of New York
Newark, N.J.: The Newark Museum

FURTHER READING

The Collector's Encyclopaedia of Dolls by Dorothy S., Elizabeth A., and Evelyn J. Coleman, New York, 1968.
Antique Collector's Dolls by Patricia Smith, 1975.
The Warner Collector's Guide to Dolls by Jean Bach, New York, 1982.

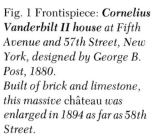

Fig. 1 Frontispiece: **Cornelius Vanderbilt II house** at Fifth Avenue and 57th Street, New York, designed by George B. Post, 1880.
Built of brick and limestone, this massive château was enlarged in 1894 as far as 58th Street.

Fig. 2 **Drawing-room** *of the William H. Vanderbilt house at Fifth Avenue between 51st and 52nd Streets, New York, decorated by Herter Brothers in the 1880s.*
Far less flamboyant architecturally than the house of his son, William K. Vanderbilt (Fig. 6), William H. Vanderbilt's house was no less rich in furnishing and decoration.

Bred from the French academic tradition and Ruskinian Gothic, a curious and elaborate architecture began to adorn the streets of New York in the later nineteenth century

It was not until the middle of the nineteenth century that stately mansions began to appear in America, heralding the arrival of a new class of citizen. In a country which had prided itself on its republican virtues and democratic spirit, the capitalist-*entrepreneur* appeared as something of a new breed. The older rural and agrarian society gave way to newer urban orientations.

Developments in New York City were central to this shift of orientation. 'New York', wrote James Fenimore Cooper in discussing the 'Emporium' of the New World, 'is essentially national in interests, position and pursuits. No one', he insisted, 'thinks of the place as belonging to a particular State, but to the United States'. New York was, at this moment in mid-century, largely the product of the tremendous expansion of the 1840s. During the decades immediately prior to the Civil War, the city was

undergoing a trying adolescence that would result in its becoming the financial capital of America and its empire city. The population of the city expanded rapidly as a great influx of immigrants pushed the settlement pattern to the northern reaches of Manhattan Island and into the adjacent areas in Brooklyn, Williamsburg and New Jersey.

The living conditions brought about by this tide of urban poor threatened to wipe away all that had once been heralded as beautiful about city life. Immigrants and displaced agricultural workers provided the manpower for rapidly expanding engines of commerce and industry. The contrasts of poverty and wealth not only filled popular literature, but also provided a cause for a variety of humanitarian enterprises.

There also emerged a peculiar stimulus to the expression of private wealth, for it was increasingly stated that if the rich applied their fortunes to noble, edifying or tasteful enterprises, the poor would learn by example. In the face of expanding slums and increased occupancy of tenements and boarding-houses, the sudden creation of palatial private homes found a curious rationale. Yet it was out of poverty that many millionaires traced their successful inspiration, and their homes might well be viewed as a final shaking of the fist at the demons of want and deprivation.

The Civil War proved an extraordinary stimulus to

Fig. 3 *William B. Astor house (foreground)*, 1856, *and A. T. Stewart house*, 1864–69, *at Fifth Avenue and 34th Street, New York. Astor's traditional brownstone was gallingly overshadowed by the grand, marble, Second Empire hôtel of his chief rival, Stewart.*

manufacturing and commerce, and the men who emerged at the head of new industrial and commercial enterprises possessed the typical ambitions and aspirations of the *nouveaux riches.* Among those who had turned shopkeeping into merchandising and big business, was the Scottish-Irish immigrant Alexander Turney Stewart, whose dry goods business had an annual retail volume of ten million dollars during the War. Supplementing this was a wholesale operation and a range of business investments which made Stewart, by the post-War decade, a contender for the title of 'richest man in America'.

It was probably with the knowledge that his chief competitor was William B. Astor that Stewart

Stewart had broken the mould in which the wealthy cast their lives. His house, while ornamenting and giving relief to the otherwise dreary stretches of brick and brownstone fronts, had by no means violated the notions of the propriety of street architecture and must have appeared dignified and restrained when measured against the elaborate pictorial solutions already being adopted for commercial and public architecture.

The dual loyalty to the lacy polychromy of Ruskinian Gothic and the sculptural massing of the French Second Empire style had given birth to the unique architectural forms which have become synonymous with the 'Gilded Age'. American

Museum of the City of New York: Byron Collection

Author's Photo

Fig. 4 *Senator Clark house at Fifth Avenue and 77th Street, New York, designed by Lord, Hewlett and Hull and K. Murchison in consultation with H. Deglane, built 1898-1904.*
Erected for the copper magnate Senator Clark from Montana, this striking example of lavish spending was demolished in 1927.

Fig. 5 *William B. Astor house at Fifth Avenue and 65th Street, New York, designed by Richard M. Hunt, built 1891-96.*
So great became the pressure to pioneer architecture that in the 1890's even the Astors moved from their brownstone house (Fig. 3) to this splendid double house uptown.

Fig. 6 *William K. Vanderbilt house at Fifth Avenue and 52nd Street, New York, designed by Richard Morris Hunt, built 1879–81.*

decided to erect a grand marble mansion on the north-west corner of Fifth Avenue and 34th Street, directly opposite Astor's more traditional brownstone residence. At this time, when men of Astor's long-standing fortune were still content to live in such self-effacing structures, Stewart's house must have appeared magnificent beyond description. Erected and furnished at a cost of around three million dollars, the Stewart house was an uneasy compromise between the severity of the Italian *palazzo* style and the recently introduced French Second Empire style. The exterior merely hinted at the elaborate richness of the interior, which displayed all those apartments considered essential for a gentleman of means: formal hall, reception-room, drawing-room, music-room, picture-gallery and library. The furnishings, like the owner's taste, were acquired principally during the period of the construction of the house.

At a time when the popular press was calling for the wealthy to endow the city with significant architectural monuments, the house was warmly received. Addressing a national audience in *Harper's Weekly*, one enthusiastic critic wrote: 'There is one edifice in New York that, if not swallowed up by an earthquake, will stand as long as the city remains, and will ever be pointed to as a monument of individual enterprise, of far-seeing judgment, and of disinterested philanthropy'.

architectural loyalties were undergoing a shift from the picturesque and largely rural styles derived from English sources to the urban architectural models of Paris as rebuilt by Napoleon III. The 1870s saw the establishment of the first American architectural schools and the emergent pre-eminence of French academic canons which, in the 1890s would finally dominate. Given the strong emphasis on convention in French academic training, it is ironic that it was the first American to study at the Ecole des Beaux-Arts in Paris who finally broke the assumptions of propriety in street architecture and introduced essentially rural models to the urban scene. In the process, Richard Morris Hunt helped make the millionaire's mansion an ancestral home and a fashionable palace.

Hunt's house for William K. Vanderbilt at the north-west corner of Fifth Avenue and 52nd Street was based on sixteenth-century *châteaux* of the Loire Valley. Built of Indiana limestone, a material that was suitable for both fine detailed carving and broad unornamented surfaces, the house demonstrated Hunt's mastery at massing and articulate detailing. While the detail and ornament was based on historical prototypes, its use here was dictated by the design rather than by the desire to load the structure with symbolic detail.

The palatial interiors of this house were largely designed by the architect. The elaborately carved

7

8

Fig. 7 **Interior,** *possibly the morning-room, of the A. T. Stewart house (see Figs. 3 and 8), decorated 1864-69.*
The grandiose exterior of Stewart's house merely hinted at the lavishness of the interior decoration. The furnishings, like the owner's taste, were acquired during the construction of the house and filled all the apartments considered essential for a gentleman of means.

Fig. 8 **Sunshine and Shadow in New York,** *late nineteenth century. Engraving.*
This title-page from a contemporary piece of social commentary shows the A. T. Stewart house (Fig. 3) in sharp contrast to the squalor of the poor. Although Stewart's house was well received by architectural critics, it encouraged the feelings of social injustice current in New York.

Caen stone main hall and staircase gave on to the splendid parlour, dining-hall, library and Moorish Room, composed of stucco, tile and onyx. Fashionable taste of the day preferred the styles of the Renaissance, Louis XIV and Louis XVI, yet even houses of this scale were subject to fits of redecorating and the Vanderbilt house was no exception. The French renaissance detailing of the parlour and library gave way to a more discreet Louis XV decorative scheme before the entire establishment fell under the wrecker's ball in 1926.

While William K. Vanderbilt had allowed his architect to design much of the decoration of his home, his father, William H. Vanderbilt, commissioned a decorating establishment to supply the architectural plans for his twin brownstone homes on Fifth Avenue between 51st and 52nd Streets. His houses were less daring architecturally but no less rich in furnishing and decoration than those of William K. Vanderbilt.

Since the mid-century, decorating establishments had begun to replace the older furniture manufactories and warehouses as creators of a wide range of furniture types and styles as well as purveyors of the cherished *objets de vertu* which formed a significant adjunct to any decorative scheme. Among those firms operating in the 1880s, Herter Brothers were the leaders. Although fashion declared the French style supreme, Herter Bro-

Museum of the City of New York: Byron Collection

Author's Photo

Author's Photo

Fig. 9 *The Japanese Parlour in the W. H. Vanderbilt house (see Fig. 2), decorated by Herter Brothers in the 1880s. The Japanese taste was popular in America from the 1860s and found one of its most complete expressions in this magnificent room.*

Fig. 10 *Andrew Carnegie house on Fifth Avenue, New York, 1900–01 by Babb, Cook and Willard. Of the mansions, châteaux, palaces and quasi-monastic enclaves which spread up Fifth Avenue, this is one of the few to survive.*

Fig. 11 *Drawing-room of the William H. Vanderbilt house. The catholic taste of the 1880s embraced a variety of historical and exotic styles. This mixture of motifs was often replaced by correct period schemes favoured by later generations.*

thers were particularly proficient at the creation of furniture showing the influence of English design reform movements. Frank expression of construction and ornament restricted to flat surfaces and low relief were evident on both exterior and interior of the William H. Vanderbilt houses.

The Japanese taste, which provided both ornamental and compositional motifs for the Aesthetic Movement, found expression in the Japanese Parlour of the Vanderbilt house. Nearly seven hundred artisans were employed to complete the decorations of the house and, of these, two hundred and fifty were assigned to the marquetry and carving. As in the case of the neighbouring William K. Vanderbilt house, much of this decoration gave way to the Louis XV style in the early years of the twentieth century; the last part of the twin houses was demolished in 1947. At the same time as these houses were being erected, another son of William H. Vanderbilt, Cornelius II, was building a massive *château* further up Fifth Avenue.

It has been estimated that over fifteen million dollars were expended on the construction and decoration of this suite of Vanderbilt houses. Certainly they were responsible for the expenditure of a great deal more as the waves of influence caused by their building activity not only spread up Fifth Avenue for forty blocks, endowing the street with a miscellaneous collection of mansions, *châteaux,*

palaces and near monastic enclaves, but eventually penetrated the fashionable spas and country retreats favoured by the well-to-do.

Money in New York had sought to magnify its name through a combination of socially acceptable forms and personal eccentricities. The pressure towards outward show triumphed in the great mansions begun by the Vanderbilts, and finally even the Astors moved uptown to a splendid double house designed as a French *château* by the reigning academic master, Richard M. Hunt.

The more elaborate and monumental these houses became, the more fragile they proved to be, subject to an increasingly fickle taste and the unwillingness of succeeding generations to live as their parents had. Further discouragement to the maintenance of such vast establishments came with the introduction of personal income tax in 1913.

Perhaps the most striking example of the conspicuous in late nineteenth-century architecture was the house erected for Senator Clark of Montana, the copper magnate. This granite pile designed by Lord, Hewlett and Hull and K. M. Murchison, in consultation with H. Deglane, took six years to construct. The house stood for only twenty-three years at the corner of 77th Street and Fifth Avenue before it fell victim to what critics of nearly a hundred years earlier had dubbed New York's 'pull down and build over again' spirit.

The Rookwood Pottery

Founded by the socialite daughter
of a wealthy Cincinnati family,
the Rookwood art pottery rose
to great artistic heights and
won widespread recognition

The Rookwood Pottery, because it was founded by a woman in the days when there were few women *entrepreneurs*, probably received more gratuitous publicity during the first twenty years of its existence than any other American enterprise.

The magazine and newspaper writers of the period seemed to delight in telling how Mrs. Maria Longworth Nichols started the venture because she was unable to find a suitable place elsewhere in which to conduct her experiments in china painting and under-glaze pottery decoration, which had been stimulated by the widespread interest in the subject following the Centennial Celebration of the United States in 1876.

The fact that Mrs. Nichols was the socially prominent daughter of one of the wealthiest families in Cincinnati and the wife of the president of the Cincinnati College of Music made her good local copy. Newspaper-writers of the city reported in detail how she spent the summer of 1880 converting a little schoolhouse, given to her by her father, into a pottery; how she named it 'Rookwood' after the name of her father's estate, and because, she said, 'it reminded one of Wedgwood', which she felt lent a certain prestige to the new enterprise.

The newspapers also recorded that the first kiln was drawn on 25 November, 1880, and that Mrs. Nichols emphasised that her primary interest was in the production of a better art pottery rather than the achievement of a commercial success. They told how three of Mrs. Nichols' friends: Edward P. Cranch, a lawyer with artistic talents; Clara Chipman Newton, a former schoolmate; and Laura A. Fry, a skilled woodcarver and china-painter, joined with her to form the nucleus of a decorating department; they described the Rookwood School for Pottery Decoration, which Mrs. Nichols organised in the expectation that it would provide a training-ground for future artists for her pottery.

Mr. Joseph Bailey, an experienced English potter who had migrated to the United States in 1848, gave some sound advice to Mrs. Nichols in the initial stages. In 1881, he joined the enterprise as factory superintendent.

During the first three years of its existence, expenses greatly exceeded income and Mr. Joseph Longworth, Mrs. Nichols' father, continued to make substantial contributions toward financing the venture. In spite of this and other difficulties, the little business grew steadily.

In 1883, Mr. William Watts Taylor, an old friend of Mrs. Nichols, was named manager of the pottery.

Fig. 1 *Rookwood ceramics, late nineteenth century.*
From the left: *Ewer with dragon motif, initialled by Albert R. Valentien.* **Vase** *with portrait of Chief Joseph of the Nez Percés, signed by W. P. McDonald, height 14 ins.* **Bowl** *with Japanese flower motif.*
(Metropolitan Museum of Art, New York. Gifts of W. M. Sawyer, 1945, and E. J. Kaufman Fund, 1969.)

Museum Photo

Under his direction the production of art pottery was expanded. New designs were introduced, and those that did not sell well were eliminated from the line. He also streamlined sales, appointing as national sales agent Davis Collamore & Co., a leading distributor of fine china, glass and crystal; and he instituted a policy of selective distribution, permitting only one leading retailer per city to handle the Rookwood line. In an effort to trim losses, he discontinued the pottery school. As a result of these changes the operation showed a modest profit by 1886, and by 1889 it had recouped all its earlier losses.

During its first three years, the production of the Rookwood Pottery was divided between art pottery, the primary interest of Mrs. Nichols, and commercial and utility wares, which were made solely to help defray expenses. The early output of art pottery was characterised by a variety of techniques as the organisation groped for a distinctive style. Among them were carved, incised, stamped and impressed designs, applied decoration in high relief, frequent embellishment with gilt, over-glaze painting and slip-painting under the glaze. This latter style, aided by the development of the airbrush technique for applying evenly blended backgrounds in rich, warm colours, soon became the most popular and was referred to as 'Standard Rookwood'.

From a few limited colours which would withstand the heat of the kiln, the pottery succeeded in developing a wider range, and also employed tinted glazes and coloured clay bodies which added to the beauty and variety of its wares. In 1884 came the accidental development of an aventurine glaze having bright golden crystals appearing deep under the surface. The effect was given the name 'Tiger Eye', but this result could not be produced with certainty and what caused it to occur remained undiscovered.

Many visitors were attracted to the Rookwood pottery on the banks of the Ohio River

The widespread publicity Rookwood received attracted many visitors to the pottery. Prominent Cincinnatians as well as visitors to the city called to inspect this 'new art industry' on the banks of the Ohio River. Oscar Wilde and Seymour Hayden, an English etcher, were among the early travellers who are known to have toured the pottery.

Mrs. Nichols' husband died in 1885, and the following year she married Bellamy Storer, a well-known Cincinnati lawyer. From that time on, her interest in the pottery gradually declined until, at the end of 1889, she transferred the ownership of the business to Mr. Taylor and moved with her husband to Washington D.C. when Mr. Storer was elected a member of the United States Congress.

Under Mr. Taylor's management the production of art pottery continued to expand and new shapes were added to the line each year. The manufacture of commercial and utility items had been phased out except for infrequent orders that came in for souvenirs or for pieces commemorating special events. Floral decorations on the rich brown, orange and yellow blended backgrounds of Standard Rookwood and on the cool pink and white grounds of a style designated as 'Cameo', dominated the output of the decorating department which had

2

K. Hoddle

3

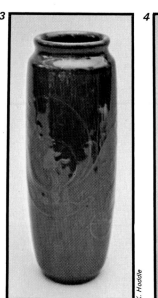

K. Hoddle

4

K. Hoddle

5

K. Hoddle

Fig. 2 *Jar, decorated by H. Wilcox with lilies on a green ground, Rookwood, shape no. 892B, 1900. (Bethnal Green Museum, London.)*

Fig. 3 *Vase, decorated by A. R. Valentien with dragons on an aventurine ground, Rookwood, shape no. S1363, 1898. (Bethnal Green Museum.)*

Fig. 4 *Vase, decorated by Constance A. Baker with poppies on a black and brown ground, Rookwood, shape no. 17C, 1900. (Bethnal Green Museum.)*

Fig. 5 *Bottle-shaped vase, decorated by K. Shirayamadani with a pattern of arrowhead flowers, Rookwood, shape no. 654C, 1900. (Victoria and Albert Museum.)*

grown to a staff of thirteen full-time artists.

Mr. Taylor's first moves on taking over the ownership of the pottery were to incorporate the business and to lay plans for its further expansion. As it had thoroughly outgrown the facilities available at the little schoolhouse, he designed the layout for a complete new pottery housed in an attractive English Tudor-style building. It was constructed on the top of Mount Adams, overlooking the central business district of Cincinnati, and operations were transferred to the new location in the spring of 1892. The decorating department was immediately expanded by the addition of six new artists.

The following year Rookwood was prominently displayed at the World's Columbian Exposition, more popularly known in the United States as the Chicago World's Fair. Here it attained added recognition by receiving the award for art pottery and was praised as 'an indigenous American art'. Several European museums acquired examples of its production for their collections.

While most of the output continued to be Standard Rookwood, three new styles were introduced:

'Iris' was the name given to ware having light blue, grey and white blended grounds under a high glaze; 'Sea Green' designated a 'limpid opalescent sea-green effect with a favourite decoration of fish moving under water' under a high glaze; 'Aerial Blue' denoted a bluish-tinted high glaze used over decorations on light blue and grey blended grounds.

Although floral themes continued to be the most characteristic during the 1890s (Figs. 2, 4 and 5), other decorative styles appeared. Among the innovations were: under-glaze, slip-painted portraits of American Indians (Fig. 1); Negroes; cats, dogs and other animals. Figures taken from Old Masters such as Van Dyck, Rembrandt, Franz Hals, Caravaggio and others were painted on vases and plaques; and wares were embellished with silver overlays applied by the Gorham Manufacturing Company of Providence, Rhode Island, one of the country's leading silversmiths. Under the influence of the developing Art Nouveau trends, several of the artists attempted to interest the pottery in making sculptured art forms, but this style apparently proved unpopular in the salerooms and was not encouraged by the management.

Rookwood Pottery

6

Rookwood
Pottery
1881

ROOKWOOD
1882

℞

℞

℞

IV

706 B

A·R·V·

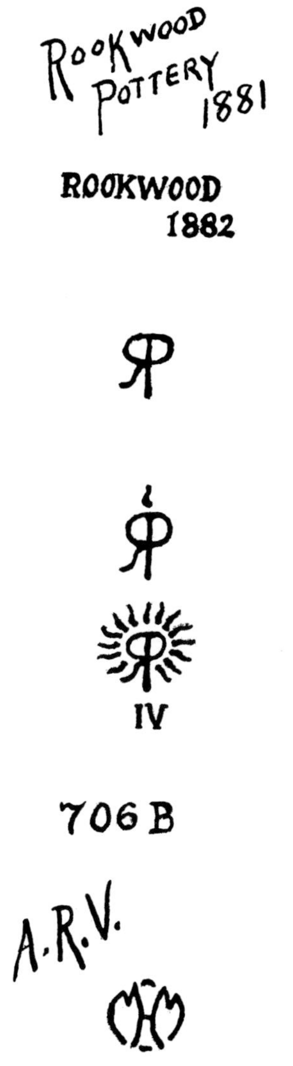

Fig. 6 **Principal Rookwood pottery marks.** From the top:
1880–81, painted or incised.
1882–86, impressed.
1886, reversed R-P officially adopted although used by the decorator Brennan from 1883.
1887, one flame point added for that year and an additional one for each year until 1900.
1904, Roman numeral added below the R-P mark with fourteen flames to indicate the year of the new century, as here for 1904.
Shape number *impressed on the bottom of each piece. When followed by a letter, it showed that shape was made in two or more sizes.*
Initials and monogram *of two artists. These are usually found incised, impressed or painted on individually decorated pieces.*

During the summer of 1897, the pottery was visited by the English writer Rose G. Kingsley, who told the Rookwood story in an article which appeared in the December 1897 issue of the prestigious *Art-Journal*. The management at Cincinnati was highly pleased and ordered a supply of reprints for use in Rookwood's promotional activities.

In 1899 the building on Mount Adams was enlarged by the addition of more studio-space for the art staff, more space for the salerooms, which were attracting an increasing number of visitors, and more work-room for the potting department. The work-force was expanded and the art department increased to thirty-six members.

When Rookwood was awarded the Grand Prix at the 1900 *Exposition Universelle* in Paris, its position as America's foremost art pottery was assured. Many more European museums acquired examples of its wares, and the Pottery from that time on seldom missed an opportunity to publicise its international recognition and acceptance.

During the 1890s the Pottery had sent several of its more talented decorators to study in Europe, believing that this would be directly in the Pottery's 'artistic interests'. Rookwood had never lost sight of the original goal of its founder, the making of better art pottery, although it no longer emphasised that this interest exceeded the desire for commercial success.

One of the artists sent abroad was Artus van Briggle, who later founded the Van Briggle Art Pottery in Colorado Springs. When he returned to Cincinnati, he brought back the idea of a dull or matt glaze which he had seen in Europe. Although Rookwood began experimenting with matt glazes as early as 1896, it was not until 1901 that matt-glazed ware became a regular part of the Pottery's production. Several styles of matt-glaze decoration were developed and were described as 'Mat Glaze Painting', 'Incised Mat Glaze', 'Modeled Mat Glaze', and 'Conventional Mat Glaze'. In 1904, a transparent matt glaze known as 'Vellum' was perfected. Its use encouraged the painting of detailed landscapes and seascapes on vases and plaques. These proved popular and their production was continued for many years, although they were sold at comparatively high prices as they were costly to produce.

The development of a matt glaze also gave rise to the manufacture of decorative tiles and medallions for architectural use, a field that gave promise for further development. This led to the second expansion of the pottery's facilities on Mount Adams. A new addition was built in 1904 to house the architectural department. During the next decade Rookwood architectural products were supplied for more than seventy prominent commercial and office buildings throughout the United States, and hundreds of Rookwood mantels and facings for fireplaces and coloured-tile bathrooms were installed in private residences. But the large staff required to design and make the architectural products, coupled with the low selling-prices forced by competition, kept the profit margin down, and the operation of the architectural department proved a disappointment to the management.

Until approximately 1910, Rookwood art pottery was almost entirely confined to pieces individually decorated by the artists, who customarily signed their work with their initials or monogram. Exceptions were the ware having the 'Tiger Eye' or aventurine effect which did not require further ornamentation. Each piece was also dated, a feature which distinguishes Rookwood from most other art pottery, and given a number which identified the shape (Fig. 6). All artist-signed pieces were unique creations and never duplicated; even matched pairs differed slightly in execution.

Several years after the development of matt glaze, however, the company began to make ware in which the design, either incised or modelled in relief, could be cast directly in the mould. Such pieces could be duplicated in quantity and the method was employed with greater frequency as the demand increased for items which could be sold at lower prices.

William Watts Taylor, who had guided the Rookwood Pottery to its greatest achievements, died in 1913. Following his death, the Pottery continued to trade on the reputation and acceptance it had built up during his leadership, but it never surpassed its earlier successes. The new management lacked Mr. Taylor's perception and his business judgement, and a series of mistakes, coupled with the Great Depression of the 1930s, led to the bankruptcy of the firm in 1941 and the eventual suspension of production.

The last few years have seen a renewed interest in art pottery in general and a new appreciation of Rookwood in particular which has stimulated the demand by collectors for the products of America's foremost art pottery.

MUSEUMS AND COLLECTIONS

Rookwood pottery may be seen at the following:
Cincinnati: Cincinnati Art Museum
New York: Brooklyn Museum
Cooper Hewitt Museum
Metropolitan Museum of Art
Washington, D.C.: Smithsonian Institution

FURTHER READING

'Rookwood Pottery in Foreign Museum Collections' by Herbert Peck in **The Connoisseur**, London, September 1969.
'Some Early Collections of Rookwood Pottery' by Herbert Peck in **Auction Magazine**, New York, September 1969.
The Book of Rookwood Pottery by Herbert Peck, New York, 1968.
Pottery and Porcelain of the United States by Edwin Atlee Barber, New York, 1979 reprint.

ART NOUVEAU & AMERICAN GRAPHIC DESIGN

Fig. 1 *Scribner's Fiction Number. August by Maxfield Parrish (1870–1966), 1897. Colour lithograph, 19¾ ins. x 14½ ins.*
As the practice of importing foreign designs declined, Scribner's *and* Century *magazines turned to the work of two young artists, Louis Rhead (Fig. 7) and Maxfield Parrish. Parrish, who was to become one of America's most popular illustrators, sounded a note of paganism in his poster work. (Library of Congress, Washington, D.C.)*

Fig. 2 *Lippincott's for January by Will Carqueville (born 1871), 1895. Colour lithograph, 19 ins. x 12½ ins.*
Trained in his father's lithography firm, Carqueville came to work for Lippincott's *in 1895 when they decided to issue posters of their own. This design is typical of his work in which objects and people are reduced to flat areas of bright colour. (Library of Congress.)*

Firmly rooted in the European Art Nouveau movement, the poster style in America swept away the tired conventions of the nineteenth century in a few years of intense creativity

After two generations of repudiation, Art Nouveau again enjoys an enthusiastic popularity. A re-examination, begun in the 'fifties and continuing today, has taught us that Art Nouveau was not a single style but that it had several stages of development and many, though related, geographical variations on the basic themes of the whiplash curve and rhythmic surface movement.

In the 1890s, stylistic trends travelled quickly and were rapidly assimilated. The role of the graphic arts in linking the art of regions and continents, and as a carrier of this new style, cannot be underestimated. This is certainly true for the United States, where the poster movement and Art Nouveau graphic design are almost synonymous; arriving at the same time, the one reinforced by the other. Significantly, the noted American painter John Sloan, in reminiscing about his early work in the Art Nouveau style, refers to it as the 'poster' style.

Elements of Art Nouveau design occur in American illustration prior to the poster movement of the 1890s, but examples are few and appear mainly in a small number of finely produced books where the artist, usually a painter, might have been allowed a comparatively free hand. Although the influence of the Pre-Raphaelites, of the Arts and Crafts Movement and of the teachings of William Morris was important in establishing an American crafts movement, which played a decisive role in American Art Nouveau decorative arts, the American publishing industry remained virtually untouched by the private press movement until the later 1890s.

The few painters and etchers interested in making fine prints in the 1880s and '90s were either strongly Whistlerian in style, or were committed to realist traditions in American painting. Although the burgeoning publishing industry employed many illustrators, their work remained tied to the style of the 1860s and the wood-engravers. Basically conservative in outlook, publishers and illustrators were careful not to go beyond the aesthetic limitations of their public.

An important exception to the rule, and some of the earliest work in American illustration to approach Art Nouveau stylisation, were the illustrations by Elihu Vedder (1836–1923) for Fitz-Gerald's translation of the *Rubáiyát of Omar Khayyám*, published by Houghton, Mifflin and Co. in 1884. Introduced to the poem by his friend Edwin Ellis, a follower of the Pre-Raphaelites, Vedder's imagination was aroused by the romantic imagery of the work. After considerable difficulty, Vedder was able to persuade the hesitant Houghton and Mifflin to undertake the kind of finely printed, profusely illustrated edition he envisaged. In a letter to a friend written at the time, he speaks of wishing '. . . to make it something like a richly illuminated manuscript'.

The work of Elihu Vedder approaches Art Nouveau

Vedder's ties with the Pre-Raphaelites were strengthened by his long-standing friendship with Walter Crane, and it is possible that his concept of the *Rubáiyát* as an illuminated manuscript may have been influenced by a knowledge, through Crane, of an Omar manuscript owned by Lady Burne-Jones, with illuminations by William Morris and Burne-Jones. In any event, Vedder found in the *Rubáiyát* a perfect vehicle for his visionary spirit, and in the designs for the cover, the notes and the end-papers he stepped beyond romantic symbolism to flat, decorative, non-objective forms approaching mature Art Nouveau in their stylisation. Although the book was both an artistic and, to the surprise of Houghton and Mifflin, a commercial success, it did not alter the course of American publications. 'Vedder's Monument', as the *Rubáiyát* was called, remained a singular achievement.

One of the most prolific and honoured illustrators of the latter part of the century was Edwin A. Abbey (1852–1911). Although known chiefly for his mural paintings, he began his career doing countless drawings for *Harper's Weekly*. Much of his illustration was concerned with a meticulous reconstruction of the past, but on the 1882 cover for Herrick's *Hesperides* he went beyond his usual narrative style to create an inventive design which approaches Art Nouveau in its pulsating forms and freely stylised hand lettering.

Although more akin to the Kelmscott style than to Art Nouveau, the work of Howard Pyle (1853–1911) in the late 1880s and early 1890s should be mentioned as bringing to American illustration a simple, strong, black-and-white style. Pyle, who wrote and illustrated books chiefly on medieval themes had an excellent command of balanced darks and lights, harmonious with the printed page and in the tradition of Morris and the fifteenth-century German woodcut-artists.

These artists remained the exception, however,

until later in the 1890s, when a younger generation of poster-artists, illustrators and publishers embraced the new European styles in graphic design with eagerness and distinction.

The beginning of the poster movement in America can be put with some certainty at 1889, when Harper and Brothers, publishers, commissioned the Swiss-French artist Eugène Grasset (1841–1917) to design a cover for *Harper's Bazaar* and posters for the Christmas issue of the magazine. The editors of *Harper's* were undoubtedly aware of the growing popularity of the art-poster in Europe and decided to use a special design by a foreign artist of repute as a means of distinguishing themselves from their competitors.

Widespread public education in America had created by the end of the century an enormous reading public eager for information of all kinds, and the numerous magazines and newspapers which sprang up in the second half of the century vied for the attention of this vast reading public. In the 1880s publishers had issued small, shop-window-sized posters to announce special holiday numbers, but these were of little artistic merit, overburdened with literal details and haphazard typography. The

experiment in advertising had established a precedent, however, which Grasset's great success helped to make a tradition.

The choice of Grasset to design the poster was shrewd and satisfactory. His work had a modern flavour, yet was not too *avant-garde* for the American public. Again, in 1892, Grasset was commissioned to do a poster for the Christmas issue of *Harper's* and, a short time later, the decision was made to issue a new poster every month. *Harper's* lead was soon followed by its main competitors, *Lippincott's*, *The Century Illustrated Monthly Magazine* and *Scribner's Magazine*. In the absence of a strong American tradition in illustration and poster-design, the new generation of poster-artists turned to European prototypes and to the vital, new, decorative

Fig. 3 *Arabella and Araminta by Ethel Reed (born 1876), 1895. Colour lithograph, 27 ins. x 15½ ins. At the age of twenty-one, Ethel Reed became the most celebrated woman poster-artist and illustrator in America, but she vanished from the artistic world after the turn of the century. (Library of Congress.)*

Fig. 4 *Chap Book Thanksgiving Number by Will Bradley (1868–1962), 1894. Colour lithograph, 20¾ ins. x 14 ins. The best of the 'little magazines', Chap Book was particularly distinguished by the work of Will Bradley. He was a printer and self-taught artist on whom the influences of Walter Crane, Burne-Jones and Beardsley were strong. The most Art Nouveau in character of the poster designers, Bradley was an original and intellectually committed artist. (Library of Congress.)*

style emerging in Europe – Art Nouveau.

Edward Penfield (1866–1925) was the young artist selected from the staff of *Harper's* to create the first in their new series of monthly posters, and again the editors of *Harper's* chose wisely. Penfield's initial effort, done, by accounts, almost overnight, was a success. *Harper's*, and later other magazines, rejected the English tradition of repeating the same basic cover-design in favour of a new cover for each issue, reproducing the covers, often in a larger format, as posters. Penfield continued to design a new cover for *Harper's Monthly* each month for the next six years.

Although Penfield's unusual viewpoints and the decorative use of flat areas of colour outlined in bold black, red and green were certainly derived from Toulouse-Lautrec and Steinlen, he quickly developed a very personal, unmistakably American style. His clean-cut, upper-class young men and women, amusing themselves in the most innocent pastimes, established types very much like the Gibson Girl and her escorts. Penfield achieved an international following, with the production of his posters often exceeding, by demand, that of *Harper's* magazine.

Another young artist, Will Carqueville (born 1871), was chosen to be Penfield's counterpart at *Lippincott's* when this magazine decided to issue posters of its own. Carqueville had been trained in his father's lithography firm in Chicago, but left the business in 1895 to work for *Lippincott's*. The pensive girl he depicted on the cover of the January 1895 number is typical of his work (Fig. 2) – objects and people are reduced to abstract areas of bright colour, subtly balanced with background voids and with the lettering. Carqueville's obvious interest in French poster-art led him to leave his job with *Lippincott's* the next year to study in Paris. He was succeeded by J. J. Gould, a young artist with less stylistic assurance who imitated first Carqueville and later Penfield.

Rhead and Parrish – two promising young artists

The Century Illustrated Monthly Magazine and *Scribner's Magazine* preferred to commission a number of different artists to design their covers. Grasset was called on by *Century* in 1895 for two posters publicising William Sloane's *Life of Napoleon,* but the practice of importing designs declined as more promising young artists appeared. Two of the most interesting to work for *Century* and *Scribner's* were Louis Rhead (1857–1926) and Max-

Fig. 5 **The Inland Printer** *by Will
Bradley, Christmas 1895.
Letterpress, 12½ ins. x 8½ ins.
This cover design for a Chicago
trade journal dates from
Bradley's years as a freelance
illustrator. He also designed
posters, small magazines and
book illustrations during this
period.
(Museum of Modern Art, New
York. Gift of Joseph H. Heil.)*

Fig. 6 **Orient Cycles Lead the
Leaders** *by Edward Penfield
(1866–1925), 1890s. Colour
lithograph, 42 ins. x 28 ins.
Although clearly influenced by
Toulouse-Lautrec and Steinlen,
Penfield soon developed a
personal and unmistakably
American style. His upper-
class young men and women
achieved for him a dramatic
rise to international success.
(Library of Congress.)*

field Parrish (1870–1966). Rhead, an Englishman trained at the South Kensington Art School, left England in the early 1880s to work for the publishing firm of Appleton's in New York; but returned to Paris and London for further study from 1891 to 1894.

Rhead's poster style, undoubtedly formed from the works of Grasset and the Pre-Raphaelites, makes much use of the decorative possibilities of graceful contour lines. The delightful field of flowers in the poster for *Century's* Midsummer Holiday number (Fig. 7) recalls the richly ornamented border designs of William Morris. In addition to *Century*, Rhead also designed for *Scribner's*, various newspapers and occasionally for manufacturers. A one-man exhibition at Wunderlich's on his return to New York in 1895 and at the 1897 Salon des Cent in Paris placed him at the forefront of American graphic designers.

In contrast to the pure maidens of Rhead's posters, Maxfield Parrish's young nymphs set among flowers and tracery-like trees strike a certain note of paganism. Much of Parrish's poster style was derived from his strong training in the classical tradition, but it is softened by his delicate colour harmonies and a very personal, poetic imagery. Parrish continued to work in illustration long after the poster movement had lost its momentum, becoming one of America's most popular illustrators.

The demand for posters and artists grew as manufacturers and newspapers recognised the advertising value of the artistic poster. Bicycle manufacturers, in particular, used the poster extensively, even organising poster competitions and exhibitions. Much of the early work by John Sloan (1871–1951) was in the form of illustrations and visual puzzles for newspapers. Sloan also worked for *The Echo*, one of the many 'little magazines' which were popular at the time and whose *avant-garde* designs added zest to the poster movement. These literary magazines were in close touch with European movements and, aimed at the limited audience of the intelligentsia, could afford to be more daring. Beardsley and *The Yellow Book* had much to do with the movement, according to Sloan, but Sloan was personally more attracted by the work of Walter Crane and Steinlen and Japanese woodcuts, which had been known for some time in America.

Of the many 'little magazines' – *Gil Blas, Echo, Moods*, to name only a few – the *Chap Book* holds first place. Published by Stone and Kimball bi-monthly from May 1894 to July 1898, it was founded to promote the finely printed books of Herbert Stone and Hannibal Kimball, but soon became a leading force in the 'poster craze', publishing articles on poster-artists and selling posters by American and European artists. Their own posters were particularly distinguished from 1894 to 1895 by the work of Will H. Bradley (1868–1962).

Bradley, possibly the most creative and original of the graphic designers of the 1890s, was also the most completely Art Nouveau, not only in style, but

Malcolm Varon, N.Y.C.

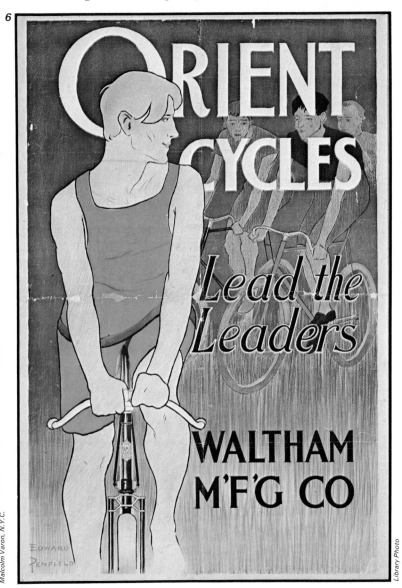

Library Photo

Fig. 7 *Century Magazine Midsummer Holiday Number* by Louis Rhead (1857–1926), 1895. Colour lithograph, 14½ ins. x 19¾ ins. *An Englishman trained in London and Paris, Rhead worked for much of his life in New York. (Library of Congress.)*

Fig. 8 *Harper's March* by Edward Penfield, 1897. Colour lithograph, 14 ins. x 19 ins. *Rejecting both the English tradition of repeating the same cover every month and their previous use of foreign artists, Harper's were wise to choose Edward Penfield. His first cover was a success overnight, and he continued to design them monthly for six years. (Library of Congress.)*

also in outlook. While other artists assumed the 'poster style' during its heyday before going in other directions, Bradley was an intellectually involved artist – committed to an aesthetic ideology of establishing good graphic design and fine printing in the United States. Bradley became, in later years, one of America's best typographers.

A printer's apprentice from the age of eleven, Bradley was a self-taught artist. In 1886 he decided to leave his job as staff-artist with Rand-McNally in Chicago to become a freelance illustrator and for the next few years designed monthly covers for the *Inland Printer*, a Chicago trade journal, as well as posters for manufacturers, small magazines and illustrations for books. Burne-Jones and Walter Crane were early influences, but later the influence of Beardsley was to earn him, at least in his own country, considerable criticism as a slavish imitator of the shocking Englishman. The criticism was untrue, however, and was recognised as such outside America where Bradley's work was acclaimed in numerous articles and his posters were eagerly collected.

A deep interest in the hand-printed books of William Morris and the Kelmscott Press led Bradley to leave Stone and Kimball in 1895 to establish the Wayside Press in his native Massachusetts. There, in Springfield, he published *Bradley: His Book*, a small magazine concerned with art, literature and theories of fine printing, and illustrated with original woodcuts by Bradley. Like many of the 'little magazines', it was unfortunately short-lived, closing in 1897.

Bradley's place at Stone and Kimball's was assumed by Frank Hazenplug (born 1873), who designed posters for the *Chap Book* and book-covers and illustrations for the firm's books. A very talented young artist, he unfortunately dropped out of sight at the end of the poster movement.

Two other concerns active in fine printing at the end of the century should be mentioned: Copland and Day, the American publishers of *The Yellow Book*, and Lamson, Wolffe and Co. Both houses employed a young woman, Ethel Reed (born 1876), who became at twenty-one the most celebrated woman poster-artist and illustrator in America, and also received international attention in *The Yellow Book* and the *Studio*. But she, like Frank Hazenplug, vanished from the artistic world after the turn of the century.

The poster style lasted only a few years in America. By the turn of the century, most artists associated with the movement had turned in other directions. John Sloan was to become a celebrated painter, a leader of the so-called 'Ash-can School' of realism. Bradley was to devote more time to typography and pure design. Others, like Ethel Reed and Frank Hazenplug, became almost forgotten figures. But, brief as the movement was, the impact of Art Nouveau on the future direction of design in America was great and of lasting significance. American designers had borrowed from Europe but went beyond mere imitation. In a few intense years of creativity, Art Nouveau swept away the tired conventions of the nineteenth century and prepared the way for the major developments of the twentieth century.

7

8

Library Photo

MUSEUMS AND COLLECTIONS

American Art Nouveau posters, prints and illustrations may be seen at the following:

Cambridge, Mass.: Department of Printing and Graphics, Harvard University
Chicago: Art Institute of Chicago
New York: Museum of Modern Art
New York Public Library
Washington, D.C.: Library of Congress
Wilmington, Del.: Delaware Art Centre

FURTHER READING

World and Image: Posters from the collection of the Museum of Modern Art, text by Alan Fern, New York, 1968.
American Art Nouveau, The Poster Period of John Sloan, collected by Helen Farr Sloan, Lock Haven, Pennsylvania, 1967.
'Will Bradley' by Robert Koch in **Art in America,** No. 3, 1962.
Maxfield Parrish Prints by Marian S. Sweeney, 1975.
Perceptions and Evocations: The Art of Elihu Vedder by Joshua C. Taylor, 1979.

Tradition and Reform in Furniture

Fig. 1 *Organ by the Mason & Hamlin Company, Boston, 1876. Engraving from* The Masterpieces of the Centennial Exhibition, *1876.*

As times and mood changed towards the end of the nineteenth century, the exuberance of American furniture design gave way to a sobriety and solidity which reflected the English Arts and Crafts Movement

Most of the furniture produced in the United States between the Civil War and the end of World War I is characterised by the revival of a variety of past styles, in particular the rococo and the renaissance styles. In reaction to the excesses of these tastes and a decline in quality of craftsmanship came the innovatory furniture made by followers of the Arts and Crafts Movement which had originated in England with Ruskin and designers such as Bruce J. Talbert and William Morris.

Exhibitions demonstrated that much revival furniture was pretentious and vulgar, but it has too often been judged on the basis of its excesses. The organ in Figure 1, made by the Mason & Hamlin Company of Boston, was exhibited in the United States Centennial Exhibition at Philadelphia in 1876. Although many of the exhibitors showed pieces which clearly demonstrated the influence of the Arts and Crafts Movement, this firm evidently was not interested in reform. *The Masterpieces of the Centennial International Exhibition* praised the sounds that the organ made and claimed that it was an object 'that attracted the attention of the ear as well as the eye', and '. . . is a grand and massive design, in harmony with the music which will issue from its pipes . . . Just as organ music suggests lofty, noble and grand themes, so the instrument itself should be built on noble lines . . .'.

The library-table shown in Figure 2, made of solid – not the usual veneered – rosewood, and with finely carved applied decoration, is by one of New

Fig. 2 **Library table** by
*Alexander Roux (c.1813–86),
New York, 1850–57. Solid
rosewood with finely carved
applied decoration,
height 29½ ins.
A Frenchman who came to
America in 1837, Roux was one of
New York's best cabinet-
makers. This fine piece
effectively combines rococo
elements with renaissance motifs.
(City Art Museum of St. Louis,
Missouri. Decorative Arts
Society Funds.)*

York's best nineteenth-century cabinet-makers, Alexander Roux (c.1813–86), a Frenchman who came to the United States in 1837. In 1850 a contemporary of Roux wrote: 'In New York, the rarest and most elaborate designs, especially for drawing-room and library use, are to be found in the warehouses of Roux, in Broadway'. The firm worked almost to the end of the century, producing furniture in all the revival styles. This piece effectively combines renaissance motifs, seen in the strap-work, turnings, volutes, medallions and finials, with naturalistic rococo elements.

Less popular than the rococo and renaissance revivals was the Egyptian, the origins of which go back to the Napoleonic Egyptian campaign of 1798; this interest was furthered by later archeological discoveries. The Egyptian theme recurred at intervals throughout the nineteenth and the first part of the twentieth centuries, and the armchair in Figure 4 in this taste, produced in about 1870, is a brilliant example. Part of a set of furniture, the chair was possibly made by the New York chair manufacturer Ingersoll, Jewett & Co., since 'Ingersoll' is inked in large letters on the top of the frame underneath

surround an oval relief depicting a figure in a garden. Also produced in cast iron were architectural ornaments and fences; its most important use however, was in architecture, as seen in numerous cast-iron fronted commercial buildings in American cities. In addition to cast-iron pieces, American manufacturers produced furniture which utilised mechanical devices in their construction, especially pieces which contained movable parts.

The reform movement in America was popularised by Charles Lock Eastlake (1836–1906), a keeper of the National Gallery of London, whose *Hints on Household Taste*, published in 1868, was influential in England and America (there were eight American editions between 1872 and 1890). In fact, in the United States, his name has been given to the style he advocated, a simple rectangular form with rich decoration and excellent craftsmanship. Another name for this reform furniture was 'art furniture'. Transferred across the Atlantic, it is seen in the ebonised cabinet in Figure 6. Its form is simple, flat and rectangular (in opposition to the revived rococo), but rich ornamentation is seen here in the inlays of light woods, *eglomisé* panels, bird's-

Fig. 3 **Garden bench**, *Shickle,
Harrison & Company, St. Louis,
Missouri, c.1868. Cast iron,
height 3 ft. 4½ ins.
Innovations in machinery and
technique during these years
enabled manufacturers to
experiment with materials other
than wood; cast iron was one of
the most popular. This bench was
copied from an English design.
(City Art Museum of St. Louis.)*

Fig. 4 **Armchair**, *probably from
New York, c.1870. Gilt and
veneered wood and brass.
Height 3 ft. 2 ins.
This superb example of the
Egyptian revival style may have
been made by the New York firm
of Ingersoll, Jewett & Co.,
although the name 'Ingersoll'
inked on the frame may refer to
an owner.
(Art Institute of Chicago.
Suzanne Walter Worthy Fund.)*

the upholstery. The name might alternatively refer to an owner. Egyptian motifs adapted here include the bird's claw-and-ball feet, the terminals of the arm supports in the form of pharaohs' heads, and the elaborate, imaginative design of the needlework upholstery.

Both the Egyptian chair and the Roux table characterise the best of nineteenth-century revival furniture and uphold traditional taste – excellent craftsmanship and a free deployment of past styles in an overall design which succeeds in its own set of aesthetic terms.

Although machine and technical innovations of the industrial age provided the means of mass producing furniture of poor quality, they also enabled the ingenious manufacturer to experiment with making furniture from materials other than wood; cast iron, as in the handsome garden-bench in Figure 3, was one of the most popular. The manufacturers, Shickle, Harrison & Co., of St. Louis, copied an English design at the request of the philanthropist Henry Shaw, in whose extensive gardens in St. Louis the bench was used for many years. Shaw's botanical interests are reflected in his choice of design, the back of the bench being conceived as flowing vines, flowers and buds which

eye maple interior and the spindled bracket. The fashion for Japanese taste is seen in the scenes painted on the panels.

Japanese art was to be seen at the London International Exhibition of 1862, the Japanese bazaar at the Philadelphia Centennial and the Japanese showroom in New York. New York was the centre for firms producing art furniture, in particular Christian Herter and his brothers, whose firm was as well known to the rich of the 1880s as was Tiffany & Co. in the twentieth century. Other firms followed the lead of Herter and by 1900 the major United States cities had art-furniture companies, although usually not up to the standard of Herter's; the word 'art' was a commercial prefix applied to almost anything produced.

Although quantities of furniture were cheaply mass produced in the nineteenth century, a small minority of craftsmen demonstrated tremendous skill, as seen in the cabinet-bookcase in Figure 5 designed by Isaac E. Scott (c.1845–1920), who was first listed in the Chicago Directories for 1873. Before coming to Chicago, Scott worked in Philadelphia. Because his work is closely related to the work of English designers of the period, such as Alfred Waterhouse, William Burges and Richard

Fig. 5 **Cabinet-bookcase,**
designed by Isaac E. Scott
(1845–1920), Chicago, late
nineteenth century.
Height 15 ft. 7 ins.
First listed in the Chicago
directories for 1873, Scott came
there from Philadelphia and, as
may be seen from this piece, his
style of design has affinities with
the English Arts and Crafts
Movement.
(Chicago School of Architecture
Foundation. Gift of Mrs. Charles
F. Batchelder.)

Fig. 6 **Cabinet,** *New York,*
1875–85. Ebonised wood with
inlay, bird's eye maple and
eglomisé panels, height 5 ft.
The style of this elaborate
piece of furniture derives from
C. L. Eastlake.
(Private Collection.)

4

Museum Photo

5

Owner's Photo

Author's Photo

7

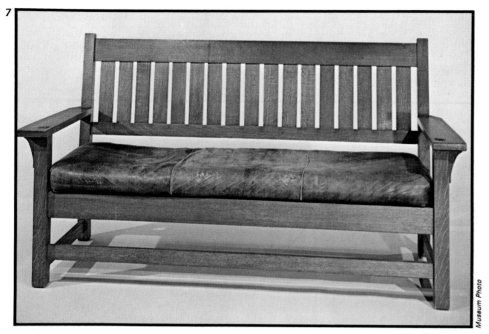

Museum Photo

8

Museum Photo

Fig. 7 **Settle**, *designed by Gustav Stickley (1857–1942), Eastwood, New York, c.1909. Oak with leather cushion, height 3 ft. 3½ ins. (Art Institute of Chicago. Gift of Mr. and Mrs. John J. Evans.)*

Fig. 8 **Library-table**, *designed by Frank Lloyd Wright (1867–1959) for the Ray W. Evans house, Chicago, c.1908. Oak, height 28¾ ins. Wright's designs were organic, but he used machine techniques. (Art Institute of Chicago. Gift of Mr. and Mrs. F. M. Fahrenwald.)*

Fig. 9 **Tall clock**, *designed by George Grant Elmslie (1871–1959) for the Henry B. Babson house, Riverside, Illinois, 1912. Height 7 ft. 4 ins. (Art Institute of Chicago. Gift of Mrs. Theodore Tieken.)*

Norman Shaw, it is likely that he was familiar with their work. This piece succeeds in its fine proportions and superior craftsmanship. Its Gothic-inspired architectural form is interspersed with gothic as well as naturalistic motifs, seen in the finely carved birds and vines in the frieze.

In 1888 the Tobey Furniture Company formed a subsidiary, the Tobey and Christiansen Cabinet Company, which specialised in high-quality, hand-made furniture, frequently made to order. Charles Tobey (1831–88) was of New England origin; his partner, William F. Christiansen, was Norwegian. Norwegian craftsmen were employed by the firm, and they adhered to the tenets of William Morris and the Arts and Crafts Movement.

Art Nouveau was not as popular with cabinet-makers in the United States as it was with those in Europe, and there seem to have been no American counterparts to French Art Nouveau designers such as Louis Majorelle and Hector Guimard. Perhaps the most innovatory American furniture which derived from the English reform movement – in particular the ideas and work of William Morris – was the 'craftsman' furniture designed by Gustav Stickley (1857–1942). Born on a farm in Wisconsin, Stickley worked in furniture factories and stores.

This great midwestern industry, found primarily in Chicago, Cincinnati and Grand Rapids, produced quantities of cheap mass-produced furniture which was turned out daily to supply the demands of a rapidly increasing population. Stickley's simple furniture, such as the sofa in Figure 7, presents a strong contrast to the traditional pieces. Whereas factory-made furniture was generally over elaborate and cheaply made, simple craftsman furniture was sturdily constructed in the craft workshops near Syracuse, New York.

Perhaps as important as Stickley's actual furniture was the publication of *The Craftsman* magazine, which helped to spread his ideals throughout the country for amateurs as well as numerous furniture-making firms. Equally influential was Stickley's contemporary Elbert Hubbard (1856–1915), whose Roycroft Shops in East Aurora, New York, produced an array of hand-made items.

Like their English counterparts, Stickley and Hubbard were interested in the application of democratic ideals to the arts; Morris wrote: 'One day we shall win back art – that is to say, the pleasure of life – to the people'. Stickley's designs were popular with the public, and furniture factories throughout the country copied his designs so that the so-called 'Mission-style' furniture was seen in many American houses. These techniques, however, did not always lend themselves to the popular democratic ideals advocated by the Arts and Crafts exponents, since in most cases the labour and material required to produce quality furniture raised its price beyond the means of the masses, and it was acquired by an intellectual and moneyed elite. Stickley's 'do-it-yourself' craftsman books, however, were an attempt to enable the masses to possess his furniture.

The Chicago architect Frank Lloyd Wright (1867–1959) designed furniture for many of his houses; such is the library-table (Fig. 8) designed in 1908 for the Chicago house of Ray W. Evans. Wright came to Chicago in 1887 from Wisconsin at a time of great building activity in the city. After working for Adler and Sullivan, he established his own practice in 1893.

In contrast to the Beaux-Arts tradition seen in the World's Columbian Exhibition in Chicago in 1893, Wright's furniture designs follow his precepts of architecture. Basic to his philosophy of architecture was the idea that buildings should be organic (appearing to grow from their sites and harmonising with nature), and furniture for his houses was to be closely related to the architecture. He wrote: 'The most truly satisfactory apartments are those in which most or all of the furniture is built in as a part of the original scheme considering the whole as an integral unit'. Much of the furniture of the Evans house, and of other houses designed by Wright, was built-in.

In the construction of furniture, Wright did not adhere to the techniques advocated by members of the Arts and Crafts groups. Instead, he proclaimed the virtues of the machine: 'The machine is here to stay. It is the forerunner of the democracy that is our dearest hope. There is no more important work before the architect now than to use this normal tool of civilisation to the best advantage instead of prostituting it as he has hitherto done in reproducing with murderous ubiquity forms born of other times and other conditions and which it can only serve to destroy'.

Museum Photo

The criteria of craftsmanship was still important: 'The furniture takes the clean cut, straight-line forms that the machine can render far better than would be possible by hand . . . and the nature of the materials is usually revealed in the process'. Previously the machine had been abused and 'they plowed and tore, whirled and gouged all wood to pieces . . .'. The top of the library-table (Fig. 8) is veneered; 'These treatments all allow wood to be wood at its best and the machine can do them all surpassingly better than they could be done by hand, a thousand times cheaper'.

Wright's contemporaries included George Maher (1864–1926) and George Grant Elmslie (1871–1952). Although Elmslie worked for Wright, he was one of the Prairie School architects, so named because their houses conformed to the flatness of the midwestern prairie. Like Wright, Maher and Elmslie were interested in an architecture which created a unified whole, and both turned their attention to interior furniture, rugs and drapery as well as exterior designs.

The tall clock in Figure 9 was designed by Elmslie for the Henry B. Babson house in Riverside, Illinois. This house had been designed in 1907 by the Chicago architect Louis H. Sullivan (1856–1924) for whom Elmslie had worked from 1889 to 1909. In fact, it was Elmslie who designed a large part of the Babson interior when the house was enlarged and service buildings were added in 1912. It was at this time that Elmslie designed a number of pieces of furniture for Babson, including this tall clock. Its architectural style is related to the exterior of the Elmslie additions to the house, and in its simple rectilinear form it is a reflection of the Prairie School architecture, as well as in the tradition of reform furniture. Of particular note is the fine casting of the face, made from a mould by the Chicago designer and craftsman Robert Jarvie. The original hands of the clock were made by the artist-craftsman Kristian Schneider.

By the beginning of World War I, the impact of the Arts and Crafts Movement had subsided, although the Movement has lingered on even until today. The same polarity between tradition and reform occurs as a theme in the decorative arts of the twentieth century.

MUSEUMS AND COLLECTIONS

Late nineteenth-century American furniture may be seen at the following:

Chicago: Art Institute of Chicago
Dearborn, Mich.: Henry Ford Museum
New York: Brooklyn Museum
Cooper-Hewitt Museum
Metropolitan Museum of Art

FURTHER READING

Nineteenth Century American Furniture and Other Decorative Arts, a Metropolitan Museum of Art exhibition catalogue, New York, 1970.
American Furniture of the Nineteenth Century by Celia Jackson Otto, New York, 1965.
Furniture of the American Arts and Crafts Movement: Stickley and Roycroft Mission Oak by David M. Cathers, New York, 1981.
Frank Lloyd Wright to 1910: The First Golden Age by Grant C. Manson, 1979.

TIFFANY GLASS

Sotheby Photo

Sotheby Photo

Sotheby Photo

Fig. 1 **Flower-form vase**, Tiffany, c.1900. Green striated glass with an iridescent sheen on the inside, the base engraved 'L.C.T. T290', height 11¼ ins. (Sotheby's Belgravia, London.)

Fig. 2 **Wisteria lamp**, Tiffany Studios, c.1900. Leaded marble glass outlined in a verdigris with verdigris bronze base and four light-fittings marked 'Tiffany Studios New York 26854' and with the mark 'Tiffany Glass and Decorating Company' impressed, overall height 27 ins. (Sotheby's Belgravia.)

Fig. 3 **Vase**, Tiffany, c.1900. Pale green lustre glass decorated with a trailing band of lily-pads in high blue-gold iridescence over black inlaid glass, the base engraved 'L.C.T. U1862' and with a Tiffany-Favrile trade-label, height 3¾ ins. (Sotheby's Belgravia.)

Fig. 4 **Tulip lamp**, Tiffany Studios, c.1900. Leaded marble glass, the leading given a gilt-bronze patination, marked 'Tiffany Studios New York 1596', with three light-fittings and gilt-bronze base marked and numbered '587', overall height 23½ ins. (Sotheby's Belgravia.)

Fig. 5 **Vase**, Tiffany and Fabergé, c.1900. Favrile glass with peacock-feather decoration in high gold, mauve and green lustre, the 'eyes' of inlaid green glass with darker centres, marked 'Louis C. Tiffany 07233'; the silver-gilt Fabergé mount by Johan Viktor Aarne. Overall height 7¾ ins. The prefix 'O' to the number of the glass body indicates a special order. The vase was given by Louis C. Tiffany at the wedding from the White House of Miss Julia Grant to Prince Michael Cantacuzene. It was taken with other Tiffany pieces to their home in Russia, where Fabergé was commissioned to make the mount. Tiffany's peacock vases of this type represent the ultimate achievement in his technique of glass-blowing and decoration. (Sotheby's.)

In producing his beautifully designed and executed art glass, Louis C. Tiffany was largely instrumental in giving an identity to American craftsmanship

Louis Comfort Tiffany was born in 1848. His father, Charles Louis Tiffany, had by then established himself as a jeweller and silversmith, having founded the firm of Tiffany & Young in 1837. By the year 1870, when L. C. Tiffany had reached the age of twenty-two, his father's was the smartest shop in the country and was able to present for sale what was possibly the largest collection of gems in the world. The firm's own silverware was of a very high standard and had won prizes in European exhibitions, including the Paris Exhibition of 1867.

This was a booming period for the United States. New families appeared with what seemed like limitless fortunes. The Vanderbilts, the Astors, the Goulds and the Havemeyers were in competition to dispose of vast sums, often, sadly, with more money than taste.

The young Louis Comfort, to his father's chagrin, took little interest in the business and seemed to have no enthusiasm for the commercial side of it. In 1866, he declared his desire to study art rather than go to college. His first leaning was towards landscape painting and he developed a very romantic view of nature as the pupil of one of America's leading landscape-artists, George Inness. The winter of 1868–69 was spent in Paris with Léon Bailly, who was to take Tiffany on a visit to Spain and North Africa, instilling in him a fascination for Islamic, North African and Moorish art, all of which styles he was later to adapt in his eclectic decorative schemes. An important influence on the young Tiffany was one of his father's chief designers, Edward C. Moore. Moore was a great admirer of oriental art and was, in turn, admired by Samuel Bing, the Parisian dealer and critic, whom Tiffany met on a visit to Paris and who was to become the French agent for Tiffany's work.

Bing supplied Tiffany and Moore with examples of oriental art and started them off as collectors.

Tiffany had devoted most of the 1870s to painting. However, he was the first to admit his shortcomings in this field and it was Edward C. Moore who encouraged Tiffany to devote himself to the applied arts and interior decoration. In 1879, Tiffany finally determined to go into decorative work professionally and formed a partnership with Samuel Colman and Candace Wheeler, which he called 'Louis C. Tiffany and Associated Artists'.

He very quickly won a high reputation, and his pre-eminence as America's leading decorator was acknowledged in the winter of 1882–83, when he was invited to redecorate parts of the White House. The highlight of his decorative scheme was a vast opalescent glass screen regrettably destroyed in 1904, when Theodore Roosevelt, redecorating the White House, gave the order to 'break in small pieces that Tiffany screen'.

From surviving photographs and accounts, one can piece together the style of the Associated Artists. Their decorative work was still essentially high Victorian in feeling; their sources were many, although they were successful in achieving a sense of harmony, blending Islamic art with their own embroidered hangings and painted friezes and with tiling and panelling in the coloured glass in which Tiffany was becoming interested.

These domestic applications of glass were Tiffany's introduction to the medium – he became tremendously involved and broke up his old partnership to devote his energies to glassmaking. His former associate Candace Wheeler recalled: 'I think Mr. Tiffany was rather glad to get rid of us all . . . for his wonderful experiments in glass iridescence . . .'.

During his travels, Tiffany had formed a collection of glass – his particular fascination was with ancient glass with its marvellous nacreous iridescence, caused by decomposition while buried, and by the effects of metallic oxides. Tiffany also loved the pitted and corroded effects caused by decomposition. He saw the beauty of what were essentially imperfections in the glass. It became his ambition to learn so much about glass and its reactions to various chemicals that he would be able

6

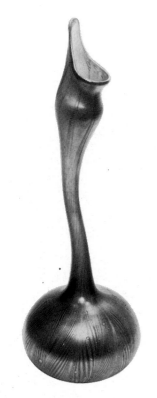

Sotheby Photo

Fig. 6 **Gooseneck vase**, Tiffany, c.1900. *Gold iridescent glass enriched with green feather lines, the base engraved '803T. L.C. Tiffany-Favrile', height 14½ ins. The form of this vase is organic, and, like much of Tiffany's work, it is of Persian inspiration. The word 'Favrile', derived from the Old English word 'fabrile', meaning 'hand-made', appears on many of Tiffany's glass pieces. (Sotheby's.)*

Fig. 7 **Lava vase**, Tiffany, c.1900. *Dark purple-blue iridescent glass with gold lustre decoration, height 5 ins. Pieces of this particularly interesting range of Tiffany glass have abstract decoration in trailed gold or silver lustre. (Sotheby's.)*

Fig. 8 **Paperweight vase**, Tiffany, c.1900. *Two layers of tinted glass decorated between the layers with swirling green leaves and red poppies with* millefiore *stamens, the inside with a green-gold lustre, the base engraved '8520 N. L.C.Tiffany Inc. Favrile', height 6 ins. The finest paperweight vases were those of this type, with sliced and embedded* millefiore *canes. (Sotheby's Belgravia.)*

to control these accidental imperfections.

Coloured glass fascinated him; the art of stained-glass windows was a challenge he could not resist, but he was horrified by those craftsmen who were content to apply painted decoration to the glass. On this point, Tiffany felt most strongly – that any decoration in his glasswork should be integral to the glass body. If, for instance, he wanted a glass vase to be decorated with flowers, he felt it would be abhorrent to paint flowers on the vase; their presence should be represented by the texture and the colour of the glass itself.

Tiffany was further inspired by the simplicity of the forms of ancient glass, just as he was horrified by nineteenth-century efforts to mould or cut glass into shapes more appropriate for bronze or porcelain. Tiffany was pleased by the irregularity of form of a good deal of ancient glass and, as a result, one finds that much of his own glassware has a certain, probably intentional, asymmetry (Fig. 6).

One should bear in mind that not all the glass that bears his name was made by Tiffany himself, although he kept a close supervision on everything that left his workshops. Certain pieces are the result of serious experiment and their technical invention is of significance in the history of art glass. A good deal of Tiffany output, however, tends to be of more commercial quality, for he had a very large and enthusiastic clientele.

This market was kept happy with the plain gold lustre pieces which form the largest single category, designed mostly as decorative tableware – one finds vases, sets of beakers, glasses, *tazze*, bowls, finger-bowls and stands. In a patent-claim filed in 1880, Tiffany described the essential method of producing iridescent glass: 'The metallic luster is produced by forming a film of a metal or its oxide or a compound of the metal on or in the glass, either by exposing it to vapors or gasses or by direct application. It may also be produced by corroding the surface of the glass, such processes being well known to glass manufacturers'.

Tiffany found how cobalt or copper oxides could colour glass blue; how iron oxide resulted in green; how manganese oxide produced shades of violet; how gold or copper produced red; how coke, coal or other carbon oxides gave an amber colour; and how manganese cobalt and iron could combine to give a black glass. The distinctive gold lustre was achieved with gold chloride either suspended in the glass or sprayed on while the glass was still hot from the furnace. Twenty-five dollar gold pieces were used as the base. After the plain gold glass, one finds in order of frequency blue, green, white, yellow, brown, amethyst, black and red. Samuel Bing's purple prose on the subject of Tiffany's lustre glass is almost too enthusiastic to be true: 'They captivated the eye by reason of both their wonderful matt softness and, at the same time, a nacreous richness over which played, according to the breaking of the light, an infinite variety of tones in which were opalised radiations so subtle, delicate and mysterious that the water of an exquisite pearl can alone be compared to them'.

The second most numerous category is the decorated iridescent ware, although this is a fairly broad heading as it includes all types from the superb 'peacock feather' vases (Fig. 5) and the flower forms (Fig. 1) to the simpler vases decorated with a few trailing ivy-leaves or lily-pads (Fig. 3). Samuel Bing, although full of the same sense of rapture, is more

helpful in the following passage where he describes the craftsman at work on the decorated glass. 'Look at the incandescent ball of glass as it comes out of the furnace; it is slightly dilated by an initial inspiration of air. The workman charges it at certain pre-arranged points with small quantities of glass, of different textures and different colours, and in this operation is hidden the germ of the intended ornamentation. The little ball is then returned to the fire to be heated. Again it is subjected to a similar treatment (the process being sometimes repeated as many as twenty times), and, when all the different glasses have been combined and manipulated in different ways, and the article has been brought to its definite state as to form and dimension, it presents the following appearance: the motifs introduced into the ball when it was small have grown with the vase itself, but in differing proportions; they have lengthened or broadened out, while each tiny ornament fills the place assigned to it in

7

advance in the mind of the artist'. Tiffany's 'Peacock-feather' vases are the ultimate achievement in this technique and they are often further enhanced by inlaid 'evil eyes' of dark coloured glass (Fig. 10). Similarly, one finds inlaid glass in lily-pad vases such as the one illustrated (Fig. 3).

Another group that presented comparable technical problems were the 'paperweight' vases in which the floral decoration was trapped between two layers of glass. An initial form would have been blown and into its warm, soft surface would be pressed coloured glass to form flower-patterns; these would be rolled until smooth and the whole would be cased in a further layer of glass, thus giving to the surface of the object an illusion of great depth which was sometimes enhanced by a light internal iridescence. Perhaps the finest quality paperweight vases are those which incorporate *millefiore* glass – glass canes are sliced and then embedded in groups in the inner layer of glass and rolled into the surface. These are *millefiore* canes of a type used in traditional French paperweights, but Tiffany's application is all the more remarkable in that he was able to create so good a three-

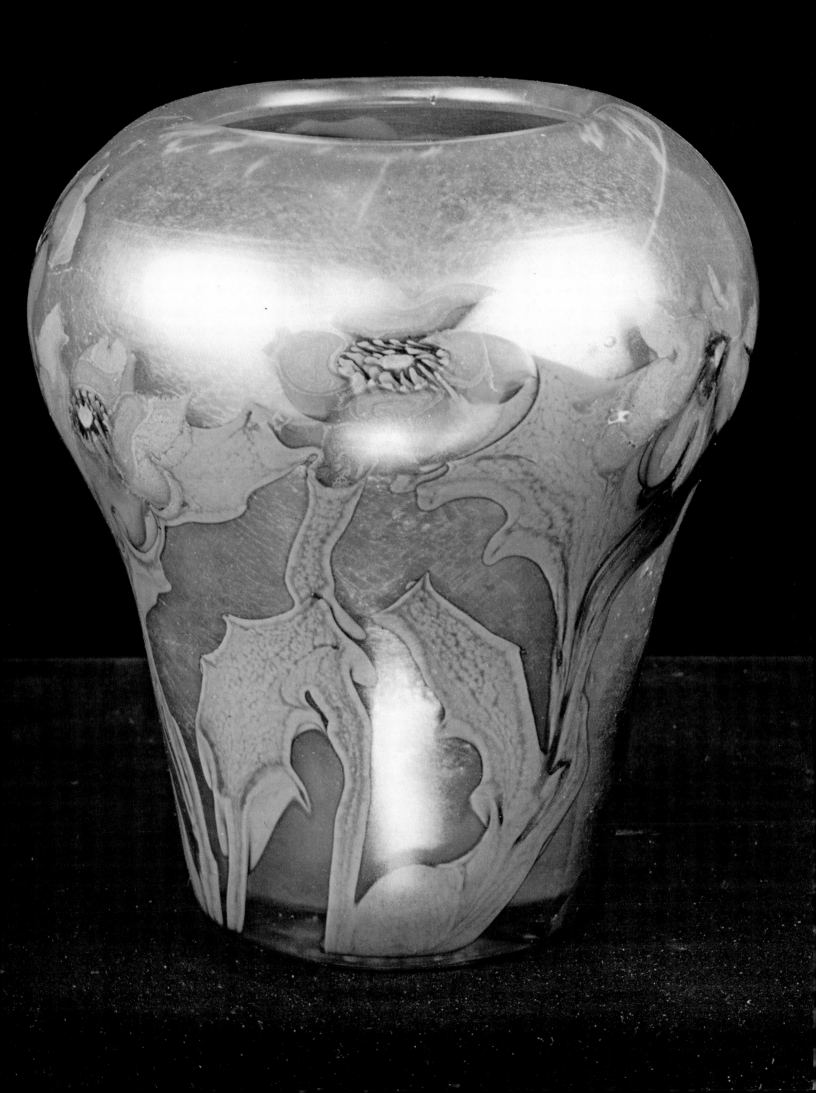

Fig. 9 **Favrile Cypriote vase,**
Tiffany, c.1900. *Opaque green
glass with a partly pitted surface,
numbered 'K 1379' and with a
Tiffany Glass and Decorating
Co. trade-label and the original
verdigris bronze base, height
$13\frac{1}{2}$ ins.*
(Sotheby's.)

Fig. 10 **Peacock vase,** *Tiffany,
c.1900. Glass body decorated
with a combed peacock-feather
design of pale green and gold
iridescence, the three 'evil eyes'
of dark green iridescence, the
base engraved '06580', height
$13\frac{1}{4}$ ins.*
(Sotheby's.)

Fig. 11 **Marks** *used by Louis C.
Tiffany at the Tiffany Studios.*

9

Sotheby Photo

10

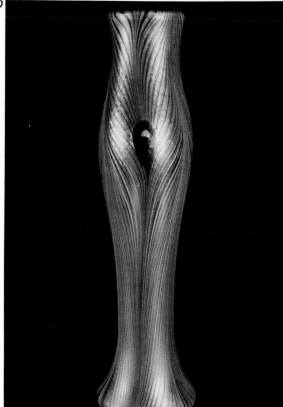

11

dimensional effect with so thin a body.

'Cypriote' was the name given to a type of glass
most closely inspired by the corroded textures of
excavated ancient glass. Nearly always found in
brown or blue opaque glass, Cypriote ware is
characterised by its crusty surface. This effect
was achieved by rolling the body over a marver
covered with pulverised crumbs of glass. Cypriote
pieces are often haphazard in form and are often
larger than other types of vase (Fig. 9).

Lava glass is the self-explanatory name of a
particularly interesting range of Tiffany glass
(Fig. 7). These pieces are generally of a dark blue
lustre body with voluptuous, abstract-organic,
trailed or poured, gold lustre decoration. In their
very free conception of form, they are among the
most revolutionary of Tiffany's works.

There are other categories such as Agate ware
(coloured glasses are run together and then polished
down to resemble agate) and Marblized ware
(colours are blended to resemble the texture of
marble), and the various glasses used in the series
of leaded shades for table-lamps which helped more
than anything else to make Tiffany's name a
household word. From the quantity produced, and
from contemporary reports, one must assume that
no well-decorated (or at least fashionably decorated) home in America was complete without one.

In this series of lamps, Tiffany found a means
of adapting the principles of stained-glass
windows to electricity in an unobtrusive as
well as a very decorative way. The lamps vary
a good deal in quality; some are far more elaborate
and far more subtle in the tones of glass used. The
large Wisteria lamp illustrated in Figure 2 is a very
good example, conceived in a fully naturalistic way.
Here we have, not a lamp decorated with wisteria
blossom and trees, but a lamp which is in the form of
a wisteria tree. Other types have the shades
decorated with dragon-flies or their bases modelled

in full relief as clusters of lily-pads.

Louis Comfort Tiffany was no great social
theorist; his influence, however, was very great in
giving an identity to American craftmanship. At the
back of his mind was always an ambition to become
a kind of American William Morris, but he found it
all too easy to indulge his taste for the luxurious and
the exotic. There was no return to simplicity,
although there was a return to nature and
inspiration from organic form. In this sense he can
be called an Art Nouveau designer, but he was
never attached by any dogma to the Art Nouveau
movement as such. His range was far wider.

Samuel Bing concludes significantly: 'If we are
called upon to declare the supreme characteristic
of this glassware, we would say it resides in the
fact that the means employed for the purpose of
ornamentation are sought and found in the vitreous
substance itself, without the use of either brush,
wheel, or acid. When cool, the article is finished'.

MUSEUMS AND COLLECTIONS

Tiffany glass may be seen at the following:

New York: Metropolitan Museum of Art
            Cooper-Hewitt Museum

FURTHER READING

Artistic America, Tiffany Glass and Art Nouveau
by Samuel Bing, reprinted with an introduction by
Robert Koch, Cambridge, Mass., and London, 1970.

Art Glass Nouveau by R. and L. Grover, Rutland,
Vermont, 1967.

Louis C. Tiffany, Rebel in Glass by Robert Koch,
New York, 3rd ed., 1982.

SIDELIGHTS

SIDELIGHT

Collection Robin Wyatt: A. C. Cooper

TYPEWRITERS

The first successful commercially built typewriter appeared in 1874. It was invented by an American, Christopher Sholes. He took his designs to Remingtons of New York, who, because the Civil War was over and there was a slump in the sale of arms, were looking for a new product. Typewriters were originally marketed for people such as church officials, ladies and gentlemen for their personal correspondence, and authors. In 1875, a year after its invention, Mark Twain used and extolled the virtues of the typewriter. The *Universal* keyboard we use today was devised for the first Remington machine; the reason for the layout of the keyboard was that the typebars clashed when the typewriter was being operated at even moderate speed unless the letters that frequently occurred together were placed well apart in the works. Other, later manufacturers tried to improve the keyboard layout, but because of Remingtons' early lead their ideas never really came to anything.

During the decade between 1890 and 1900, the great office potential was discovered and from then on hundreds of makers entered the scene, each being careful not to infringe their rivals' patents. By this time, Remingtons had sold off

their typewriter company to independent interests. The social change caused by the sudden need for typists, and the huge influx of young women into offices which began at this time, is a study in itself. From the collecting point of view, the most interesting machines are those built before 1900, when they were still in the process of being improved and developed.

Collecting Hints

Make sure that the enamel paintwork and decorations are original. The plated parts should be good, too; renickeling is expensive.

Above: Left, **Fitch**, *1886, was almost the first typewriter which wrote within vision.*
Right, ***Chicago***, *1892, with type-wheel and hammer.*
Below: Left, **Lambert**, *produced by Gramophone and Typewriter Co. c. 1900.*
Centre, ***Columbia***, *1886, the first with differential spacing.* Right, **Blickensderfer.** *1893–1910.*
Opposite: **Hammond.** *c. 1895, with the 'Ideal Keyboard'.*

Collection Robin Wyatt: A. C. Cooper

Collection Robin Wyatt: A. C. Cooper

SIDELIGHT

BERLIN WORK

In the Victorian period, in both the United States and Europe, Berlin work was popular until about 1870. It got its name because it originated in Berlin, very early in the 19th century. During the Victorian period it virtually outran all other forms of embroidery as a form of decoration and amusement. Cross- or tent-stitch were the only skills required, and the heaviest worsted wools were the usual materials. Berlin work was known in England after the Napoleonic wars; Ackermann's repository in 1814 included engravings of several wool-work patterns, 'from designs by Herr Wittich, of Berlin'. By 1840, if the Countess of Wilton's *Art of Needlework* is to be believed, there were more than ten thousand different designs to be copied. The principal source was Wilke's Warehouse in Regent Street, which began to import both patterns and, oddly, materials direct from Berlin after 1841. In the 1850s, there was a fashion for what was called 'German Embroidery', which was simply wool-work heavily ornamented with beads of coloured glass. All the earlier examples of Berlin work used the harshest colours available—viridian, scarlet and magenta being among the favourite. With the vogue for greater ornamentation, however, the colours became more united. In the 1860s, much of the bead-work was discarded, and the fashion died away completely in the 1870s. Most of the designs reflect the Victorian preoccupation with the Gothic, whether in design features or historical scenes. Sir Walter Scott's novels were a favourite theme, as were the paintings of Landseer. Berlin work was used widely for cushions and stools of all sorts, and came to be used on screens, slippers, book-covers and chairs as well.

Collecting Hints

Berlin work is such an obtrusive form of decoration that the smallest objects are often the most attractive. Pin-cushions and foot-stools are less easy to find than fire-screens and chairs, but more worthwhile. Floral and pictorial patterns naturalistically rendered were particularly popular between about 1830 and mid-century.
If Prussian blue is the predominant colour, it is safe to assume that the article was made sometime after 1870.

Where To Look

Most antique shops tend to stock a few examples, if only to give a little colour to set off a dark interior.

What To Buy

Much depends on the condition of the article, and on how it is mounted. If set in a chair, for example, it will merely add to the cost of the chair.

Above: **Stool top.** Unmounted, wool on canvas, 1 ft. square. This piece shows a typically complex design in garish colours.

Below: **Rug,** c. 1860. Wool on canvas, 4 ft. 8 ins. × 2 ft. 9 ins. This superb example in near-perfect condition is quite valuable.

Over page: **Panel for a firescreen,** unfinished, wool and beads on canvas, 18 × 25 ins. This fine piece displays the full range of Berlin work techniques: common wool stitches such as cross- or tent-stitch; tufted work cut into petal shapes; and beads for variation of colour and texture.

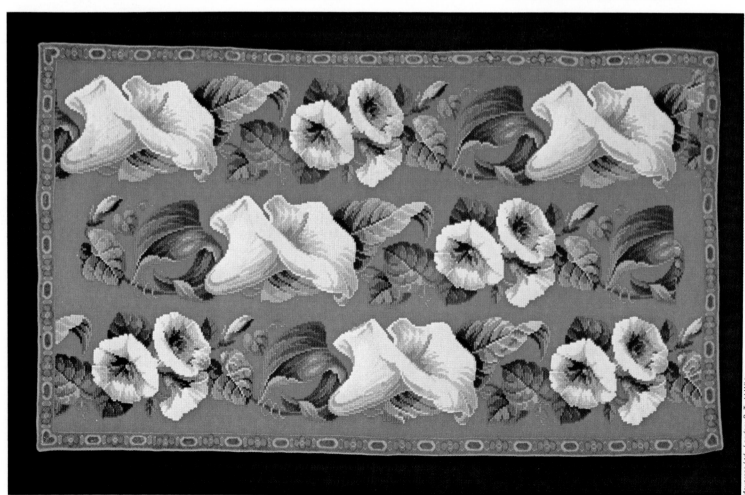

Embroiderers' Guild, London : R. Todd-White

SIDELIGHT

RECRUITING AND LIBERTY LOAN POSTERS OF THE GREAT WAR

Private Collection: A. C. Cooper

Above: *The most famous of all American posters, designed by James Montgomery Flagg in 1917.*
Above right: *A poster for the Third Liberty Loan campaign by C.H. Leyendecker, the Saturday Evening Post cover artist.*
Right: *A 1917 poster emphasizing the importance of the workers in the shipyards and munitions factories.*
Opposite: *A 1917 recruiting poster by Howard Chandler Christy, an artist famous for his portrayals of beautiful women.*

During World War I men were required for service in unprecedented numbers and at very short notice. The success of recruiting depended on the effectiveness of government propaganda and persuasion, and recruiting posters were used extensively for this purpose. Posters were also produced in great numbers to raise vital money through the various Liberty Loan campaigns urging people to buy U.S. war bonds. The great artists of the day gave their services for the cause, and you will find posters signed with famous names.

Some posters tended to reflect an equal partnership between the man in the French trenches and the men in the factories at home, emphasizing the interdependence of front-line soldiers and munitions workers. The exigencies of wartime production inevitably meant that recruiting posters were often printed on coarse and easily perishable

paper. It is important, therefore, to treat them with the utmost care. Posters should be kept flat if possible, as the edges may be damaged by taking them out of tubes.

SIDELIGHT

FOUNTAIN PENS

'Nature's noblest gift – my grey goose quill;
Slave of my thoughts, obedient to my will;
Torn from thy parent bird to form a pen,
That mighty instrument of little men'.

Thus did Lord Byron apostrophise his pen, which was most likely to have been one of Joseph Bramah's cut quills. Bramah divided his quills into several pieces, fitting them together to make different kinds of nib. In 1818, Charles Watt developed this process by gilding the nibs to make them last longer, and in the following year James Lewes invented the first 'calligraphic fountain pen' with an ink-flow controlled by a silver lever. Between that year and the 1850s were patented a great many 'self-supplying' pens of this sort. Very few of them were as efficient as a good quill, although George Poulton developed a pen in 1827 which found favour with the Duke of Wellington. In 1853, Charles Goodyear developed a pen of vulcanised rubber with an ink-flow controlled by a metal screw. This process was amplified by John Darling in the 1860s, who filled the tubular part of the pen with a tube of soft India rubber. Between 1870 and 1885, there were thirty-two different types of pen patented. In the 1880s, the names still associated with pen-making today first came into prominence. The earliest of the commercial Waterman pens was produced in 1884 by a New York

Right: Parker pens, from the left: ***Ivory dip pen*** of commonplace design. ***Glass 'Exhibition' pen, 1851.*** ***Gold and vulcanite pen*** with eye-dropper filling mechanism, c.1890. ***Early fountain pen*** by John Jacob Parker (no relation to the Parker Pen Company), 1832; one of the first developments in the evolution of the fountain pen and plunger, made of silver.

Below left: Waterman pens, from the left: ***Unusually long feed-fill pen*** ($6\frac{1}{2}$ ins.), c.1910. ***Safety pen,*** c.1920; reputedly used during Prohibition for the storage of illicit liquor. ***Early self-filler*** with lever mechanism, c.1912.

Below right: Waterman pens, from the left: ***Self-filler*** with experimental piston mechanism, c.1900; the earliest known of this type. ***Four feed-fill pens*** of the type perfected by Waterman, c.1890–1905; vulcanite with 14 ct. gold nibs; the second is silver-mounted and inscribed 1903.

Over page: ***Three Waterman safety pens,*** c.1920–30; vulcanite with decorative silver mounts and gold nibs. In order to avoid spilling the ink, the nib of a safety pen only appears when the cap is screwed on to the base. The centre pen of these three is shown half retracted.

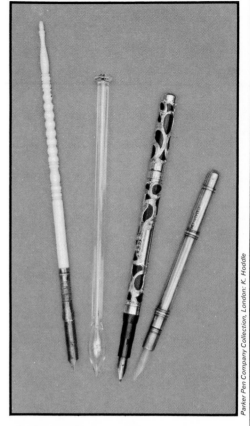

Parker Pen Company Collection, London: K. Hoddle

solicitor and insurance broker, Lewis Edson Waterman and, by 1890, 'Parker' and 'Swan' were already household words. Until that time, pen-making was largely a German monopoly. The best-known types were Oidtmann, Kollisch, Schmackelsen and Reisert. In the 1890s, however, alongside Swan, Parker and Waterman, there were Moor's early non-leakable safety-pen favoured by Mr. Gladstone, Shaw's automatic pen and Eyre & Spottiswoode's 'Commercial'

pen. The external furnishings of these pens do not differ greatly. It is rather the internal mechanism which attracts collectors.

Hints To Collectors

Always examine a pen minutely before purchasing it as it is very likely that it will have been repaired at some stage of its career. The repair may be just as interesting as the original, although making it worth less.

Waterman Pen Company Collection, London: Miki Slingsby

Waterman Pen Company Collection, London: Miki Slingsby

SIDELIGHT

Collection Mrs. A. Freeman: Liz Hay-Brown

VALENTINE CARDS

When, in 1870, a writer referred to 'those pretty and gorgeously-bedecked missives which fly about in all directions on 14th of February, telling in all sorts of metres of love's young dream', the craze for sending valentine cards had reached its peak. Valentines had achieved popularity in the last few decades of the previous century, especially in England and America, as a natural development of the little pictorial visiting cards which had become fashionable. The high cost of postage limited their sale at first, but by about 1815 most towns had introduced a local penny post and the sending of elegantly engraved pictorial valentines with 'paper lace' floral borders turned 14th February into the postman's busiest day of the year.

The hand-made valentines of this period with, for example, the motif of 'the endless knot of love' and a few lines of verse, were often beautifully designed. But despite the existence of many 'Valentine writers' to provide inspiration, the craftsmanship of the verses rarely approached the virtuosity of the design. Vulgar, and often bitterly cutting valentines were commoner than might be realised nowadays, because naturally a lovesick maiden would not preserve for posterity a card referring to her as 'a withered flower' or 'Miss grey hairs and wrinkles'!

The charm of the early hand-made and lithographed cards was exchanged for the lavishness of the mid-Victorian mass produced cards. 1840 to 1870 was the golden age of the Valentine. Card manufacturers ensured that the public would never forget 14th February by introducing eye-catching novelties each year—cards with perfumed sachets, movable cards, topical cards and so on. Specially designed envelopes were produced to match the sentimental enclosures. These charming envelopes are now hard to find.

Valentines of extraordinary complexity enjoyed a vogue in the 1860s, when a famous manufacturer, Jonathan King, affixed to his cards everything from pressed leaves and shells to artificial jewels and pheasants' feathers. Yet the craze was in decline by the 1880s and despite the Edwardian substitute of Valentine postcards, and a mild revival in the 1920s, St. Valentine's Day today is an unexciting affair when compared with its former status.

Collecting Hints

The beautiful and sentimental valentines of the mid-Victorian era are naturally attractive to the would-be collector but the cheaply printed and vulgar cards of the same period should not be scorned. Indeed, they are probably rarer, since they had less chance of being treasured at the time. But the collector should always try to avoid imbalance within his collection. The cruel and the comic deserve a place alongside the elegant and the charming. Among the more artistic variations of valentine art, mention must be made of the much sought-after 'cobweb' designs, where a short cotton string is lifted to reveal a picture or a verse beneath intricate cut-out paper work.

Other valentines worth searching for are those with a military or naval theme (such as those resulting from the Napoleonic Wars or the American Civil War). Cards or envelopes with a musical design and those in a format similar to early Victorian ballad sheets are popular. More complicated cards of the 1860s, with their fragile accessories, are difficult to find in good condition.

Where To Buy

Still available at fairly low prices, valentines are most often found in albums or trays of cards in general antique shops.

Mansell Collection

Mansell Collection

Top: **Christmas valentine** *in the shape of a fan, decorated with flowers and love poems.*

Above left: **Valentine from a realistic lover** *The pineapple can be lifted up to reveal a cartoon figure and an insulting verse.*

Above right: **'Drink to me only with thine eyes'**, *a humorous valentine. It was fashionable to decorate cards with pressed flowers or feathers, such as these owl feathers.*

Overpage: **Valentine** *with two scenes of lovers in pastoral settings and quotations below which express true devotion.*

Bottom left: **Decorative valentine** *trimmed with ribbon and lace.*

Bottom right: **Highly ornate valentine** *based on the age-old theme of music and love.*

I DO LOVE NOTHING IN THE WORLD SO WELL AS YOU: IS NOT THAT STRANGE.— *SHAKSPERE*.

I'LL SING TO THEE, AND LOVE THEE TOO FONDLY, AND WITH AFFECTION TRUE.

Collection Mrs. A. Freeman: Liz Hay-Brown

Mansell Collection

Mansell Collection

SIDELIGHT

MONEY-BOXES

Money-boxes for the purposes of distributing alms to the poor were used from the earliest Christian times. The earliest known money-box, however, is Roman and it certainly did contain a hoard worth saving—thirty-three gold pieces.

Thrift has persisted—as a virtue, if not a necessity—from that day to this, promoted, like many other disciplines, by the Victorians. Some of the prettiest and most ingenious boxes date from the nineteenth century; Staffordshire cottages resembling pastille-burners, or the mechanical ones based on an American invention.

The more traditional of money-box shapes are symbols of saving. The pig is a most rewarding animal, cheap in the rearing, lucrative in the selling because it is edible from the trotters to the ears. In some places the fish enjoys the same sort of regard as the pig, and in rare cases the characteristics of both animals are combined in the same box. Curiously, few boxes have the solid, business-like appearance that might be expected of a miniature safe. Perhaps the reasoning was that a pretty ornament or a fascinating toy was more likely to attract attention—and savings—than a grimmer-looking object.

Collecting Hints
Apart from searching for the obviously desirable pottery cottages and mechanical boxes, remember that quite recent boxes will probably be valuable one day,

especially souvenir boxes from exhibitions and holiday resorts. Even the ones that have been designed for collecting vital parking-meter money might be interesting rather than hateful one day.

Below left: *Fish/pig, Sussex, seventeenth century. **Staffordshire cottage**, nineteenth century. **Staffordshire dog**, nineteenth century. **Slipware pig**, date unknown.*

Below right: ***William Tell**, designed by Stevens, American, 1896.*

Bottom; (left) ***Pony trick**, designed by Stevens, 1885. The coin is deposited in the manger. (right) **Always did 'spise a mule**, designed by Stevens, 1879. The boy is kicked off the bench by the mule.*

Leonard W. Dunham Collection: A. C. Cooper

Leonard W. Dunham Collection: A. C. Cooper

Leonard W. Dunham Collection: A. C. Cooper